Practitioner Series

Springer

London
Berlin
Heidelberg
New York
Barcelona
Hong Kong
Milan
Paris
Santa Clara
Singapore
Tokyo

Other titles in this series:

The Politics of Usability
L. Trenner and J. Bawa
3-540-76181-0

Electronic Commerce and Business Communications
M. Chesher and R. Kaura
3-540-19930-6

Key Java
J. Hunt and A. McManus
3-540-76259-0

The Project Management Paradigm
K. Burnett
3-540-76238-8

Distributed Applications Engineering
I. Wijegunaratne and G. Fernandez
3-540-76210-8

Finance for IT Decision Makers
M. Blackstaff
3-540-76232-9

Middleware
D. Serain
1-85233-011-2

The Renaissance of Legacy Systems
I. Warren
1-85233-009-0

Java for Practitioners
J. Hunt
1-85233-093-7

David Benyon, Thomas Green
and Diana Bental

Conceptual Modeling for User Interface Development

Springer

David Benyon, PhD
Computing Department, Napier University, Edinburgh EH14 1DJ, UK

Thomas Green, PhD
Computer Based Learning Unit, Leeds University, Leeds LS9 2JT, UK

Diana Bental, PhD
Computing and Electrical Engineering Department, Heriot-Watt University,
Riccarton, Edinburgh, UK

ISBN-13: 978-1-85233-009-5   e-ISBN-13: 978-1-4471-0797-2
DOI: 10.1007/ 978-1-4471-0797-2

British Library Cataloguing in Publication Data
Benyon, David
    Conceptual modeling for user interface development.--
    (Practitioner series)
    1. User interfaces (Computer systems)—2. Computer software – Development
    I. Title—II. Bental, Diana—III. Green, Thomas
    005.1'2
Library of Congress Cataloging-in-Publication Data
Benyon, David.
    Conceptual modeling for user interface development–/–David Benyon,
    Diana Bental, and Thomas Green.
        p.——cm.
    Includes bibliographical references and index.
    1. User interfaces (Computer systems)—2. Human-computer
interaction.—I. Bental, Diana, 1960—.—II. Green, Thomas, 1941—.
    III. Title.
QA76.9.U83B46—1999   98-51145
005.4'28–dc21   CIP

Typesetting: Midlands Book Typesetting Company, Loughborough
34/3830-543210 Printed on acid-free paper   SPIN 10673944

Contents

Preface

In 1989 Thomas Green presented a paper at the British Computer Society's 5th Annual Conference entitled "Cognitive dimensions of notations" (Green, 1989). Green was already well known for his work on TAG – a Task Action Grammar (Payne and Green, 1986) but had come to realize that highly detailed techniques such as TAG were not solving some important problems in human-computer interaction (HCI). Accordingly he had been working on a much "higher level", broad brush technique – the cognitive dimensions – which could be used to criticize and evaluate human-computer interfaces (and other notations). The thinking behind this move was that designers and users of systems would have a set of "dimensions" in which to describe and discuss alternative designs.

In 1991, at the British Computer Society's 7th Annual Conference, he introduced the idea of a "structure map", based on entity-relationship modeling (Green, 1991), which could be used to understand some of these dimensions. He had read David Benyon's book on data modeling (Benyon, 1990) and later in 1991 they began to correspond, exchanging ideas on how effective entity-relationship modeling could be in representing aspects of interfaces. Although entity-relationship modeling had been used in software engineering, database design and knowledge representation for 15 years, it had not previously been applied to interface design.

Discussion between Benyon, Green and his co-worker on cognitive dimensions, Marian Petre, led to a proposal to the UK government-backed initiative in cognitive science and human-computer interaction to develop the idea of entity-relationship modeling of information artefacts (ERMIA). The proposal presented the rationale behind this development:

"Part of the motivation for this proposal is our conviction that although HCI is creating many interesting techniques and devices, there is a huge gap left unfilled. Much of HCI is not providing types of analysis that are relevant to immediate problems. In the real world most people are not concerned with the niceties of the artefact; they are concerned with how much effort it takes to get the job done. We have all had first-hand experience of artefacts which are incomprehensible or difficult to use. The problem is, how do we portray our experience? We have an impoverished vocabulary within which to describe even the most straightforward of difficulties ... Our conviction is that HCI should give the users and designers a vocabulary in which to present their analyses at an appropriate level of discourse. Such a vocabulary needs to be adopted into common parlance, but it also needs to have a secure underpinning. In other sciences, terms such as 'elasticity' or even 'velocity' are now part of everyday life and help non-specialists to produce accurate reasoning. Although usually used casually, these terms are supported by precise theoretical definitions and a body of practical knowledge. HCI currently has no such terminology."

The project ran from 1992 until the end of 1995 with Denise Whitelock working full time as the research fellow. During the project the researchers developed and criticized a wide range of information artefacts, from the interfaces to standard word processors to the notation for citing references, trying to understand the problems and benefits of using ERMIA to describe the cognitive dimensions of notations. Martin Stacey, Diana Bental and others contributed to the discussion and the results of the work were presented at a number of research meetings.

As with much research, the project took a number of different directions and we did not complete the cognitive dimensions "vocabulary". Work continues in this area. However, we did discover that ERMIA worked well as a technique for cooperative design and evaluation as it forced designers to be explicit about their ideas. We also discovered a number of difficulties in using the technique and worked to find ways in which the technique could be presented more effectively so that designers and users of computer systems can gain an insight into alternative designs. As the project neared its conclusion we felt that we should provide tutorial material so that the technique can be picked up and used "in anger" by designers.

We produced a small book on ERMIA that was read and criticized by several colleagues (in particular, detailed comments were provided by Alison Crerar and Steve Hitchman). The book was used as the basis of lecture courses on ERMIA and as a tutorial presented by Benyon and Green at the British HCI group's Annual Conference, HCI 98, in 1998. Several papers were published (Benyon and Green, 1995; Benyon, 1995; Green and Benyon, 1996) describing various aspects of the technique and a major case study was undertaken by Mike Jackson (Jackson, Benyon and Lowe, 1998). The result of this work is presented in this book.

Who Should Read this Book?

This book is intended for systems designers, computer system users and practitioners of user interface design. It introduces the technique of entity-relationship (ER) modeling to interface designers, who will find it complementary to techniques such as GOMS, UAN, Z and heuristic evaluation. For those already familiar with ER modeling it shows how the technique can be applied to interface issues.

We do not assume that the reader has any prior familiarity with entity-relationship modeling. This book explains those aspects of ER modeling which are relevant to ERMIA, and it presents the extensions to the notation that are necessary for modeling interfaces. It does not present all aspects of entity-relationship modeling, for which the interested reader should seek other texts in the field of data modeling and database design (e.g. Benyon, 1997).

By aiming the book at both interface designers and at software developers we hope to bridge a gap in the development of interactive systems. Too often, when software is being developed, the software engineers do not sufficiently consider how easy the system will be to learn and use. One of the reasons for this, we believe, is that they do not want to learn yet another notation. They do not have a readily available vocabulary in which to express these aspects of their designs. On the other side, interface specialists tend to express their concerns in ways which are either too detailed to be readily understood or in ways which are difficult for the software developer to imple- ment. We hope that ERMIA provides a set of concepts which can be used equally easily by software developers and interface designers.

Users are another group who need a language in which to express their ideas. Users have a different set of requirements from a software system than the experts. They have different background knowledge which can lead them to experience difficulty with elements of the system. When developers sit down to discuss their designs with the users, we hope that they will be able to share ideas through ERMIA models.

The book is aimed at students and commercial systems developers alike. It provides an insight into some of the most important ideas in human- computer interaction and it provides a detailed tutorial on entity-relationship modeling.

What Is ERMIA?

Designers and prospective users need to have some basis for choosing one design rather than another. One of the many different criteria that designers have to consider is, how difficult is it to find things and change things in the system that is being considered? This book describes ERMIA, an analytic modeling technique which helps to answer that question.

ERMIA is a data modeling approach to human-computer interfaces. It is based on entity-relationship modeling, which is a familiar technique from information modeling and database design. Using the ERMIA formalism, designers and analysts can present an appropriate abstraction of the informa- tion that can be obtained from a device, and they can identify potential pitfalls and problems in retrieving the required information. ERMIA provides a notation in which analysts, designers and users can all discuss an interface and the information it presents.

ERMIA is not only a design technique, it is also a useful technique for analyzing existing interfaces. It will be useful to potential users of computer systems, when they try to evaluate which of several possible interfaces will most easily present the information that users will need in order to do the work they want to do. ERMIA is also a useful technique for analysing competing designs for interfaces. An ERMIA analysis of an interface design will help to evaluate whether a proposed interface does indeed capture and make available all the information that is needed for all the users' activities.

By extending ER modeling into interface design, ERMIA offers a common language in which to describe both the external aspects of the interface and the conceptual structure of the information which is being stored, presented and sought.

ERMIA is mainly applicable to computer-based interfaces which present information that is needed for particular activities. These may be electronic, mechanical or paper-based. It is also applicable to control switches and to interactive devices such as cash dispensers, where the objective is not only to receive information but to use the information to achieve some goal. We have chosen to present examples from these fields, as well as from computer systems.

ERMIA and Software Engineering

One of the important aspects of interface development that ERMIA addresses is how to integrate HCI with software engineering (SE). The concerns of HCI – the usability, utility and effectiveness of computer systems to enable people to do the things that they want to do – and the concerns of software engineering – the efficiency, functionality and maintainability of computer systems – are sometimes difficult to reconcile. ERMIA provides a bridge between HCI and SE because it highlights HCI issues using a notation familiar to software engineers.

Of course there are many different methods and approaches to software engineering, and currently the object-oriented (OO) approach is most widely used, notably through the Unified Method Language (UML) (Booch, Rumbaugh and Jacobson, 1998). In UML the structure of the software system is represented as an object model and user interactions with the system are described as "use cases". The entities in ERMIA are analogous to the objects in UML, and ERMIA makes use of the use case construct when describing user interaction scenarios. An important difference between entities and objects, however, is that entities do not explicitly include a description of their behaviour. This is advantageous when looking at human-computer systems because we want to focus on the structure and representation of the information in the whole human-computer system. As the design of some device continues, and the user activities are identified and defined, then the entities of ERMIA can be mapped onto the objects in UML.

ERMIA is an extension of traditional ER modeling and includes the ideas of inheritance and encapsulation that are found in OO methods. The entities in ERMIA have relationships with one another in the same way that objects have relationships with other objects. In short, anyone familiar with object modeling will find ERMIA fits easily into their ways of working. What ERMIA offers the OO systems developer is a complementary modeling technique that highlights aspects of the system that could otherwise be overlooked.

Structure of the Book

This book is divided into three main sections. The first four chapters provide the motivation for ERMIA and introduce the basic concepts and notation. The following four chapters describe searching for information and show how ERMIAs can be used to represent and derive information about search. The final four chapters explore methodological and practical issues to do with developing ERMIAs.

Chapter 1 introduces the idea of modeling in user interface design and development, the various models that are appropriate and where ERMIA fits into user interface development. Chapter 2 introduces the concept of an information artefact and shows how ERMIA can help to create and identify designs that allow users to find the information they need. Chapter 3 describes the fundamental components of ERMIA – entities, attributes and relationships – and how to represent them. Chapter 4 explains the need to represent both perceptual and conceptual structures in ERMIAs.

Chapter 5 introduces the problem of searching for information in an artefact and presents some additional notation for describing search. Chapter 6 shows how complex relationships influence search, while Chapter 7 explores search that traverses many relationships and shows how ERMIAs can identify standard patterns with their implications for finding information. Chapter 8 shows how information artefacts are built upon each other to provide different views onto the information, and it examines the effect that different views can have in making information accessible.

Chapter 9 presents guidelines and a methodology for developing ERMIAs and presents a case study in which ERMIA is used to compare different designs. Chapter 10 encourages the reader to gain experience in developing ERMIAs. It offers many exercises and detailed worked examples. Chapter 11 presents a case study of the use of ERMIA during the development of a major piece of software. Finally Chapter 12 presents a number of other HCI techniques which are complementary to ERMIA and outlines the design areas where ERMIAs are most likely to be of use.

Acknowledgements

We are grateful to many colleagues and friends for discussion of these issues, notably Denise Whitelock, Martin Stacey, Marian Petre and Darrell Raymond. Alison Crerar and Steve Hitchman provided detailed comments on an earlier draft of the text. The ERMIA project was funded by the Joint Council's research initiative on Cognitive Science and Human-Computer Interaction.

1. *Modeling in User Interface Development*

Aims and Objectives

User interface development is concerned with producing computer-based systems and other 'information artefacts' that are effective and easy to learn and use for the intended users. During the process of developing user interfaces, the designer will need to produce a number of abstract representations, or models. There are a host of different modeling techniques that are used in user interface development and more generally in software engineering. This chapter reviews these and discusses the principles of models in design.

After reading this chapter you should be able to:

- understand the role of models in the development of user interfaces
- understand the processes involved in user interface development
- distinguish the different types of models required
- understand the difference between models of structure, models of dynamics and models of function
- understand where ERMIA, 'Entity-Relationship Modeling of Information Artefacts' fits into developing user interfaces.

1.1 User Interface Development

The user interface to an artefact, device or system is all the parts of the system that the user of that system comes into contact with. This includes the physical aspects of the system such as buttons, knobs and levers, perceptual aspects such as icons, messages, colours and pictures and the conceptual aspects such as what these icons and messages represent or what we think the levers and knobs do. A well-designed user interface will make a system easy to use and will ensure that the system is effective in enabling people to do things that they want to do with the device.

All manner of systems have user interfaces. My bicycle has a user interface which includes the pedals, seat, handlebars, brakes and gear levers. My alarm clock has a user interface consisting of a small display and two buttons to set the time and the alarm. Video cameras, the remote control to your TV, even a train timetable or a tourist map of a city have user interfaces.

Question: List some of the components of the user interface to a car.

Comment: The steering wheel, brake, clutch and accelerator pedals, gear stick, indicator arm, light switch, dip switch, and so on.

As computer-based systems have become more complex and more ubiquitous, so the need for efficient and effective user interfaces has become increasingly important. As more and more of the way an artefact does things is hidden in software, so the need to reveal information about it through the user interface becomes more important. At least when my bicycle goes wrong I can see how it works. With computer-based systems, an effective and well-designed user interface is crucial.

A user interface provides the connection between people and some underlying system. In most of the cases with which we are concerned this will be a computer-based system that is being, or has been, developed by software engineers. Software engineers use a whole range of methods to develop their systems such as object-oriented methods, structured methods or rapid application development methods. Nowadays the Unified Modeling Language (UML) (Booch, Rumbaugh and Jacobson, 1998) is widely used, but structured methods such as SSADM (Downs, Clare and Coe, 1991) are still popular in some organizations as are relational database systems or approaches using rapid development methods.

One of the aims of this book is to provide software designers with a method that enables them to develop effective user interfaces and which fits in with their way of developing and programming the underlying system. (Other aims include helping users and 'choosers' of systems to evaluate them.) The method is called ERMIA, Entity-Relationship Modeling of Information Artefacts.

1.2 Principles of Design

As with the production of any artefact, user interface development involves two major activities: understanding the requirements of the artefact to be produced and developing the artefact. Understanding requirements involves looking at similar products, discussing with the people who will use the product what their needs are and analyzing any existing systems to discover the problems with current designs. Development may include producing a variety of representations until a suitable artefact is produced, with different representations being more or less useful at different points.

For example, a garden designer discusses with clients the use they will make of the garden, what they do and do not like about their existing garden. The garden designer might show pictures of other gardens, draw sketches of possible arrangements and perhaps use a computer simulation of possible garden designs to show how the garden will look during different seasons. A dressmaker will show a bride-to-be different fabrics, discussing the price and look of alternatives. The bride-to-be might watch videos of people wearing different wedding dresses and examine various patterns in a catalogue. A software designer might sketch a few screen designs on paper and show them to the future system users to get comments. When the users seem happy with one of the designs the designer might develop detailed screen layouts using a prototyping tool.

✳ Example A car designer has been commissioned to produce a new luxury sports car. He/she doodles a few designs on paper and shows them to the other designers. They make certain comments and criticisms and as a result changes are made to the designs. Finally the designer is satisfied with one of the designs and draws up detailed blue-prints which are given to the firm's model maker. Plastic scale models of the design are produced and are sent to marketing and sales for customer reaction. The models are also subjected to wind tunnel experiments to investigate the aerodynamics of the design and the results are used in a computer program which will calculate the car's speed and fuel efficiency.

The designer is using four different models in at least four different ways:

- The original models represent a clearing of the mind. In this case they are "doodles" and sketches which are used to generate new ideas, examine possibilities and prompt for questions.
- The blue-prints given to the model maker and the scale model given to the marketing and sales departments are suitable models for accurately expressing ideas to others.
- The wind tunnel experiments show models being used to test ideas.
- The computer model is used to make predictions.

In all these cases the developer of the artefact – a garden, a wedding dress, a software system, a sports car – uses various simplified representations of the final artefact in order to understand the requirements and progress the development of the artefact. The various representations that are used – sketches, patterns, videos, simulations, screen layouts, blue prints and so on – are used where appropriate during the development process.

Developing suitable representations, or models, of an artefact is fundamental to all design activities. The representations employed may be formal or informal, precise or vague and may be used for very different purposes within the overall design activity. One of the skills of the designer is selecting an appropriate representation for the task at hand. Another is making good use of that representation.

1.2.1 Conceptual and Physical Design

Another general principle of design that is important in user interface development is the distinction between conceptual and physical design. At the conceptual level, the designer is concerned with what the system has to be like if it is to meet its purpose, with the structure and functions that are needed. At some point the designer must decide what the system will look like, how it will do the things that it needs to do and how the parts of the system are linked together. This is the stage of physical design. Between conceptual and physical design is the process of task allocation; deciding which things the underlying system will do and which things the users will have to do.

Question: Think of some conceptual design activities that a garden designer might undertake.

Comment: The garden designer might discuss with the client whether the garden should have a pond, a lawn and a barbecue area. This would be considered to be conceptual design because the designer is identifying the main components, but is not saying what these things will look like.

Distinguishing between conceptual and physical design does not proscribe a method for the design. Analysts and designers will iterate between these two levels of description and will fix on certain physical design decisions in order to understand the conceptual level better. This iteration will involve various kinds of testing (or evaluation) with users in order to check that the design really does meet their needs.

1.2.2 Conceptual Design of User Interfaces

In user interface design, the conceptual level involves analyzing users' needs in terms of the activities that need to be accomplished using a system and the objects and operations which a user has to employ to accomplish the tasks. For example, the designer of a company's Web site might decide that there needs to be information about the products that the company sells, a way for potential customers to register their requirements and links to the company's parent organization. The designer must define the conceptual objects – the pages, the registration form, the links and so on and consider how specific or general these conceptual objects should be. As a general principle, the designer aims to minimize conceptual complexity in the system by using familiar concepts, by having as few concepts as possible and by making methods of interaction as simple as possible. The result of conceptual design is an abstract representation, a conceptual model, of the whole human-computer system.

Question: Suppose you were asked to develop a ticket machine for a train station. What sort of conceptual objects and operations would be needed?

Comment: The machine would need to provide information about train destinations and departures and the cost of journeys. It would have to accept payment and deliver a ticket.

1.2.3 Physical Design

Physical design concerns embedding the conceptual model of a system in a physical structure so that users can communicate with that system. Physical design, unlike conceptual design, needs to focus on when and where actions and decisions are taken, which actions may be repeated, which actions are optional and the sequence in which actions are undertaken. Physical design is concerned with what the final system looks like, with what people have to do and what they have to know about.

Operational Aspects

The operational aspects of physical design concern packaging conceptual operations into a 'dialogue' – deciding what the system displays, what the user has to do and the order in which things have to be done. How is data going to be input by the user and how is information to be displayed by the device?

Many systems can be in different 'states' at different times. For example, a video recorder can be in a state of 'playing', 'recording' or 'timed recording'. Only certain interactions are possible depending on the state of the system. Hence, the designer needs to consider how the system can reveal the state it is in, how to make clear what actions the user can take and what the system responses (that is, feedback) will be.

Thinking about the design of the registration form for a Web site, for example, the designer will have to make decisions about the order in which the information is filled in, the need for a 'submit' button, how to request further information if the user does not provide everything that is required and so on.

Question: Think of some issues concerned with the operational aspects of the physical design of a ticket machine.

Comment: One aspect is the order in which people specify the destination and type of ticket and pay for the ticket. Another aspect would concern what people do if they have made a mistake, or want to buy several tickets.

Question: Assuming that the ticket machine requests (i) "specify destination", (ii) 'specify ticket type' and (iii) 'make payment' in that order, what states can the machine be in?

Comment: Probably exactly the three states numbered (i), (ii) and (iii) above.

Representational Aspects

In addition to specifying the operational aspects, the designer needs to design what the system will look like – the representational aspects of design. Details of exactly how to display information, such as where to position items on the screen, how to use colour and how to label items needs to be considered. The design of buttons, screen displays and so on should make it obvious that certain actions such as pressing, clicking, touching and so on are possible.

1.2.4 Function Allocation

Moving from the conceptual to the physical level of design requires the designer to decide who or what is going to undertake particular functions. This is the process of task, or function allocation. It is important to remember that designers create tasks for users by allocating some of the conceptual functions to people, and others to the computer. The tasks which people have to do as a result of a design should match the tasks that users consider to be tasks as much as possible. Another important aspect of function allocation is to take account of the cognitive processing and emotional demands of any particular design. Such things as how much the user will have to remember, how stressed might people get if things go wrong or whether people have to figure out complex problems in using the system all need to be taken into consideration.

1.2.5 Summary

User interface design is a complicated business which draws on many areas such as aesthetics, psychology and software engineering. User interface designers need to make decisions about what the interface will show, how it will show it, what people have to do and have to remember and about how they will do things. The user interface has to communicate both with the users and with the underlying software system.

However, like all design activities, user interface design is concerned with understanding and specifying the requirements, with producing various representations of the final system and with testing those representations with the system users. Design will include conceptual design, physical design and the allocation of functions.

1.3 Models in Design

As we mentioned above, during the design of any artefact, the designer will make use of models. A model is a representation of something constructed and used for a particular purpose. A good model is accurate enough to reflect the features of the system being modeled, but simple enough to avoid confusion. A good model adopts a style of presentation and uses a medium which is suitable for its purpose. In software engineering many models are paper-based, but some might use computer animations or simulations. In the previous section there were examples of different media being used for models: plastic models, the use of pictures and the use of video. Choosing and constructing appropriate models is a difficult but vital part of the designer's job. The designer must always bear in mind how the model is to be used, who is going to use it and must choose a modeling technique appropriate to the required level of abstraction and intended recipient.

Models are devices for understanding, communicating, testing or predicting some aspects of some system. They provide an abstract representation of a domain of interest by hiding some details so that the important aspects stand out. Models provide a certain perspective on the domain by employing abstraction mechanisms that are reflected in the content and the structure of the concepts employed by the model.

The analytic, explanatory and communicative power of a model arises from the structure, operations and constraints which that model is able to capture. A model must also have suitable physical characteristics: the notation employed by the model, the medium used and its overall usability for the purpose at hand and the intended recipient.

Question: Think about the car designer example above. Which models in the example are being used to explore the problem? Which are being used to communicate ideas?

Comment: The initial 'doodles' are used for the purpose of exploring the problem. The blue-prints and scale model are used for communication.

Question: Why does the designer need two different types of model to communicate ideas?

Comment: Because it would be inappropriate to show blue-prints to get a reaction from marketing since the blue-prints do not convey the shape of the car well. The model maker needs a clear, formal specification in the form of a blue-print.

1.3.1 Aggregation and Classification

The definition of a model given above is that it is an abstract representation of something which suppresses unnecessary detail. This suppression of unnecessary detail can be achieved in two ways. First, a model can group related things together and represent just the aggregate object, thus suppressing details. Another technique is to represent a whole class of objects as a single object, thus suppressing details of the individual objects. The first of these techniques is known as aggregation and the second as classification. Together they produce abstractions.

Aggregation is the process of collecting together a number of characteristics of something and treating it as a single thing. For example, when I talk about my car, I do not need to explain that it has wheels, a body, an engine and so on. By 'car' I mean the aggregate of all these various properties. A dialogue box on a computer is the aggregate of all the buttons, boxes, sliders and scroll bars that make up the dialogue box.

Question: What sort of aggregation would I mean if I use the word 'house'?

Comment: By 'house' I mean the aggregate of the properties doors, windows, rooms and so on.

Classification is the process of recognizing that various objects share certain characteristics and can therefore be treated as a single thing. For example, I might classify cars, lorries, buses and tractors as vehicles. I might classify houses, libraries, factories and barns as buildings. We are able to classify things in this way because we recognize that they have certain shared characteristics (restricting the characteristics to those things which are of interest for the purpose at hand). For example, I am able to classify houses and barns as buildings because I am not considering the use of the building as part of the classification scheme.

Question: What sort of assumptions am I making if I classify all the windows that pop up on your computer screen as 'Windows'?

Comment: I am not distinguishing between windows with scroll bars and those without. I am not distinguishing between fixed and movable windows.

Classification of objects means that we can represent and discuss a complex situation in simpler terms. From the examples above it should be apparent that there are many levels of classification. As we deal with the more abstract concepts, we make generalizations about things and as we move towards the more concrete objects we make specializations. So "car" is a generalization of Fords, Nissans, Vauxhalls and so on. Ford is a specialization of car. Ford Mondeo is a further specialization of Ford and the Ford Mondeo parked outside my house is a specialization of Ford Mondeo. Moving in the opposite direction – towards the more abstract classification – vehicle is a generalization of car.

Selecting appropriate classes or categories and identifying the defining properties which determine whether or not something belongs to a class is an area which has been studied by philosophers over many years. One of the most famous examples is Wittgenstein's (1953) discussion of the class of games – see if you can find the defining properties which allow us to treat football, chess, card games, board games, ring-a-ring-a-roses as a single class: games. You will find many overlapping properties, but not a single property which connects them all. More recently George Lakoff has discussed classification in his book *Women, Fire and Dangerous Things* (1987) and highlighted how different people classify things in different ways. Indeed the title of his book is chosen because these seemingly diverse things are classified as belonging to the same category by the Australian aboriginal language, Dyirbal.

The importance of this philosophy is that user interface developers need to think very hard about how things are to be classified – what are the attributes of the things which are going to be used as the basis of deciding whether one thing is in the same class as another? Will the designer's ideas about how things are classified be the same as the users ideas? Designers also have to think about how the properties of things are going to be grouped together – what is the basis for the aggregation? Clearly these aspects are related and together determine the abstractions which will be appropriate for a particular situation.

✳ **Example** Classification is a central part of user interface development. Consider the problem of menu design and where the designer should put particular functions. One word processor that I use has eleven menu headers visible – File, Edit, View, Insert, Format, Font, Tools, Table, Window, Work, Help. Where would you expect to find the Sort command? Another word processor has eight menu headers – File, Edit, Format, View, Special, Graphics, Table, Help. Where would you expect to find the Sort command in this system? The answer is that there is no Sort command in the second system (as far as I can tell). In the first system Sort is under the Table menu, even though it applies to paragraphs and other objects in addition to tables! I would expect Sort to be classified as a 'Tool' or to appear as one of the Edit or Format commands. It is also interesting to notice the different names that the designers have used for the menu headers.

1.3.2 Structure and Function

In addition to using abstraction, models may focus on different aspects of the artefact being modeled. The modeler can look at the structure of the artefact, the functioning of the artefact or at the way the artefact changes when things happen to it.

A structural view of some artefact or system focuses on the main entities or objects which are in the system and how those objects are related. For example, the structural view of a car would describe a car in terms of the main components – engine, gearbox, drive shaft, brakes and so on.

A functional view focuses on how some substance, or some object moves through the system. In the example of a car, we could look at how fuel flows though from the fuel tank to the engine, how it transformed into exhaust gases and flows out through the exhaust system. Another functional view might focus on the braking system and the flow of hydraulic fluids.

The third view of a system focuses on the dynamics of the system, how it moves or changes from one state to another. This view is concerned with how the structure and functioning of the artefact are related and the behaviour which results. Thus, a car has an initial state of 'engine off'. Following an event of 'ignition' the petrol flows through the engine, is mixed with air and ignited which puts the car in the state of 'running'. Following an event of 'put in gear' various functions occur and when the 'release brake' event happens then the car will be 'moving'.

The three views of systems described above are complementary and interrelated. Notice how the different views interact. Certain functions can only occur when the system is in certain states and certain functions change the state of the system or of certain objects in the system. The appropriate view and the appropriate level of abstraction at which to describe a system will depend on the purpose of the modeler. So looking at a system from one point of view can help provide a perspective on another view.

1.3.3 Three Views of User Interfaces

In order to understand and design user interfaces we will need to consider these three views – the structural, the functional and the dynamic. We will also have to think about the whole human-computer system as a single thing. This is because we want to think about both what the artefact does and what the user of the artefact does. Moreover, the human-computer system may include lots of information artefacts and lots of people, so we want to be able to think about how all these people and information artefacts work together as a whole system.

The three views of people interacting with computers appear in a whole host of guises in books on human-computer interaction and user interface development. Some authors prefer one sort of model, others prefer another sort and others something different. To reiterate the point above, the central thing about a model is that it uses constructs and notations that are suitable for the purpose to which the model is being put.

Different models can capture more or less information about artefacts and the ways in which they are used. Some models are based on a psychological theory of how people use devices, others are based on theories derived from sociology and others from more pragmatic requirements of building robust and re-usable software systems. We return to a discussion of ERMIA and other specific models in Chapter 12.

1.4 User Interface Development: The Functional View

In HCI there are lots of aspects of the functioning of the human-computer system that we can model. We might look at how data flows between processes, at the data which is necessary for processing to occur and at who or what has to supply that data. Dataflow diagrams (DFDs) are useful models here (Benyon, 1997). We can build models of the movement of physical objects such as documents and focus on the control flow (i.e. the sequencing of actions) of particular implementations. We can represent the different mouse clicks, dragging and highlighting that goes on in a graphical user interface, or we might model the physical actions that people have to undertake and the things that they have to think about, or remember.

1.4.1 Tasks

In HCI research and practice, task models have been popular for many years. Task models concentrate on the mental and physical actions which users and systems perform given a particular design. Although they can be used in a more abstract way, to describe generic tasks in a domain, task models tend to be quite detailed. An example of the GOMS task model is discussed in Section 12.1.1. Other methods such as MUSE (Lim and Long, 1994) and STUDIO (Browne, 1994) use a graphical representation of tasks and provide detailed descriptions of task-based approaches to user interface development.

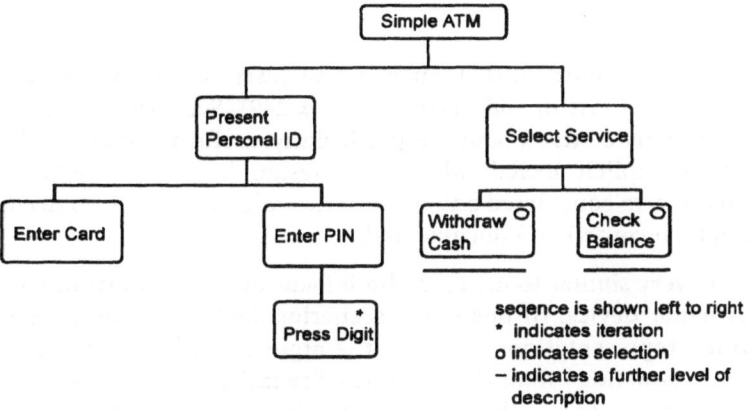

Fig 1.1 A task model of a 'Simple ATM'.

Figure 1.1 shows a MUSE task model of a 'Simple ATM' (Automatic Teller Machine). It consists of two sub-tasks which are completed in sequence: Present Personal ID and Select Service. Present Personal ID consists of two sub-tasks, Enter Card and Enter PIN, and in its turn Enter PIN consists of a number of iterations of the Press Digit action. Select Service consists of either Withdraw Cash or Check Balance. Each of these is further redescribed (indicated by the line, but not shown in this example).

1.4.2 Use Cases

Another popular way of modeling the functioning of a human-computer system is to describe the system in terms of 'use cases'. Use cases came out of developments in object-oriented analysis and design (OOAD), particularly through the work of Jacobson (Jacobson *et al.*, 1993) and now form a central part of the UML approach to systems development. Jacobson (1995) describes how use cases should present a 'black box' view of the system. A use case model defines the system's behaviour and is developed alongside, and orthogonal to, an object model (i.e. a structural model, see Section 1.6). Jacobson employs a graphical representation showing the interaction between entities outside the system ('actors') and the use cases which are inside the system. When an actor uses the system, the system performs a use case and hence the use cases describe the complete functionality of the system. Use cases each have a detailed description (e.g. see Fig 1.2) and can be used throughout the development process so that a high level case can be traced through the system to the code that implements it.

A greeting message is waiting on the display:
The customer inserts his or her card into the ATM.
The ATM reads the code from the magnetic tape on the card and checks if it is acceptable.
If the card is acceptable, the ATM asks the customer for his or her PIN code.
Waiting for PIN code:
The customer enters his or her PIN code.
If the PIN code is correct, the ATM asks the customer to select a type of transaction.
.... and so on...

Fig 1.2 A use case of a 'Simple ATM' (from Jacobson, 1995).

1.4.3 Scenarios

Scenarios are also popular in HCI. They seek to describe 'an envisioned task from a user's perspective' (Rosson and Carroll, 1995, p. 249). Scenarios make user interactions with systems concrete and are particularly useful for making the rationale behind designs explicit. Exactly why certain design decisions have been taken, the options which were considered and the criteria which were used to decide between options can be recorded and documented.

Scenarios are very similar to use cases; both focus on user actions when interacting with a particular device. In this sense, scenarios deliberately use concrete, rather than abstract, representations because, it is argued, people are better at working with concrete situations than abstract ones. Scenarios can use a variety of media such as text, pictures (when they become 'storyboards'), animation and so on.

1.4.4 Summary

There can be no doubt that it is very important for user interface designers to develop scenarios, use cases and/or task models of systems as they can highlight difficulties in particular designs which may otherwise be missed. They also enable the designer to focus on the cognitive demands that a design makes on its users and methods of evaluation of systems such as the cognitive walk-through method (Lewis *et al.*, 1990) require detailed scenarios before they can be used.

Functional models contribute to both the conceptual and physical aspects of user interface design. However, the more abstract models such as dataflow diagrams are more appropriate for conceptual design as they highlight the movement of data and suppress details of physical designs. Models such as scenarios and use cases emphasize concrete situations and are more suitable for looking at operational aspects of physical design.

1.5 Models of Dynamics

When something happens in a (human-computer) system, it is likely that the event will cause other things to happen. For example, a bank machine (an ATM) sits quietly until someone inserts a card into it, a menu in a graphical user interface remains closed up until a user moves the cursor over it and clicks a mouse button, an alarm clock begins to ring when the time the alarm is set to is reached.

All these things may be considered as 'events'; something that happens at a point in time. When an event occurs and if the system, or the part of the system which is capable of detecting the event, is in an appropriate state, some processing or functioning takes place. For example, putting the car in gear is an event, but it will not result in the car changing its state to 'moving' unless the car is already in the state of 'running'. The bank machine will have to have completed the previous transaction in order to detect the 'insert card' event.

The model of system dynamics looks at the system from the perspective of the events that can occur, the states that the parts of the system can be in and how the

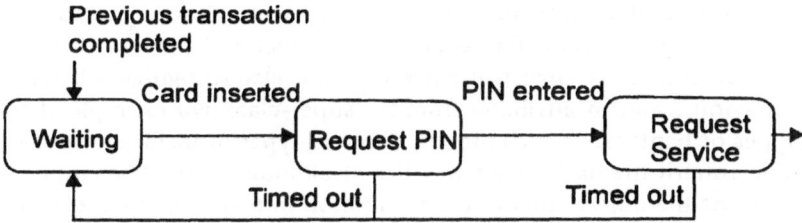

Fig 1.3 A statechart for the 'Simple ATM'.

event causes the system to move from one state to another. The most common way of representing dynamics, and the one preferred in UML is the state transition network, or a hierarchical version, the *statechart*. A statechart is a diagrammatic representation of the states of the system and the events that move the system from one state to another (see the example in Fig 1.3). Usually models of dynamics are quite detailed (like task models) but some methods of systems development do use more abstract representations just showing the major changes that occur to things; for example, the entity-life history used in structured methods of systems development.

Drawing detailed statecharts of user interfaces can be useful as they can often highlight important parts of the design that might otherwise get missed. For example, the designer may discover that the user can, in fact, engage in some interaction when the system is in a state that should not allow it. Various versions of state diagrams exist, which focus on different aspects of the events, states and transitions. From our perspective it is interesting to compare the models of dynamics with the models of function and to note the different focus provided by each.

Models of dynamics are particularly useful for evaluating and specifying the operational aspects of a physical design. As with the other models described here, it depends on the purpose of the modeler and on the nature of the system as to how important and useful the model might be.

1.6 Models of Structure

In structural models, the perspective taken is on the objects or entities that exist in the system and on the ways in which they are related. The two main traditions of structural models in software development are entity-based approaches and object-oriented approaches. Although objects are often presented as very different concepts from entities, there are more similarities than there are differences.

Both objects and entities are viewed 'from the outside' and users need not be concerned about how they are implemented. Both objects and entities have relation-ships with the other objects or entities in the system.

Objects differ from entities in that they can send and receive messages; they 'encapsulate' the structure and processing which enables them to deal with those messages. In entity-relationship approaches the structure of the thing (the entity) and the functions that are relevant to it are kept separate. Objects include, as part of their definition, the functions that apply to the object and the way that the object responds to the functions. Object-oriented methods also recognize sub-types which inherit behaviours and/or attributes from the super-class. For example, if there are various types of bank card which provide different types of facilities, these different types would inherit the basic characteristics of all bank cards. The emphasis is on the existence of the object and on its presentation in terms of the messages which it can send or receive rather than on the internal view of the structure.

UML is the best known of the object-oriented methods. It uses a notation which is very similar to an entity-relationship diagram. As with entity-relationship diagrams, boxes represent objects and lines show the relationships between objects. There are other parts of the notation which represent specific object-oriented features. An object model in UML style is shown in Figure 1.4. The objects of interest in the application – person, card, account and ATM – are shown as objects with the major messages which they can send and receive shown. The internal description of the objects (the structure of the objects in terms of the attributes which they have and the processing which the objects can perform) would be shown in separate object description tables.

Structural models are necessary at both the conceptual and physical levels of user interface design. They provide a very different perspective than the functional and dynamic models.

1.7 The Role of ERMIA in User Interface Development

ERMIA is a method of modeling structure. In ERMIA we have chosen to model information artefacts in terms of entities rather than objects because entity-relationship modeling offers a few benefits which object-oriented methods do not possess (principally the ideas of conceptual maps and connection traps, see

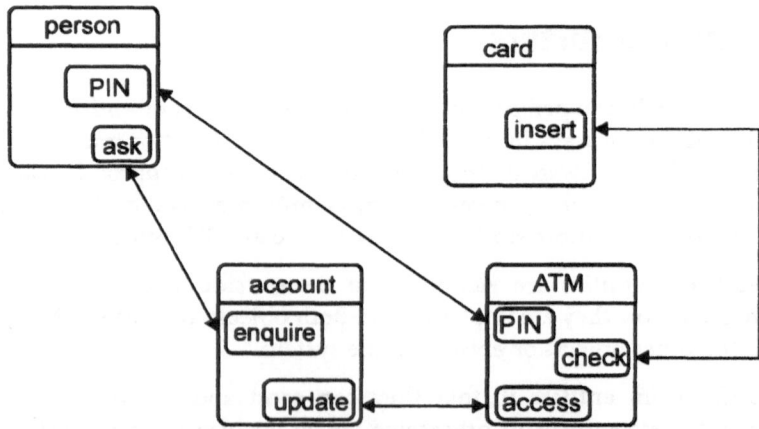

Fig 1.4 An object model for the 'Simple ATM'.

Chapter 7). ERMIA can safely be used as part of an object-oriented approach to software engineering with the entities simply becoming objects when the developer is ready to specify the system in detail.

ERMIA models things in a human-computer system by describing the entities or objects in the system in terms of the values of the characteristics (or attributes) which they have. ERMIA can show different states by showing different values of attributes. For example, an icon in a graphical user interface has the characteristic that it remains not highlighted until someone clicks on it when it changes state (or changes its characteristic of 'highlightedness') to 'highlighted'. Once it is in this state the user can do other things to it such as drag it across the screen or apply various functions to it, such as "open".

Statecharts can be used alongside ERMIA models if the designer wants to focus on the events and the effects that they have on entities. Scenarios, task models and use cases can be used with ERMIA to 'walk through' particular designs to see how much people have to remember and how many things they will have to search through in order to find out some information (see Chapter 5).

As you will see during the rest of this book, ERMIA helps you think about issues of user interface design. We think that the concepts which ERMIA uses, the operations that it allows and the constraints which it can capture make ERMIA particularly suitable as a modeling method for user interface development. The physical characteristics of the notation contribute to its usability as a modeling technique. ERMIA is not going to remove the challenges of user interface design. But it does provide a language in which user interface designers, software engineers and users can focus their discussions on the central issues of user interface development.

Summary

- *User interface development, like any design process, involves the development of various abstractions, or models, of the system.*
- *Models use combinations of aggregation and classification to simplify a complex system.*
- *Designers may choose models that focus on the structure of the system, the functioning of the system or on the dynamics of the system.*
- *Functional models in user interface development include task models, use cases and scenarios.*
- *Models of dynamics focus on how the system changes state. Statecharts are the most common model of dynamics.*
- *Models of structure focus on the objects, or entities that exist in the system and on the relationships between them.*
- *ERMIA can be used with other models to focus attention on user interface concerns.*

2. An Introduction to ERMIA

Aims and Objectives

Information artefacts need to be carefully designed so that they reveal the information which their users require. This chapter provides an introduction to what ERMIA can do to help designers and choosers of information artefacts.

After reading this chapter you should be able to:

- understand the uses of the ERMIA technique in evaluating devices
- understand that ERMIA provides a high-level, structural description of information artefacts
- define and recognize information artefacts
- understand the idea of a viewport
- distinguish between conceptual and perceptual views
- understand that there can be many different viewports onto an underlying structure.

2.1 Evaluating Designs and Devices

An information artefact is something like a calculator, a word-processor, or a spread-sheet – that is, something in which information is presented and stored or manipulated.[1] It can also be a timetable, a blue-print, or a dictionary. Even though those are paper-based objects rather than interactive devices, they store and present information. Automatic teller machines (cash dispensers), video recorders, music scores, programming languages, pages on the World Wide Web are other examples – information artefacts are diverse and multifarious.

These different objects need to be evaluated, either because their designers are trying to design good ones or because users want to choose the most suitable for their needs. There are many different viewpoints from which they can be evaluated. Aesthetically, we might want our calculator to look stylish; ergonomically, we might want it to be comfortable to hold and easy to read. The electronics engineer wants to make the hardware reliable, cheap and rugged. The software engineer tries to

---

[1]Strictly speaking it is data that is stored and manipulated, data that may become information when it is interpreted by some person (or agent). We choose to ignore this distinction in this text; a discussion about data and information can be found in Benyon (1997, p. 3-7).

make the internal programming reliable, functionally correct and – with an eye to future maintenance or upgrading – architecturally simple. Lastly, we come to the specialist in 'human-computer interaction' (HCI). HCI is concerned with the activities that people undertake using devices. What is a device used for? Can people do what they want to do easily, with a given design? Do they have to remember weird things, like which button was pressed first, or what each of the displays means; or is everything plain, easy to understand, enjoyable and easy to use?

There are many different techniques in HCI, all making their own distinctive contribution to the evaluation of alternative designs. ERMIA – 'Entity-Relationship Modeling of Information Artefacts' – is one technique which is particularly useful for some aspects of user interface development.

ERMIA has a particular advantage in that it is quite quick to do. Some of the other techniques, like GOMS (Goals, Operators, Methods and Selection rules, discussed in more detail in Chapter 12), can make very detailed predictions, but they are too expensive for routine use. Designers are usually not HCI specialists; they need a 'broad-brush' technique, something that is effective but quick and easy. Prospective users, choosing one system from a host of competitors, have even less HCI knowledge as a rule and even less time to spend on evaluating alternatives.

Unlike many of the HCI techniques, ERMIA can readily be applied to paper-based objects, such as design sketches, formal notations or timetables. Another advantage of ERMIA is that it can be used before the software is actually written, just working with the proposed design. This is good because designers need to make decisions as early as possible.

What ERMIA provides is a simplified model, a skeleton, of the data structure inherent in an application and the way that that structure is presented. Different views onto the structure can be examined and different user tasks can then be assessed for the number of steps and number of items to be remembered. Each task can be assessed very quickly, so the designer or analyst can check out quite a few different tasks.

Question: Identify four advantages which ERMIA has over other HCI design and evaluation techniques.

Comment: It is quick and relatively easy to do. It can be applied to non-interactive artefacts and to interactive devices.

2.2 ERMIA in a Nutshell

ERMIA uses an adaptation of entity-relationship modeling (about which we shall have much more to say) to describe structures. In interactive systems, such as simple drawing programs (Fig 2.1) there are two kinds of structure. First, the drawing itself, or whatever is being developed has a structure. In the example we have chosen, that structure is very simple – the drawing just consists of graphic objects.

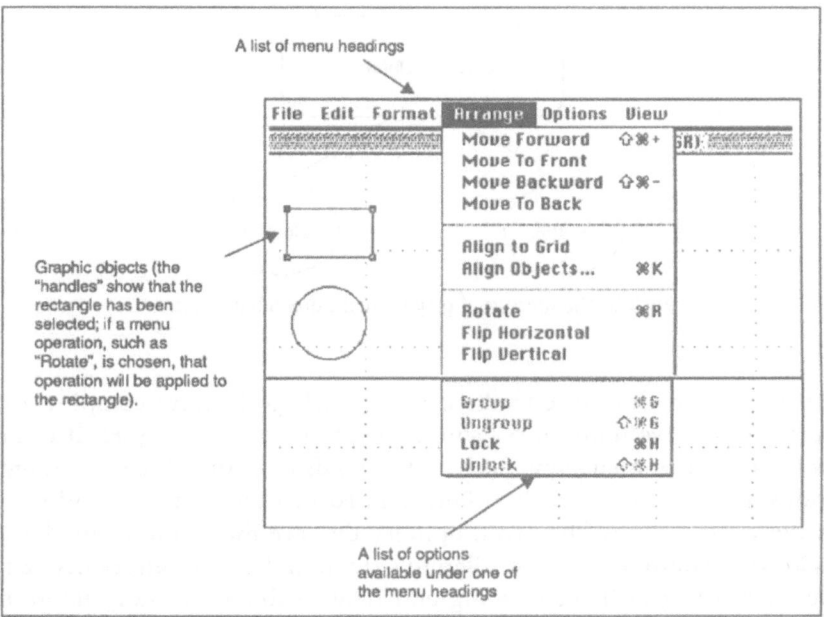

Fig 2.1 A simple drawing program, showing the document being created (a drawing, currently consisting of a rectangle and a circle) and the interface to the application.

Secondly, there is a user interface, or *viewport*, onto that structure. In Figure 2.1 the user interface is that provided by an Apple Macintosh computer. It consists of a display of the drawing, menu headers, a pull-down menu and so on.

In ERMIA, we would say that drawings have a structure comprising one kind of *entity*, called Graphic Object,[2] which has two *attributes*. One attribute is its shape, the other is whether it has been selected or not. In Figure 2.1 the rectangle has been selected but the circle has not been.

As a foretaste of ERMIA's graphical notation, Figure 2.2 shows the ERMIA model (or just 'ERMIA') describing this aspect of the drawing package. The entity is shown as a round cornered rectangle (also called a 'soft box' or 'roundtangle') and the attributes as ovals. Notice that although the drawing itself (Fig 2.1) contains two graphic objects, a rectangle and a circle, the model only contains one kind of entity, the generalized Graphic Object entity. The model is a representation of all the different *kinds* of possible things and how they are related; it is not a list of the *particular* things that turn up on an individual drawing.

Question: Does ERMIA represent all the objects which appear on a display?

Comment: No. ERMIA represents the different kinds of object. Each kind, or type of object appears only once on an ERMIA diagram.

---

[2]Names of entities have capitalized initial letters.

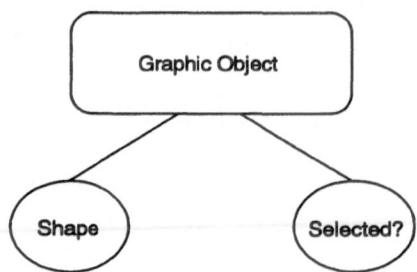

Fig 2.2 The structure of graphics in the drawing package.

The structure of the interface to the drawing package is more complex. In later chapters we shall have more to say about menus and their structure. It is enough for now to notice that menu systems have two kinds of entity. One kind of entity is the various menu headings, such as File, Edit, Format and Arrange, and the other kind is the various items, the menu options, that are found under the headings, such as Move Forward, Rotate and Align to Grid. Both kinds of entity have a name; we have chosen to call them Heading and Item in this case. More interestingly, there is a *relationship* between the two kinds of entity. Can we imagine a menu item without a menu heading? No, because there would be no way to get at it. So we conclude that every Item must be associated with a Heading. On the other hand, we *can* imagine a menu which contained no items: not much use, but not impossible, especially while the software is being developed.

It is also important to note that each menu heading can list many items, while each item is normally only found under one heading – in other words, the relationship of Heading to Item is one-to-many (written 1:m).

Question: Think about menu structures for a moment. Is it strictly true that an item can be found under just one heading?

Comment: No. As it happens, there is nothing to prevent the same menu item being listed under more than one heading. So an item like 'Format' might be found under a Text heading and also under the File heading.

So, ERMIA has already revealed something which you may not have thought about before; there is a possible weakness in the design of the Apple Macintosh interface style. The true relationship between Heading and Item is many-to-many, or m:m as it is written. The difference between the two structures is small but it may be profound. Probably at the time of designing the interface it was overlooked. Drawing ERMIA maps forces the designer to think about relationships and to be explicit.

An ERMIA model for the 1:m version of the relationship between Heading and Item is shown in Figure 2.3.

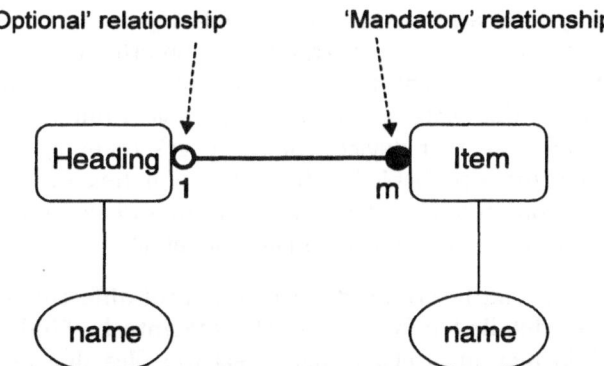

Fig 2.3 ERMIA of a menu system. The relationship between Heading and Item is 1:m (that is, each heading can refer to many items, but an item can only be associated with one heading). For items, the relationship is mandatory (that is, every item must have a heading), but a heading can exist with no associated items.

2.3 Information Artefacts

An *information artefact* is a combination of a viewport and a conceptual structure that provides information about something else. Looking at an object or a device as an information artefact means looking at it from the point of view of the information that it conveys – at what information it stores, at what information may be given to it and what information may be read from it – and at how effective it is at conveying that information or how easy it is to access the information. Many different kinds of objects can be looked at in this way, from central heating systems to pieces of paper with messages scribbled on them. More conventional examples would be spreadsheets, databases, automated bank tellers and timetables. There are objects that would be hard to view as information artefacts since they do not store or display information – for example, a blank sheet of note paper.

Question: Are there any situations in which a blank sheet of paper might be an information artefact?

Comment: One possible situation is to send a blank sheet of paper as an agreed signal, perhaps between spies.

Thinking about information artefacts means concentrating on particular aspects of the object or device. You have to focus on what information is provided by the artefact and how that information is presented.

✽ **Example** A central heating system contains a complex arrangement of physical elements, including a boiler, pipework, radiators, a pump, a pressure gauge, a timer and so on. This system might have several associated information artefacts. There are paper artefacts, such as diagrams of the boiler components and their connections, flowcharts for diagnosing faults in the system, and instruction booklets for the user. If there is an electronic timer, the LCD screen is an information artefact that displays the internal state of the current settings. Different artefacts concentrate on different parts of the system, and they may reveal different information about the same object or device. For the user's manual, the important elements would most probably be the on/off switches, the timer and the thermostat. The pressure gauge is less important and elements such as the pump do not figure in this information artefact at all.

Information artefacts may be arranged in a hierarchy of different *viewports*, each of which gives more detailed information. The Macintosh 'Finder' or Microsoft 'Windows' are information artefacts that reveal the files that are stored on the computer and the functions that the computer can perform. Each function that 'Finder' reveals will typically have another information artefact which reveals information about how to use that function. For example, the existence of a calculator function is revealed by a menu item or icon labelled 'Calculator' (see Fig 2.4) The calculator display in turn reveals more information about the calculator's functions by using a layout which looks very like the layout of a 'traditional' hand-held calculator, and which includes icons for specific functions such as '+', '−', '*' etc. These specific functions are not explained any further by information artefacts; instead the user is expected to know that (for example) '*' means 'multiply', and the user is expected to understand the effects of the multiply function without any further help.

When we consider an information artefact, we need to distinguish between two levels of description. We need to consider both the information that the artefact presents to us and the way in which the information is presented. More formally, we need a *conceptual description* (or conceptual model) of the information in the artefact and a description of the *perceptual display* (or perceptual model) of that artefact. For example, we could have a conceptual model of a clock as a device which represents time in hours and minutes. This conceptual model could have a variety of perceptual displays, such as an analog clock face, a digital clock face, or a speaking clock. Different perceptual displays (different viewports) enable different tasks to be performed more or less easily.

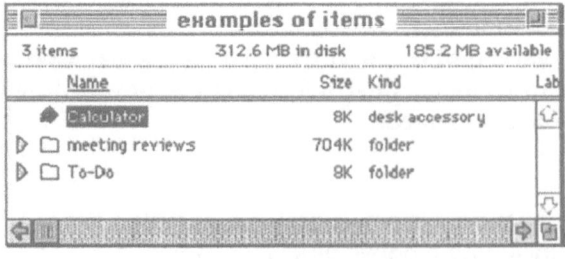

Fig 2.4 Hierarchical viewports onto information structures: the Macintosh Finder reveals the calculator icon; launching the calculator reveals another interface.

An information artefact abstracts certain aspects of an object or device and then employs some perceptual device to reveal that abstraction to the user. In a well-designed information artefact, the abstraction which is chosen highlights the important features of the object or device. Ideally, the abstraction should also be closely related to concepts that the user already knows about, and the perceptual device used to reveal the conceptualization should capitalize on the user's existing knowledge. For example, the Macintosh 'Calculator' offers similar operations, and uses a similar layout, to that of a familiar pocket calculator.

✳ Example The telephone network can be viewed in terms of subscribers who have a name, address, exchange and telephone number. The viewport onto this is usually provided by a telephone book which lists the relevant information. The telephone book presents the data in alphabetical order of subscriber name which affects the usability of this view – so searching for a particular number, not knowing the subscriber's name, becomes a nearly impossible task. Other viewports onto this structure (e.g. the 'Directory Enquiries' or the 'Call Tracing' viewport) enable other goals to be achieved.

An information artefact thus consists of:

- a conceptualization of objects in the experienced world which has the purpose of revealing some information about the underlying objects to some users (and possibly allowing changes to be made);
- a viewport which provides access to that conceptualization and which employs a method of presentation from which the user may derive information (and if necessary provides means for making changes).

As we mentioned earlier there may be several levels of information artefact each revealing some information about the artefact 'below'. Figure 2.5 illustrates the different levels of viewport provided by the calculator information artefact (see Fig 2.4). We conceptualize a number of functions provided by the computer as the calculator functions. A calculator icon provides a viewport onto this conceptual structure by revealing the existence of these functions. The calculator display provides further information – another viewport – about the functions available. Individual functions are revealed by the calculator buttons which provide a third level of viewport.

Just as there may be several levels of viewport onto the same underlying structure, so there may be different viewports at the same level (see Fig 2.6). The same information can be presented in different ways; some methods of presentation may hide certain information altogether, or they may make it quicker and easier to discover some kinds of information than others.

✳ Example A train timetable could be presented on paper (Fig 2.7) or as a talking timetable. The different methods of presentation may look

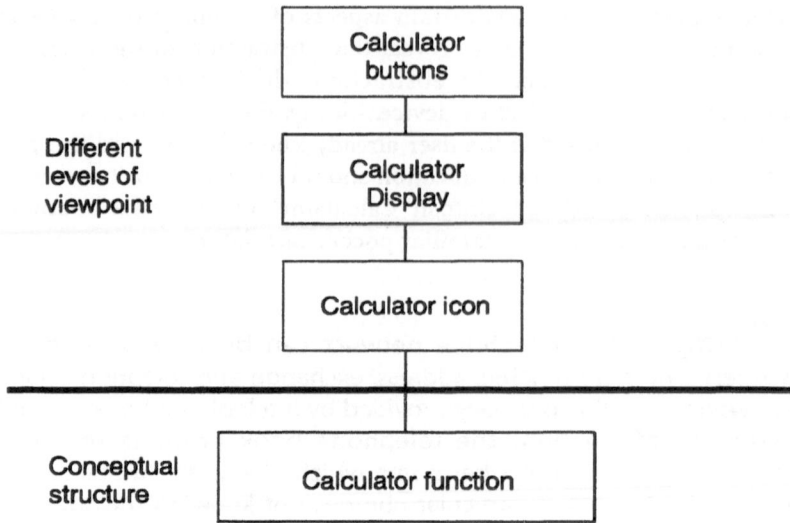

Fig 2.5 Illustrating a hierarchy of viewports for a calculator information artefact.

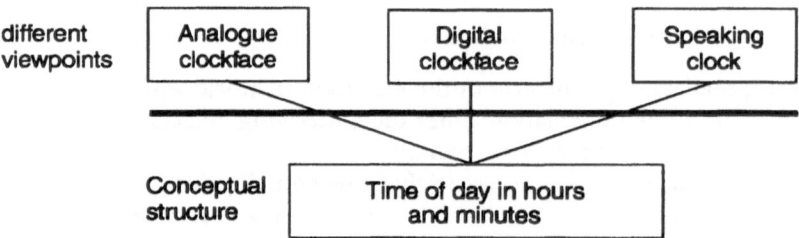

Fig 2.6 Illustrating different viewports at the same level of abstraction.

very different, but since the underlying structure of the information is the same many aspects of the different information displays will also be the same.

London	8.25	9.55	11.05
Welwyn Garden City	8.55	10.25	11.35
Stevenage	9.15	10.45	11.55

Fig 2.7 Train timetable.

A talking timetable typically gives only a summary of the departure time from one major station and the arrival time at the main destination (i.e. it hides some information), whereas a paper timetable usually gives times at the intermediate stops. With a talking timetable it can take substantially longer to find out when the evening trains leave, since the times are usually read in sequence – i.e. it is harder to discover some kinds of information.

2.4 The Uses of ERMIA

A display of information is very seldom random. Usually it has some structure. One common structure for many information displays consists of several different types of item, so that each type of item occurs several times in the display. For example, a railway timetable contains departure times and stations, and a timetable usually contains many departure times and many stations. It is important (though not always easy) to distinguish between the structure of information and its content. For example, if you look at just one page of a train timetable you can probably invent other fragments which have the same structure – a list of station names, associated with a time – even without knowing what the content should be. At any rate, when we describe a structure, we wish to do so without encumbering ourselves with details of its content. So the problem is to describe an information artefact without mentioning every instance of similar objects (such as names or numbers) and without including unwanted detail about physical appearance (but to be able to include it if thought desirable).

ERMIAs describe the underlying structure of the information that the information artefact can present. They also describe the structure of a particular information artefact, the way in which that artefact presents information to the user. ERMIAs enable a designer or analyst to describe and compare different presentations of the same underlying information, and to explore their consequences in terms of how easy it is to find particular kinds of information.

ERMIAs can describe how different users think about the same structure. So ERMIAs can be used to compare, for example what the designer thinks the structure is and what a typical user thinks the structure is (the so-called 'designer's model' and the 'user's model', see Section 4.6). In a similar fashion ERMIA can provide a comparison between different users' models (Section 8.4) and so be used to highlight misconceptions which some people have.

Because ERMIA uses the same notation to represent the conceptual structure and the perceptual structure, these can be combined on a single diagram. This can be useful for showing where various pieces of knowledge are in a whole work system.[3] For example, when using a calculator the user has to know that '*' means multiply; the information artefact does not supply that knowledge. In Section 4.5 we provide an example of this use of ERMIA.

Question: What information does the user have to know in order to use the timetable information artefact (Fig 2.7)?

Comment: There are many things, of course, such as which station in London the train leaves from. One thing which the user has to know about the perceptual display is that the rows of the

---

[3] A work system is all the people, devices and information artefacts that constitute some coherent domain of activity. For instance, the domain of withdrawing cash from an ATM (cash dispenser) includes a person, a bank card, the buttons on the ATM, the ATM display and the link to the central computer.

timetable are ordered in the same sequence as the train journey. Although you may think that is obvious, remember when you were last using an information artefact in a foreign country and how 'obvious' things were to the local population which were completely unknown to you!

ERMIA's main role in design is to analyze an existing design or a design idea. ERMIAs help a designer to identify and describe the underlying structures that are common to many different devices, and to distinguish the underlying structure from the way that the structure is presented. They help the designer to pre-empt the problems which can occur when people interact with devices.

To summarize, the advantages of using ERMIA are:

- the same notation can model both interactive devices (such as telephones, spreadsheets and cash dispensers) and static displays (such as timetables);
- the same notation can model both the underlying structure of the information required and the structure of the presentation itself;
- the notation can model different perceptions of the same structure – especially the designer's view and the user's view (or the views of different users);
- the notation can be used to show how knowledge about a structure is distributed between different artefacts and the user of those artefacts;
- an ERMIA can be used to understand what information may be read easily from a given display and what information may be difficult to find;
- the notation contains only a small number of terms, yet it still provides a clear analysis that is both visual and formal;
- it helps the designer to think precisely about the connections between the structure of a display and the purposes for which the display will be used.

ERMIA is not so good at representing processes, change, and in general anything involving transactions over time. Chapter 12 discusses ERMIA in relation to some other techniques.

Summary

- *Entity-Relationship Modeling of Information Artefacts (ERMIA) is a technique aimed at the designers and choosers of information artefacts.*
- *An information artefact is anything which provides information about something else.*
- *An information artefact consists of a conceptualization of the device and a viewport which provides a presentation of the information content.*
- *In ERMIA we develop models of both the underlying information (a conceptual model) and of the perceptual displays (perceptual models).*
- *ERMIA is primarily an evaluation technique, though one that can be used very early in the design process.*
- *ERMIA deals with the kinds of things (as opposed to the individual things) which*

are presented by an information artefact and how that presentation relates to the underlying, conceptual constructs about which it is meant to provide information.

- *ERMIA is used to help designers and choosers of systems to reason about the effectiveness of different presentations for different people and for different purposes.*

3. *The Components of an ERMIA Model*

Aims and Objectives

The aim of this chapter is to give a concise account of the elements of ERMIA diagrams. The formalism is explained and the main concepts are illustrated and discussed.

After reading this chapter, you should be able to:

- understand the fundamental components of an ERMIA model (entities, relationships and attributes)
- understand some of the more advanced features of ERMIAs (clones, behavioural attributes and participation conditions)
- read an ERMIA model of a fairly complex information artefact
- construct an ERMIA model of a simple information artefact.

3.1 The Components

There are three fundamental components in the ERMIA modeling kit. These are entities, attributes and relationships. Entities have a set of descriptors, or properties known as attributes. Entities are described by their attributes and are linked together by the relationships which they have with one another. All these components are selected by the modeler to describe an information structure.

It is important to realize that an ERMIA model is a *subjective* representation. Different modelers may choose to focus on different aspects of an information artefact. This is not a problem; rather it is a strength. When different modelers meet to discuss their representations, the differences between the models often provide useful insights into the effectiveness of different designs. We show this in some detail in Section 9.4. It is also important to remember that developing ERMIAs allows designers and choosers to reason about information artefacts. You will not draw a 'correct' ERMIA first time. You will need to analyze and revise an ERMIA until a representation which is suitable for your purpose is obtained. Section 9.2 gives some useful 'rules of thumb' for constructing ERMIAs. In this chapter, concentrate on understanding the basic components of the ERMIA technique.

3.2 Entity

An entity can be described as 'any object of interest within the area being modeled, about which information may be collected, manipulated or stored. Entities can be people, material things, events, locations or more abstract concepts and groupings' (Veryard, 1992).

ERMIA describes the relationships between *classes of entities*, not between *individual occurrences (or 'instances') of entities*. In the railway timetable (Fig 2.7) the three stations London, Welwyn Garden City and Stevenage form an entity class that we might choose to call Station. In order to distinguish the entity class from the instances of that class, we shall use capital letters as a convention to refer to an entity class, such as Station, and lowercase letters when we mean an individual instance of that class, such as station. (Of course the name of a station, such as London or Stevenage, may have a capital letter since these are proper nouns, but the station's name should not be confused with the concept of the station itself.)

Because ERMIA is about classes of entities, nothing on an ERMIA model refers to individual members of the class; the model asserts relationships (see below) between classes, not between individuals. So the model might assert a relationship between Station and Train, but it would not say anything about which train stopped at which station. It follows, therefore, that each entity class is mentioned once and only once in an ERMIA model.

Question: What would it mean if an ERMIA model mentioned the Station entity class twice?

Comment: Each assertion about the Station class is supposed to refer to all possible stations, and each assertion is supposed to describe all the ways that Station is related to other entities; so there would be no point in mentioning Station twice.

When creating an ERMIA, it is important to choose entity classes so that the entities in the class are all similar. All the entities in a class have similar types of attributes (discussed below). All the entities in a particular class should have a similar purpose in the model (and in the artefact that the model describes). For example, all stations are places where trains start and stop, where passengers can board or alight.

It is also important to be able to distinguish which entities belong in a class and which do not. There must be some clear boundary between the entities in a particular class and the entities in other classes, and there should be no ambiguity about whether an entity belongs to a class or not. For example, if Station is to be used as an entity class there must be no ambiguity about which locations should count as a station and which should not. Although this sounds easy enough, it can be the cause of many problems. For example if there are some stations which will allow people to disembark, but will not allow people to get onto the train, should these sort of stations be considered as the same type of entity as a regular station? As we will see in Section 3.2.3 there are ways of dealing with this problem.

Ideally, it should be possible to tell the different entities in a class apart in some standard way. For instance, each station has a different name. It is a principle of good design that it should always be possible to tell individuals apart. However ERMIA describes artefacts that already exist and that may be badly designed, so within ERMIA we allow for the possibility that the individual entities in a class may be impossible to tell apart. We call these sorts of entities *clones* (see Section 3.2.3).

Entity classes are drawn as soft boxes. Each entity class is labelled with a name. Since the entity represents a class of object, the name given to an entity should usually be in the singular. For example, two of the entity classes for the railway timetable are the classes of stations and of trains. These are labelled Station and Train as illustrated in Figure 3.1.

Fig 3.1 Notation for entities.

3.2.1 Conceptual and Manifest Entities

As we discussed in Section 2.3 an information artefact consists of a conceptual structure and viewport onto that structure; there may be many viewports onto the same structure. Accordingly when we construct ERMIAs we might choose to focus on the conceptual structure, the structure of the viewport(s) or both. Entities which can be perceived – that is those that exist in a viewport – are known as *manifest* entities. Entities which make up the conceptual structure are known as *conceptual* entities. (Chapter 4 discusses the differences in detail.)

When it is important to distinguish between these, conceptual entities are represented with a dotted lined box (Fig 3.2). Manifest entities are always represented with a solid lined box. However, often it is not necessary to distinguish manifest and conceptual entities since the context of the ERMIA makes this clear.

Fig 3.2 Notation for conceptual entities (when required for clarity).

Exercise 1

Identify some entities in the interface to a simple calculator (see Fig 2.4 for an illustration).

Question: Are the entities in Figure 3.1 conceptual or manifest entities?

Comment: They are conceptual entities since they refer to the concept, or idea of stations and trains and not to anything in a viewport onto that structure.

Question: Are the entities in the solution to Exercise 1 conceptual or manifest entities?

Comment: They are manifest entities since they refer to perceivable objects on the calculator display.

3.2.2 Clones

Unlike conceptual entities, sometimes it is not possible to tell the difference between individual members of a manifest entity class (i.e. the entity occurrences). In ERMIA we have to allow *clones*, several entities of the same class co-existing, without any defined means to distinguish between them. For example, unlabelled floppy discs are not distinguishable by inspection. (Even when such a means could in principle be defined, we may not wish to model it.) Clones are a necessary characteristic of the world, but can cause confusion (as anyone who has searched for a particular file on a set of unlabelled discs can verify).

There is almost always some way to identify individual occurrences of entities – even if only by remembering its position in relation to the other occurrences ("the file you want is on the third disc"). However, if the viewport of an information artefact does not easily reveal occurrences of manifest entities then the user of that artefact has to put in a considerable amount of effort in order to locate the item that they want. The problems are exacerbated if the occurrences get muddled up so that the meagre information provided by the viewport (e.g. it is the third disc) becomes inaccurate or misleading. *Near clones* can also cause problems. The display provided by the Windows 3.1 File Manager made locating a specific occurrence of a file very difficult because the icons representing the files were so similar. Although there were perceptual differences between the entity occurrences, these were difficult to discern. (Later versions of Windows have not improved on this much). In Figure 3.3

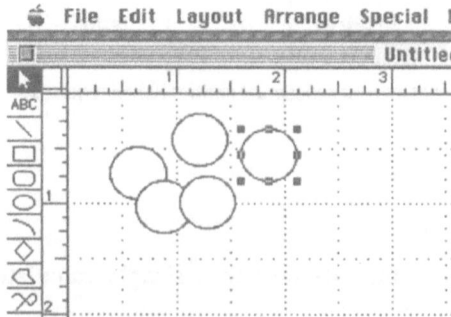

Fig 3.3 Display of circles in a window.

Fig 3.4 ERMIA of circles in a window (Fig 3.3) showing the clone notation.

there are some differences between the circles (some are filled blank and some are filled white, some are on top of others). The information display does not reveal these differences. Clones are represented in ERMIA using a filled box (see Fig 3.4).

3.2.3 Higher Level Construct: Composites and Sub-types

ERMIA allows two 'higher level' (i.e. more abstract) constructs. The first of these is useful when an ERMIA model starts to get too complex. It is then simpler to consider the relationship between entities which themselves consist of other entities and relationships. We call this a composite entity. A composite entity encapsulates a number of entities and relationships. In Figure 3.5 the modeler has developed an ERMIA of the 'Normal' display of an alarm clock (we deal with this example in detail in Section 10.2). It consists of the (manifest) entities Number and :Flash (which depicts a flashing colon on the display). The lower part of the figure shows that the whole of the normal display (i.e. the entity Normal consisting of the entities Number and :Flash and the relationships OnRight and OnLeft) has two attributes, AlarmOn and Chime.

ERMIA also allows for entities to have sub-types. In Section 3.2, the trains example was used to illustrate that some stations may be just slightly different from other stations (e.g. allowing passengers to get off the train but not to get on it). This sort of station may be called a Drop Only station. Since it shares other attributes and other relationships with all stations, it is useful to show it as a sub-type of Station. The notation for this is illustrated in Figure 3.6.

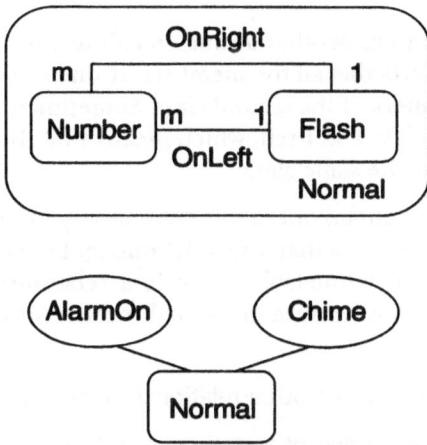

Fig 3.5 ERMIA illustrating a composite entity.

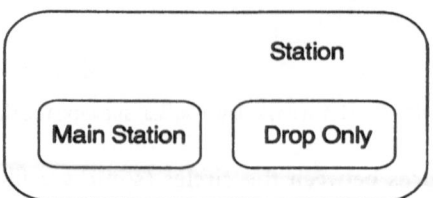

Fig 3.6 Entity sub-types.

Question: One way of modeling the calculator in Figure 2.4 would be to have an entity Button which has two sub-types called Oops (for when things go wrong) and OK (for when things go right). How would you draw this in the ERMIA notation?

Comment: A large box would be labelled Button. It would contain two smaller entity boxes labelled Oops and OK.

Question: Do you think that this would be a useful model?

Comment: Probably not as it would not distinguish sufficiently between the different types of entity which were identified in Exercise 1 namely, Number-Button; Operator; Clear; Decimal-Point; Equals-key; Display.

Sub-types need handling with care. The questions above illustrate that if sub-types are too general then the ERMIA will not be very useful. Conversely, if there are too many sub-types then the model will become cluttered. As with other features of ERMIA, sub-types need to be chosen to focus attention on important aspects of the information artefact.

3.3 Relationship

Entities are associated with each other through relationships. A relationship connects two entity classes. It asserts that all the members of one class have the same type of relationship to the members of the second class. Sometimes, there can be a relationship between an entity class and itself, which means that the entities have relationships to other entities of the same class.

The entity classes might contain one, a hundred, or any number at all of individual entities; and there may be more than one relationship between the same two entity classes. For example, in the timetable, there is a relationship between the Train entity and the Station entity, because individual trains visit individual stations.

Question: Think of some other relationships between Train and Station.

Comment: A train *arrives at* a station. A train *departs from* a station. A train *stops at* a station.

Consider a different example – books. Obviously there is an entity class called Book (and there will be various other classes depending on what aspect we want to model). Since some books mention other books, there is a relationship between Book and itself.

Relationships do not have a direction. The name of a relationship often implies a direction, but it is important to remember that whatever the name, the relationship is present in both directions. Wherever there is a relationship (such as that a person borrows a book) in an ERMIA, the reverse of the relationship is also present (the book is borrowed by that person).

We draw relationships as lines connecting entity classes. It is often useful (though not strictly necessary) to name relationships, especially when there are two or more relationships connecting the same two entity classes. The names are written onto the ERMIAs.

In our train timetable example, we might consider Train entities to be related to Station entities by the relationships Departs From and Arrives At, as shown in Figure 3.7.

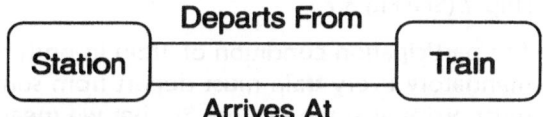

Fig 3.7 Two relationships between Station and Train.

3.3.1 Participation Conditions

There are some entities that always take part in a particular relationship, and others which may take part in a particular relationship but need not do so. These are called the *participation conditions* for the relationship. There are two main participation conditions, *mandatory* and *optional*. Mandatory participation in a relationship means that every entity in the class must participate in the relationship. Optional participation allows some or all occurrences of an entity not to participate in the relationship. Mandatory and optional participation are indicated by dots on the ERMIA model. A filled dot means that participation is mandatory. An open dot means that participation is optional (Fig 3.8).

✳ Example Consider an information artefact that represents information about library subscriptions. Each member of the library must have a card, so the relationship Has Card can be described as mandatory for Person in our database of subscribers. Every Card belongs to someone, so Has Card is also mandatory for Card:

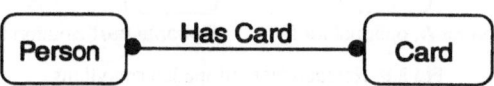

We might be using a different system in which we keep a record of cards that have not yet been issued. In this case Has Card would be mandatory for Person, but optional for Card:

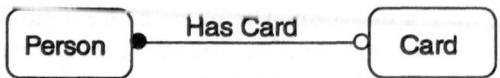

Sometimes it is useful to specify other participation conditions. We may wish to insist that an entity must participate in two or more relationships (*inclusivity*). Similarly we may want to represent that an entity may only participate in one of two or more relationships (*exclusivity*). These constraints on the participation of entities in relationships are not given special symbols. Instead they may be represented in the ERMIA diagram by text annotations.

Question: What do you think are the participation conditions for Train and Station in the Departs From and Arrives At relationships? (See Fig 3.7.)

Comment: The participation condition of Train in both relationships is mandatory. Every train must depart from some station and must arrive at some station. By that we mean that we only want to know about trains if they are associated with stations. However, the participation condition of Station is optional in both Arrives At and Departs From since we will want to assert the existence of stations without knowing which trains arrive or depart.

This question makes an important point about relationships and participation conditions. If an entity has a mandatory participation in a relationship with another entity it means that we will not allow an occurrence of that entity – that is, an individual member of the entity class – to exist unless we also know the occurrence of the entity to which it is related. This is quite a strong assertion. For example, in Section 2.2 we acknowledged that we had to have optional participation of the menu header, Heading, in the relationship with Item because we wanted to model menu systems which were still under development.

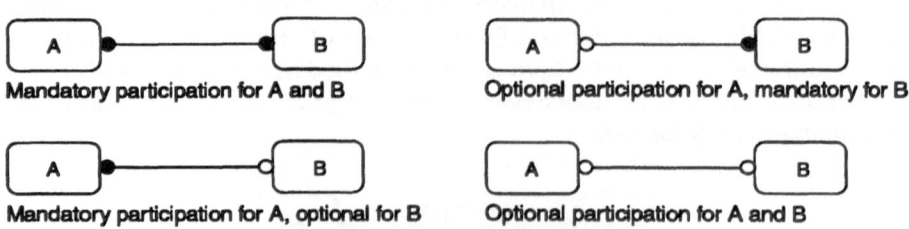

Fig 3.8 Notation for participation conditions.

Question: Can you recall why we insisted that a menu item had a mandatory participation with the Heading?

Comment: Because there would be nowhere to put the item if it had no heading. (However, this does depend on the purpose of the model and in some circumstances we may decide that we do want to recognize the existence of a menu item which we have not allocated to a menu header).

As with all aspects of ERMIA, the participation conditions depend on what the modeler is interested in. Specifying the participation conditions forces the designer to think about such issues.

3.3.2 The Degree of a Relationship

One of the key aspects of a relationship is the *degree* of the relationship, that is, how many occurrences of the entities may be involved in the relationship. Usually we are not concerned with exactly how many. We just want to know if only one entity occurrence can participate, or more than one. So, we classify relationships into three kinds: one-to-one, one-to-many, and many-to-many.

A one-to-one relationship (1:1) between entities A and B associates each occurrence of entity A with at most one occurrence of entity B, and it associates each occurrence of entity B with at most one occurrence of entity A. A one-to-many relationship (1:m) between entities A and B may associate many occurrences of entity B with each occurrence of entity A, but each occurrence of B is associated with at most one occurrence of A.

A many-to-many relationship (m:m) permits many occurrences of entity B to be associated with each occurrence of entity A, and many occurrences of entity A to be associated with each occurrence of entity B. Where the actual numbers are known in a one-to-many or many-to-many relationship, the m may be replaced by a specific number. Many-to-many relationships are potential sources of difficulty in obtaining information from an artefact. When they appear in an ERMIA, they are always worthy of further investigation, as we shall see later in Chapter 6.

✳ **Example** Consider ownership of a subscription card for a public library as a 1:1 relationship. If the system has been computerized, each person must have exactly one library card and each card belongs to exactly one person.

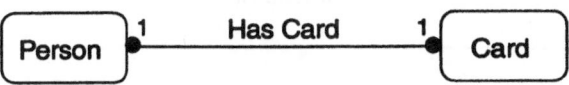

The public library system used to give several cards to each subscriber (one card for each book that the subscriber could borrow). In this system we keep a list showing that a person may hold many cards, but each card is held by exactly one person.

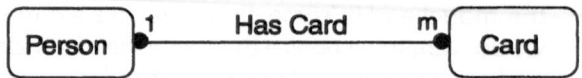

All of the people on our list are subscribers, or we would not have put them on the list, so in this case the relationship Has Card can be described as one-to-many, and is mandatory for both Person and Card.

We can think of a library where each book may be borrowed (over a period of time) by many people, and each person may borrow many books. The relationship Has Borrowed is many-to-many, but is optional for both Person and Book. Some books may not have been borrowed during the period under consideration, and some people may not have borrowed any books.

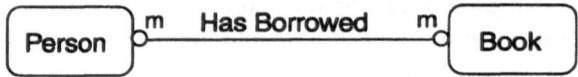

We can have a relationship Borrows that describes the books each subscriber is currently borrowing. Borrows is a many-to-many relationship, in that each person may borrow several books at once, and the same book may be borrowed by many persons. It is optional for both Person and Book. In a library where each subscriber may borrow at most six books, we can include the number 6 in the ERMIA model.

Exercise 2

Put the appropriate degree and participation conditions on the following ERMIA model.

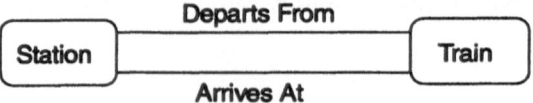

3.3.3 Relationships in Perceptual Models

One of the things that people find difficult about ERMIA is abstracting the perceptual display and producing a perceptual ERMIA of that display. This is because it is tempting to describe the physical relationships between the objects on a display; relationships such as 'is next to', 'is above' and so on. The trick is to concentrate on the meaningful relationships about the *use* of the perceptual entities and on how the perceptual entities are understood by users of the device.

So far we have encountered the drawing package display (Fig 2.1) and a simple perceptual ERMIA of that in Figure 2.2. A simplified perceptual ERMIA of the menu system was presented in Figure 2.3. In both these cases the perceptual ERMIA corresponded closely with a conceptual ERMIA of the same information artefact. If we had wanted to explore the perceptual aspects of the menu system in more detail we could have modeled the 'short-cut' keys that are shown, the fact that some items on menus have ellipsis (three dots) after the name and so on and indeed we discuss some of these aspects below (Section 3.4.2). We have also looked at the display of the Macintosh Finder (Fig 2.4) where we could have modeled the different icons, use of arrows, information about size, kind and the other entities on the display (scroll bars, re-sizing buttons and boxes and so on). Such a model would describe the entities Window, Close Box, Re-size Box, Folder Icon and so on, and the relationships between these a Window has one Re-size Button, a Window has one Close Box, a Window may contain many Folder Icons and so on.

In Exercise 1 you identified a number of perceptual entities on the calculator display. Now we want to look at the relationships between these. This is not necessarily easy, so persevere if at first you cannot think of anything sensible. If you are working with others, you will find that trying to identify relationships and discussing which are the important relationships, provide a good insight into what is important.

Question: What is the degree of the relationships between the entities Number-Button; Operator; Clear; Decimal-Point; Equals-key; Display, in the calculator example?

Comment: Number-Button to Operator is m:m (since there are many, 4, operator keys +, -, *, / and many number buttons). Clear has a many-to-one relationship with Display (there is only one Clear key but it can relate to many displays). Number-Button to Equals-key is many-to-two (since there are two equals-keys). Similarly for Decimal-Point.

Notice that, as ever with ERMIA, we are interested in types of things not occurrences of things. What is actually on the display is not important, it is the relationship between the buttons and the entity class Display. For example, Clear clears the Display.

Exercise 3

Spend five to ten minutes drawing an ERMIA of the calculator interface. At this point do not include participation conditions on your ERMIA, but you should show the degree of the relationships between the entities. Do not worry about the physical layout of the various buttons and other entities on the calculator interface, but use your knowledge of the way that a calculator works and the comment on the question above in order to show the important relationships between the interface entities.

3.4 Attribute

Entities are described by their attributes (also known as *properties* or *characteristics*). For example, a book might have an Author attribute. The value of the author will vary from book to book. A book also has a title, and a number of pages. In ERMIA, we draw in the attribute type and not the specific values that the attribute may take.

Some attributes may be used to pick out the particular occurrence of an entity that interests us. We might want to find a book with a particular title, or to find all the books by a particular author. Other attributes are simply used to provide further information about the book – for example, the number of pages. Exactly which attributes we use to pick out an entity and which we use merely as added information, will vary according to different tasks. One attribute (or collection of attributes) is often deliberately chosen so as to identify each occurrence of an entity uniquely.

We draw attributes in ovals or circles. For example, we have some attributes (Author and Title) that describe the entity class of Books (see Fig 3.9).

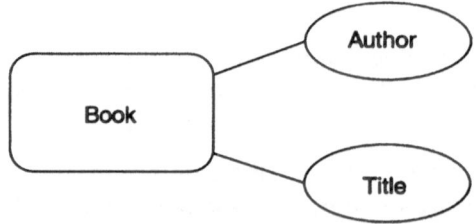

Fig 3.9 Notation for attributes.

Question: Think of some possible attributes for the entities Train and Station.

Comment: There are lots of possibilities, depending on what the modeler is interested in. Train will have an attribute Departure Time and may have other attributes such as Number of Carriages, Buffet Service (values 'yes' or 'no') and so on. Station has an attribute Name. We might also want to record details of the station's address, telephone number and so on.

3.4.1 Using Attributes to Define Entity Classes

The attributes determine how we define entity classes. All the entities in a class should have the same set of attributes, even if they have different values for that attribute. So, if we have an entity class, Book, with an Author attribute, then all occurrences of Book should have an Author attribute, although different books will have different authors. Conversely, entities from different classes should have at least one attribute that is different (although entities from different classes may have some attributes that are the same). If two different entity classes seem to have exactly the same collection of attributes, then the modeler needs to consider treating them as a single entity class.

The values of attributes distinguish between different entity occurrences in the same class (the exceptions are clones, see Section 3.2.2). Different entities have different values for some attributes. Often we do not need to know the values for all the attributes in order to tell entities apart. The attribute (or attributes) which distinguishes between the individuals in a class is known as the *identifying attribute(s)* for that entity, or the entity *identifier*. Identifying attributes are drawn with double connecting lines (Fig 3.10).

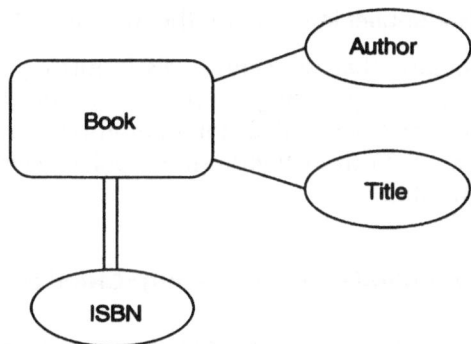

Fig 3.10 Notation for identifying attributes, showing ISBN as identifier of Book.

Question: What is the identifying attribute for Station.

Comment: Name would be a suitable identifier.

The identifying attribute is not always obvious. A naive attempt to find an identifying attribute for books might be to use the title, but of course some books may have the same title. A combination of the author and title might be better. This would be sufficient for a personal collection of books, but in a library there might be multiple copies of the same book. If the ISBN alone were used as the identifying attribute, then multiple copies of the same book would be clones – having the same author, title and ISBN – and impossible to tell apart. In most libraries, the identifying attribute for a book is usually a combination of its ISBN and a number to indicate the copy. It is quite common for identifying attributes to be created deliberately in order to ensure that we can identify each individual uniquely so that there is no ambiguity.

It is important to realize that in choosing an identifying attribute, or identifier, the modeler effectively defines the meaning of the entity. So it is important to think carefully about identifying attributes.

Question: What do you think would be a suitable identifying attribute for Train?

Comment: Departure Time is an obvious candidate, but what if two trains leave at the same time? This is quite likely if we do not refer to the name of the station from which it departs. It is more likely that the composite attribute of Departure Station Name and Departure Time taken together, e.g. 'Paddington, 15.30' will uniquely identify an occurrence of Train. A composite attribute is shown in curly brackets, {Departure Station Name, Departure Time}.

Question: Can you think of any problems with using {Departure Station Name, Departure Time} as the identifier for Train? What does this identifier imply about the meaning of Train?

Comment: It means that we cannot distinguish between trains on different days. Using {Departure Station Name, Departure Time} as the identifier for Train implies that trains such as 'The 15.30 from Paddington' will always have the same attributes.

3.4.2 Structural, Behavioural and Perceptually-coded Attributes

ERMIA recognizes three main kinds of attributes – structural, behavioural and perceptually-coded. Structural attributes describe the static characteristics of the entity. They are particularly important because they define what we mean by an entity class. For example, if we define the entity class Book to include all those objects which possess an ISBN and nothing else, this rules out many objects which we may agree are also books such as snapshot albums, a first edition of Shakespeare, student theses, etc. It is clear from this that different structural attributes will be chosen for different purposes. A database for a public library might use an ISBN to define the entity class Book, but a database for an academic library which included unpublished material might use some other attributes. Decisions about structural attributes can be changed in the light of further analysis, so long as the new definition is made explicit.

Behavioural attributes describe how the entity behaves when it interacts with another entity. For example, in Figure 2.1 we saw how handles appeared on a Graphic Object entity when it was selected. When you click on an icon on a computer, the icon is highlighted. While structural attributes refer to the conceptual characteristics of an entity, behavioural attributes refer to the physical or perceptual level of description.

Some attributes are directly visible, such as the colour and size of a book, or the height of a line on a graph. These are called perceptually-coded attributes (discussed in more detail in Section 4.3). Attributes that differ through perceptual aspects, such as shape or colour, can be recognized or discriminated faster than attributes differing in their symbolic labels, which have to be read (e.g. the titles of books).

ERMIA makes a distinction between structural and perceptually-coded attributes by drawing a thick line around the attribute oval (See Fig 3.11). Behavioural attributes can be indicated in the same way. A search process can be much faster if a perceptually-coded attribute can be used ("It was a red book"). We return to a discussion of issues concerned with searching structures in Section 5.1.

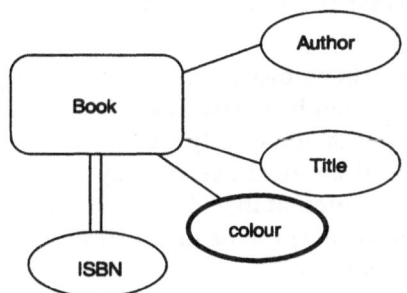

Fig 3.11 Notation for perceptually-coded attributes.

Question: Look at the example of a menu interface in Figure 2.1. Identify (i) a perceptually-coded attribute of a menu heading (ii) a perceptually-coded attribute of a menu item (iii) a behavioural attribute of a menu item.

Comment: As usual there may be more than one possible solution. We would say an example of (i) is that a menu heading is highlighted when it is selected, an example of (ii) is the ellipsis (the three dots next to some items, for example next to Align Objects) which indicates that a further dialogue is required if this option is selected and for (iii) some items are greyed out when they are not relevant to the current state of the system.

The solution to the above question indicates an important point about behavioural and perceptually-coded attributes; the two types of attribute are often linked. For example, the highlighting of the menu header can be considered a behavioural attribute (since it changes behaviour when it is clicked) or a perceptually-coded attribute (because it appears highlighted). However, some perceptually-coded attributes are not behavioural (the colour of a book, for example) and some behavioural attributes are not perceptually-coded – a fact of computer systems that causes no end of confusion for the user!

✳ Example Consider the perceptual attributes of a cursor. It changes shape from an arrow to an I-bar to a watch, or hour-glass depending on what the computer is doing. If the programmer has forgotten to instruct the cursor to change shape when the computer is busy (which happens on at least one word-processing program when the computer is checking the spelling), then the user has no perceptual clue as to what is going on and may conclude that the computer has 'crashed'.

3.5 Entity, Relationship or Attribute?

One of the important questions that arises when building an ERMIA is whether some part of the model should be represented by an entity or an attribute. If an element has many attributes then it clearly must be represented as an entity, but if an element consists only of an identifier, or only a range of values and nothing more, then it is possible to represent that element as either an attribute or an entity. The decision depends on the purpose of the analysis and on which aspects of the artefact and its use are important.

There are a number of rules of thumb which can be used to help choose whether to model some feature as an entity or as an attribute.

In general, an entity represents an item that groups information together, and an entity is a single perceptual or conceptual item that we wish to describe by several of its associated attributes and relationships. By contrast, an attribute in general only has one property, a set of values. For example, we can consider colour as an attribute if we are simply interested in a set of named colours, and if these colours describe other objects. Conversely, if we wanted to describe different aspects of a single colour such as its wavelength, or the other colours that a given colour matches or contrasts with, then it is best represented as an entity.

Attributes are more limited in their connections and relationships than entities. Attributes are only connected to entities: an attribute cannot itself have attributes, nor can it connect to other attributes. Entities can have any number of attributes and they can connect to other entities. The degree of a relationship is only represented between entities. So if the degree of a relationship between two elements is important, they must both be treated as entities.

The upshot of this discussion is that ERMIA provides a flexible, subjective modeling language which enables designers and choosers of information artefacts to think about their needs and the facilities offered by a particular design. There is no single, correct choice of entities, attributes and relationships.

3.6 Example: A Database of Papers Submitted to a Conference

✳ In this example, we consider a data structure to maintain information about papers submitted to a conference, and the people involved in dealing with them. Papers may have one or more authors. They are submitted to the conference committee for review, and they may be accepted or rejected. If accepted, then at least one of the authors will present the paper.

To begin with, we consider just the papers and their authors. Each paper submitted to the conference must have at least one author. This gives us Figure 3.12, in which the m:m relationship indicates that any given paper may have been written by any number of people, and that a single person may have submitted more than one paper. Remember that the filled circle indicates that the relationship is mandatory (a paper must relate to at least one person) whereas the open circle indicates that the relationship is optional in the other direction (a person may be in the database because he or she is the author of a paper, but he or she might be in the database for a different reason, for example as a member of the conference committee).

Fig 3.12 A person authors papers.

We now consider the attributes that these entities may have (Fig 3.13). In order to determine which particular person is referred to, the entity Person needs some attributes, such as their name and affiliation; likewise the Paper needs a title. We assume that each Person can be uniquely identified by their name and affiliation, and that each paper can be identified by its title (i.e. all papers have different titles.) These are identifying attributes. Besides this, papers need a status attribute to note if they are accepted or rejected (or still pending a decision).

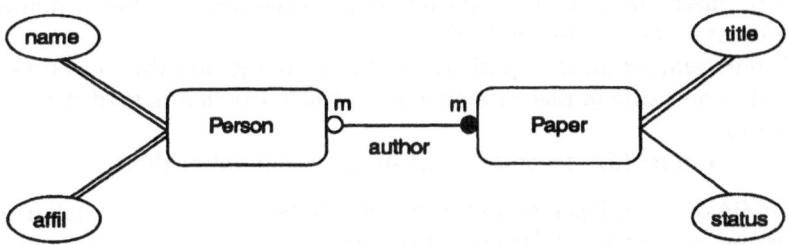

Fig 3.13 Attributes of the person authors papers example.

Things liven up when we consider more entities and more relationships between them (Fig 3.14). Each person may possibly be on the Committee, and each paper may have been accepted by the Committee; also a second relationship between Person and Paper has been introduced, that of the person presenting the paper. This relationship is optional for papers, since rejected papers will not be presented, and it is optional for Person, since some people at the conference will not present papers.

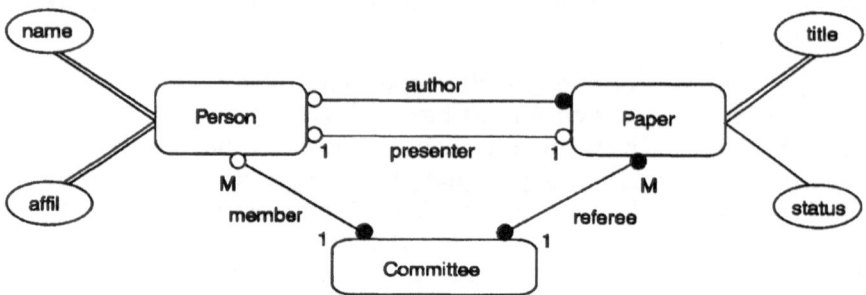

Fig 3.14 The conference structure with a committee of referees.

Some aspects of the relationships cannot be represented in the ERMIA. For example, the fact that the Person who presents a paper must be one of the authors is a constraint that cannot be represented easily on the diagram and so would require a textual annotation.

3.7 Example: Telephone Network

✳   The second example is that of the British telephone network, as seen by the lay person. (This is a much simpler view than the professional communications specialist's view).

In this example we do not need to make use of attributes, so we use an ERMIA based entirely on entities and their relationships. We have the following entities:

- Name
- Address
- Subscriber (the holder of the telephone account, who has a name, an address and a phone number)
- Phone number (made up of the exchange name and the local number)
- Exchange name (a place name, conceptually the first part of the phone number)
- Local number (the second part of the phone number, digits)

An ERMIA of the telephone network is illustrated in 3.15. The relationships illustrated show that different subscribers may have the same name or address. That is, an occurrence of Name, say Smith, can relate to many subscribers, and one occurrence of address similarly can relate to many subscribers. A subscriber has just one name, but may have several addresses. Many phone numbers are connected to a single exchange, and different phone numbers (from different exchanges) may have the same local numbers.

This ERMIA does not tell us how to distinguish between different subscribers. The one-to-one relationship between Subscriber and Phone No says that each subscriber has a different telephone number, but this ERMIA does not rule out the possibility that a single telephone number applies to several different addresses. Each phone number relates to a single subscriber who may have several addresses. In order to solve this problem, we can re-draw the ERMIA slightly and create a new entity to represent information about a Subscriber at a particular Address (as shown below in Fig 3.16). Phone No is related to the new entity, which indicates clearly that a phone number can only apply to a single address. A Phone No now relates to a single Subscriber at an Address, which relates in turn to a single Address.

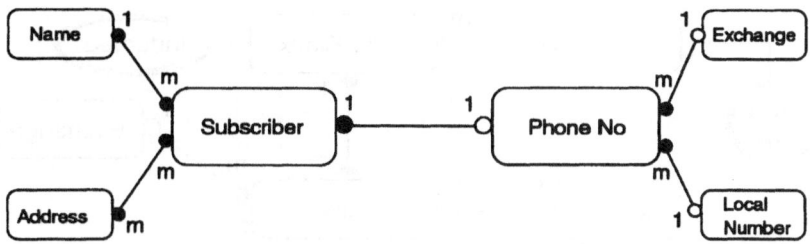

Fig 3.15 ERMIA of a lay view of the telephone network.

Figure 3.16 is an example of an ERMIA in which a many-to-many relationship has been replaced by a new entity. This process is described more formally in Section 6.1.

Now let us look at the perceptual aspects of a telephone book. The British Telecom telephone directory uses this format:

K. Lear,	Palace, Glastonbury	Glastonbury	12345
H. MacBeth,	Castle, Dunsinane	Dunsinane	13243
	The Other Castle, Cawdor	Cawdor	758

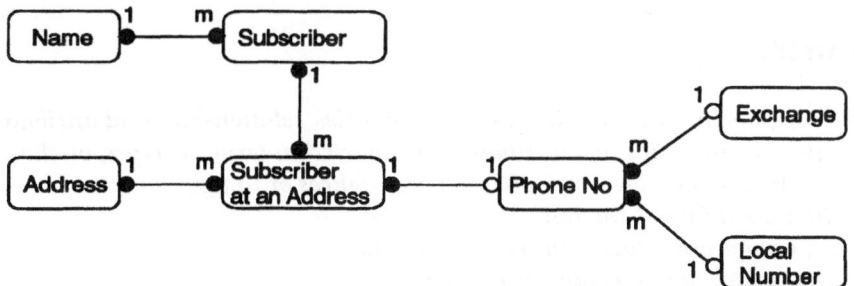

Fig 3.16 Expanded ERMIA of a lay view of the telephone network.

To construct an ERMIA showing how this conceptual model is represented by the perceptual display (see Fig 3.17), we note the following perceptual entities:

- *Name* corresponds to the conceptual entity, 'Name', distinguished by bold type
- *Address* corresponds to the conceptual entity, 'Address'
- *Exchange Name* is part 1 of the conceptual Phone No; a place name
- *Local Number* is part 2 of the Phone No; digits
- *Block Of Entries* gathers all the entries for a single Name, using typographic cues to mark the limits of the block (Lear's block has only one entry but MacBeth has two entries)
- *Entry* contains a Name, an Address and a Phone-number (omits the Name, for second and subsequent entries in a block). Normally a single line of text.

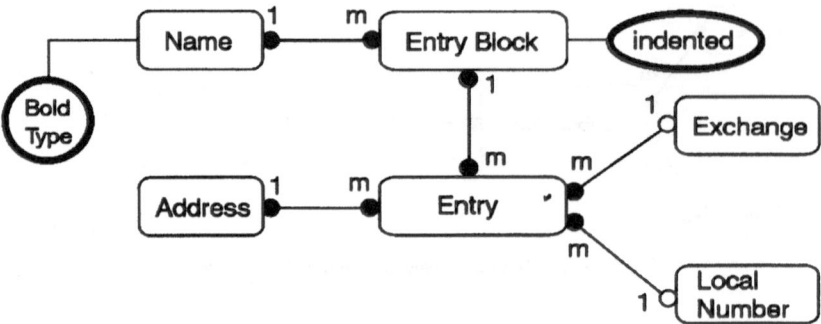

Fig 3.17 Perceptual model of telephone book.

The ERMIA diagrams in Figure 3.16 and Figure 3.17 show a very close correspondence: the Entry-block corresponds to a Subscriber, the Entry corresponds to a Subscriber at an Address, and so on. We chose this example for just this reason; a close correspondence between perceptual and conceptual ERMIAs suggests a good design.

Summary

- *The components of an ERMIA model are entities, relationships and attributes.*
- *Entities, relationships and attributes are modeled in terms of types, or classes of things. We do not represent individual occurrences of things.*
- *Entities are things of interest.*
- *Relationships are associations between entities.*
- *Attributes are characteristics of entities.*
- *ERMIA distinguishes between conceptual and manifest entities.*

- *ERMIA distinguishes between structural, behavioural and perceptually-coded attributes.*
- *The identifying attribute(s) of an entity distinguishes between occurrences of the entities and defines what the modeler means by that entity.*
- *ERMIA is a subjective representation of an information artefact focusing attention on its conceptual and perceptual structure.*

4. *Conceptual and Perceptual ERMIAs*

Aims and Objectives

This chapter aims to show how ERMIAs distinguish between the structure of the conceptual information that is contained in an information artefact, and the way that this information is made manifest to the user.

After reading this chapter, you should be able to:

- create ERMIAs that represent both the conceptual information within an artefact and the information that is manifested to the user
- use the notation to highlight purely conceptual entities and attributes that make use of properties that can be directly perceived
- draw ERMIAs showing the distribution of information

4.1 The Information to Be Displayed versus the Display Itself

ERMIAs provide a link between the conceptual information that is stored in an information artefact and the physical/perceptual way that the information appears to someone using the artefact; or to put it another way, a link between the information to be presented, and the display itself. So far, we have focused on how ERMIAs represent the information to be displayed in an artefact, and have used examples (such as the telephone book, in Section 3.7, or the menu in Section 2.2) in which the information display successfully makes these entities, attributes and relationships available to us. But sometimes the display does not succeed in conveying all the information that would be desirable, so now we start to think about how the same information can be presented in different ways.

4.2 Manifest and Conceptual Entities and Relationships

We have seen that information in an artefact is made available through *viewports*. The viewport is the actual display, or other presentation format, and different viewports may structure the same information in very different ways – for example, a paper-based train timetable compared to a 'talking timetable'. Sometimes the structure of information as shown by a viewport is very close to the underlying conceptual structure, and everything is fine. Sometimes it is similar but one or two discrepancies appear, at other times there may be a whole different structure.

To start with, consider a case where there is an entity that is 'in the mind' but is not physically represented in the viewport being modeled (although it might be represented in some other viewport). ERMIA makes a distinction between *manifest* entities (and relationships) that are directly represented by some part of the information display, and *conceptual* entities (and relationships) that are not part of the display. For example, the title of a book is manifest, since it is directly represented as part of the book; but the plot of a book (boy meets girl / Cinderella makes good / hero defeats evil, etc.) is not usually given any direct physical representation. Conceptual entities can be shown on a perceptual ERMIA represented by dotted lines, showing they are not directly represented The example of the plot of a book is illustrated in Figure 4.1.

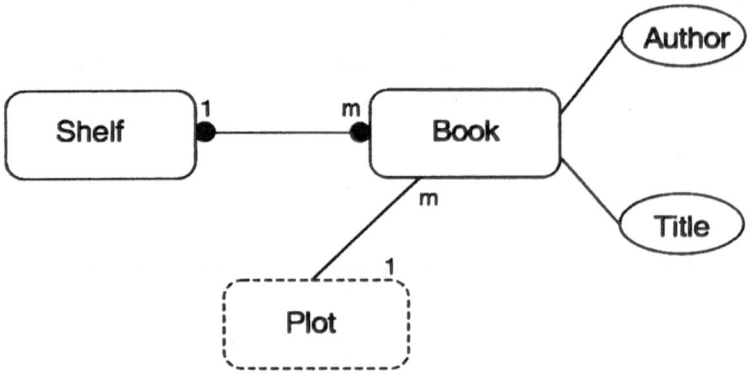

Fig 4.1 The Plot of a Book is a conceptual entity.

Sometimes it is convenient to draw entirely separate diagrams of the information display (the viewport) and the information to be displayed (the conceptual model). One reason might be to show that the viewport structure is a good fit with the conceptual structure as in Section 3.7 (the telephone book) or in Figure 4.8 (the flower list example at the end of this chapter). Another reason might be to show that the viewport structure is not such a good structure.

✱ Example Consider a typical spreadsheet. In a spreadsheet, numbers and formulae are put into the cells of the spreadsheet. Cells refer to other cells and in this way complex calculations can be quickly performed. A small example is shown below.

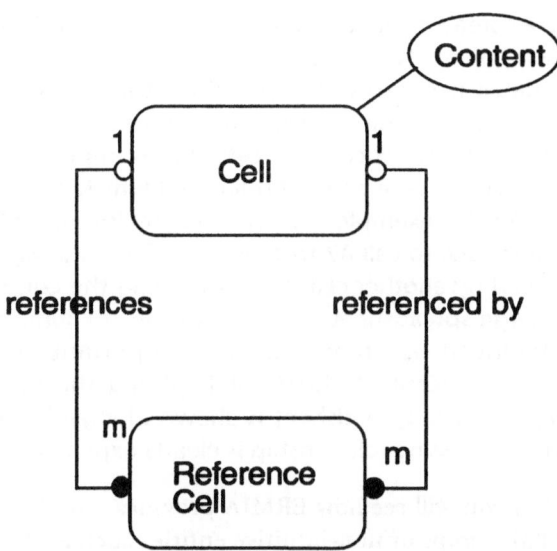

	A	B	C
1	250		
2	350		=A2-D2
3		=A7*C3	=A3-D3
4		=A7*C4	=A4-D4
5			=A5-D5
6			=A6-D6
7	=SUM(A1:A6)		
8	200		

The structure of the spreadsheet can be conceptually represented by focusing on the relationships between the cells – a cell may refer to other cells and a cell may be referenced by other cells. The ERMIA of this is shown below (Fig 4.2). It shows that a cell does not have to be referenced by other cells, nor does it have to reference other cells (optional participation – e.g. A8 above does not reference another cell, nor is it referenced by any other cell). However, a cell may both reference and be referenced by many other cells (e.g. A7 references A1 and A2 and A3 up to A6 and is referenced by B3 and B4). We can distinguish cells that are associated with other cells and those that are not by having two entity classes, Cell and Reference Cell. A reference cell must (mandatory participation) reference just one other cell and must be referenced by just one other cell.

Fig 4.2 Conceptual representation of a spreadsheet.

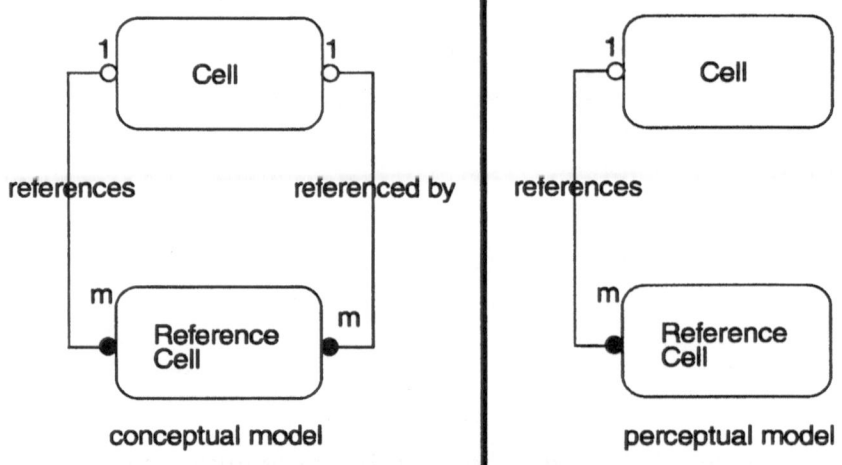

conceptual model   perceptual model

Fig 4.3 The conceptual model and perceptual models for the spreadsheet.

Question: Given the description above, what is the identifier of Reference Cell?

Comment: It is simply the concatenation of the identifiers of the two cells involved in that relationship. For example, {A7, A1}, {A7, A2} and so on. Note that the actual formula of a cell is conceptually represented as an attribute of the Cell entity (which we have called 'content'). For example, an attribute of A7 is 'Sum (A1..A6)'. The Reference Cell entity just records the existence of the relationships.

The interface to a spreadsheet does not reveal all of this underlying structure. If you were having difficulty understanding the entity Reference Cell in the conceptual model, it is because the spreadsheet interface does not make the 'referenced by' relationship explicit. The contents of a spreadsheet cell only reveal which cells reference other cells (for example, A7 references A1 through A6). There is no easy way of finding out which cells are referenced by another cell. A7, for example is referenced by B3 and B4, but there is nothing at the interface to cell A7 to show this. The only way to find which cells are referenced by another cell is by examining the contents of all the cells which in a large spreadsheet can be very time-consuming. Changing a cell that is referenced by others can have important and unforeseen consequences. The perceptual ERMIA, highlighting the manifest entities and relationships for the spreadsheet is shown alongside the conceptual model (Fig 4.3). The missing relationship is clearly exposed.

Later (in Section 6.1) you will see how ERMIA provides a useful technique to help uncover hidden relationships or non-intuitive entities such as Reference Cell.

4.3 Perceptually-coded Attributes

Many information displays present their information in a coded form, using colour, size, highlighting or line thickness, either in place of or as well as other codings. Recall (from Section 3.4.2) that ERMIA also makes a distinction between entities with perceptually-coded attributes and ones without. We show this by using our own perceptually-coded attribute – a thick line around the attribute oval. A search process can be much faster if a perceptually-coded attribute can be used ("It was a red book"). Similarly, behavioural attributes can be used to draw attention to entities which change their state; an alarm clock may 'beep', warning bells ring and so on. Recall the use of handles on the graphic object (Fig 2.1) to show that the object had been selected.

It is possible to take advantage of perceptual attributes by using them to encode other attributes or the existence of other entities. For example, some libraries attach different coloured stickers to books to indicate the kind of book (e.g. romance, crime, science fiction). Figure 4.4 shows an ERMIA of books with a perceptually-coded attribute, Colour, and Figure 4.5 shows an ERMIA of books with colour-coded covers and plots.

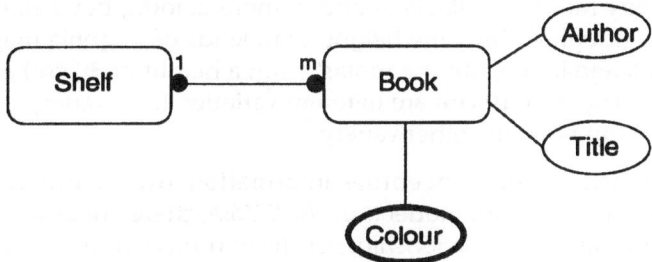

Fig 4.4 Books with coloured covers.

Question: Is there anything ambiguous about this ERMIA (Fig 4.5)?

Comment: Yes. Books and plots both have a colour, but we do not know from the diagram that the colour of Book and the colour of Plot are one and the same. The same ERMIA might describe books whose covers were coloured and whose plots were coded by a different coloured label rather than by the colour of the book itself.

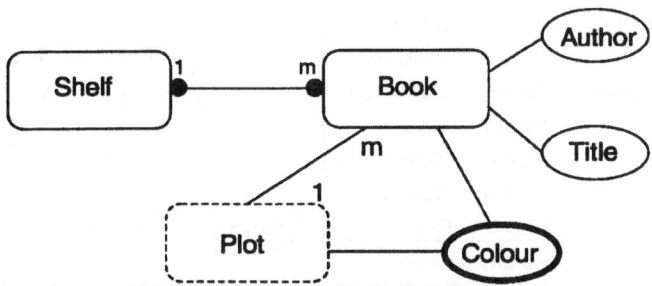

Fig 4.5 Coding the plot by colour.

Perceptual codings have a great effect on how usable an artefact will be, and so perceptual attributes need to be represented. That is especially true in cases where users have alternative strategies for the same task. A strategy that uses a perceptual attribute will often be much faster. It is obviously much faster to find out what kind of plot a book has by using the book-plot colour-coding than to dip into the book. Bertin (1981) has many examples of information displays which contain exactly the same information but possess quite different usability characteristics.

4.4 Example: A List Viewport

✱   In this example, we consider how some simple conceptual information can be structured into a list, and how this list uses perceptual cues to reveal some conceptual information. The underlying conceptual information is some information about flowers, the kind of information that we might want to present in a mail-order catalogue. Suppose that each variety of flower that we might want to order has a name, a height and a colour. A single variety may be available in one or more colours, but a single variety always has (roughly) the same height. Both kinds of begonia may be available in pink and in red, but "begonias" (with a height of 30 cm) and "dwarf begonias" (height of 10 cm) are different varieties. Each variety has a name that is different from any other variety.

Figure 4.6 shows the conceptual information (the information to be displayed) and an ERMIA model (not *the* ERMIA, there are other choices of entities, attributes and relationships) of the information structure.

Now suppose that we have created a catalogue for the convenience of garden designers. Garden designers typically want to create a harmonious collection of colours, so it is useful to present a catalogue to them ordered by colour. In this way we can provide for a conceptual model in which the information displayed is organized as a list of flowers of different colours (Fig 4.7).

We can view this list as a viewport onto the flowers information. In this viewport, the structure of the information display is a list of flowers by

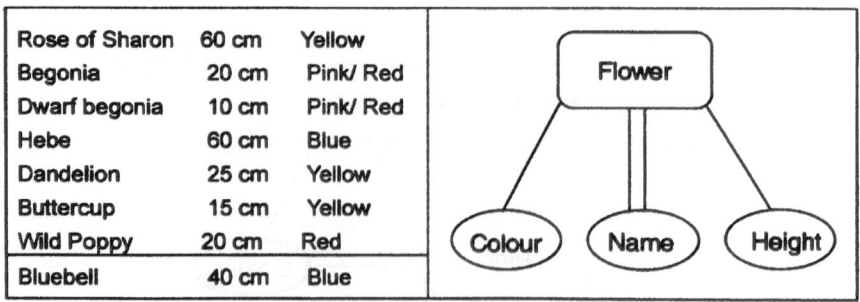

Fig 4.6 Information about flowers.

Yellow flowers
    Rose of Sharon   60 cm
    Buttercup   15 cm
    Dandelion   25 cm
Blue flowers
    Bluebell   40 cm
    Hebe   60 cm
Pink flowers
    Begonia   20 cm
    Dwarf begonia   10 cm
Red flowers
    Begonia   20 cm
    Dwarf begonia   10 cm
    Wild poppy   20 cm
Black flowers
    none

Fig 4.7 A list of flowers with headings organized alphabetically by colour.

colour, mapping cleanly onto the conceptual structure of the information displayed. Conceptually, the flowers have been sorted by their colour. This gives rise to the new conceptual entity in Figure 4.8 called Colour-group. Perceptually, the headings are distinguished from the entries by being in bold font. Each flower in the list has a name and a height, and is identified by its name. (Notice that although the list has a heading for black flowers, there are none available; that is why the Heading:Item relationship is optional for the Heading entity.

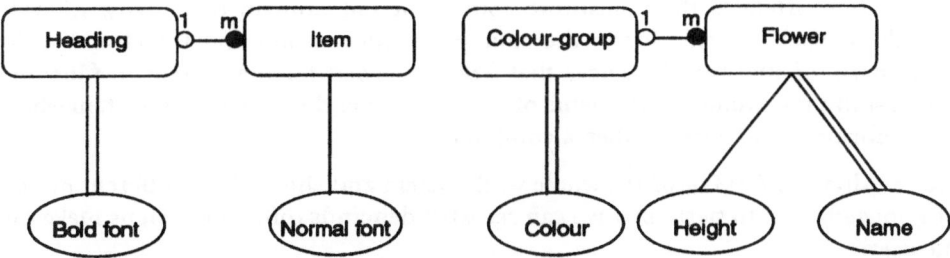

Fig 4.8 ERMIAs for a list-type viewport onto list-type information. Left, the perceptual structure (the information display); right, the conceptual structure (the information displayed).

Given this layout of the Flowers list, it is easy to choose a colour and find all the varieties of flower that have that colour. This simply means finding the Heading with the right Colour attribute and then following the 1:m relationship to find all the entries.

Exercise 4

Look again at the ERMIA in Figure 4.6 and think about the various relationships between flowers. Can you see how the Colour-group entity, that we introduced in Figure 4.8, might have been represented on Figure 4.6 as a relationship? Draw an ERMIA for this.

Question: Now suppose that our garden designer wants to choose the flowers according to their heights, while still keeping in mind their colours. Is the list structure shown in Figure 4.7 adequate to deal with this case?

Comment: No, because the conceptual information is not just a list: it is a table, in which both height and colour are represented. A list treats height as an attribute of flower, but our garden designer is interested in height as an important thing in itself; an entity (Section 3.5). We shall postpone making an ERMIA model of a table structure until Chapter 7, when a variety of structures will be compared, but it is easy to see that a simple list is inappropriate. Another solution is a list in which each colour group is sorted by height, and this will be modeled in Section 5.3.

4.5 Distributed Conceptual Information

In many situations information is not held in any one place, nor by any one person; but rather it is distributed through the work system; all the people, devices and information artefacts that constitute some coherent domain of activity. ERMIA models of such systems locate the sources of information and thereby identify some parts of the work practices that will be needed for the system to function successfully, including the problems of maintaining and repairing the system when new information arrives or when a component is lost.

We can draw an ERMIA of the whole work system and show where different pieces of knowledge lie. In particular we can see what demands different designs make on the users.

✳   Example   Smart telephones are a simple example of distributed information. These devices contain a list of short-cut codes, so that when some code sequence like #1 is keyed, the phone actually dials a full-length number. As a rule, they do not contain the information about who that number calls. It is the user's responsibility to record the relationship between names and dialling code sequences. Since surprisingly many designs have no provision for externalizing that information, we have shown it in the model in Figure 4.9 as located in the user's head. In practice, such designs are therefore frequently disfigured by sticking dialling code lists onto them, in true 'back of envelope' style. Some telephone handsets do actually contain a small notebook to record the relationship. Either way, the ERMIA model makes explicit the problem of how to store and access this information.

The ERMIA showing the overall structure is given in Figure 4.9, with the thick lines showing how the information is divided between the components of the work system.

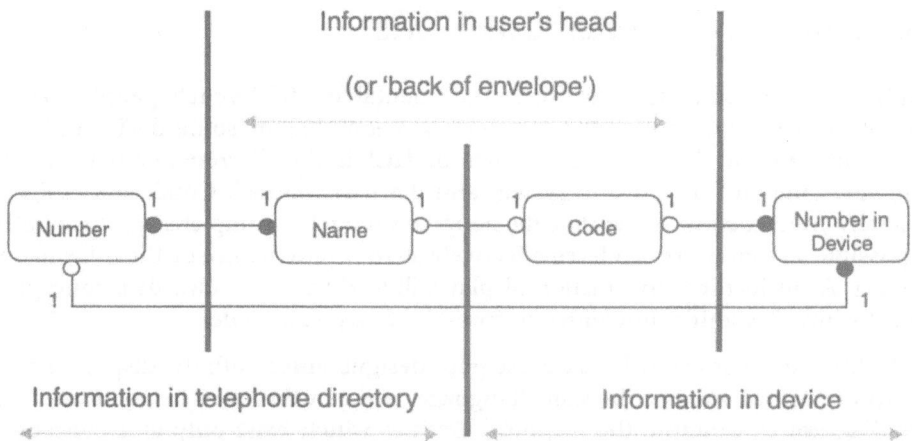

Fig 4.9 A 'smart' telephone. Every Name has a Number and vice versa, but only some Names have Codes (and vice versa). The numbers held in the smart phone (Number in Device) all correspond to real numbers, but of course not every real number is stored in the device, hence the relationship Number in Device:Number is optional on the Number's side. Nor does every Code have to be assigned to a Number in the Device.

An ERMIA of this sort which shows the location of information can help predict the consequences of the inevitable system upgrades, which enhance performance at the cost of a period of mild chaos as users discover that resources have been deleted or no longer work. In the typical scenario, a new telephone is supplied, which has not yet been customized and does not contain the dialling codes.

Question: What does a user have to do on getting a new 'smart' phone? Where can the relevant information be found?

Comment: From memory (or from the back of the envelope) the user decides which code will be allocated to which person (Jeff = #1, Devina = #2, etc.). The user must then look up the actual number for each person in the telephone directory and enter the code and real number into the device. The user will also have to record which code has been allocated to which person.

In more complex systems, information is often distributed among many people and many devices. For example, in air traffic control, the air traffic controller on the ground has information about the flight speed and flight path of all the aircraft in the area. The pilot has much more detailed information about the state of an individual aircraft, some displayed on instruments and some kept in the pilot's head. However, pilots have little direct information about other aircraft. The design of such complex systems must ensure that relevant information can be easily and successfully shared between the people and information artefacts in the whole system.

4.6 Comparing Different User Views

ERMIA is also useful for looking at the 'mental models' which people have. A mental model is the representation which someone has of some device in his or her mind. One of the recurrent themes of HCI is the discrepancy between the *designer's* (mental) model of a system and the *user's* model. Good HCI design is generally concerned with revealing the designer's model as completely and accurately as possible so that users can learn effectively about the structure of the information artefact. A misleading information display will lead the user towards a conceptual model which is significantly different from the designer's model.

An ERMIA analysis can help to expose poor designs, since both the display and the model are represented in the same 'language' and can therefore be combined into one diagram to examine the mapping. Entities which exist only at a conceptual level and have no direct representation as perceptual entities are likely to cause problems.

In order to show how ERMIA can help to expose discrepancies between the designer's model and the user's model, we have chosen for our illustration an unusual case: the card trick. Here we have an information display which is deliberately designed *not* to conform to the designer's model; the design is intended to induce an inaccurate user's model, because what the 'designer' wants to do is to deceive the 'user'.

✱ **Example** In the following trick, the magician offers the player 10 pairs of cards. The player chooses a pair, without revealing the choice, and the magician then deals the cards face up in a tableau, laying them out in a seemingly random arrangement. The player has to name the two rows in which the two chosen cards lie (or possibly they both lie in the same row). Surprise surprise – from that meagre information, the magician can identify the chosen cards.

a	b	c	b	d
e	f	a	g	e
h	f	h	i	d
k	g	k	i	c

The secret, of course, is that the tableau is far from random; it has the very special property that each of the original pairs of cards ends up in a different pair of rows. One such arrangement is illustrated. The first pair of cards (aa) goes one into row 1, one into row 2. The second pair of cards (bb) both go into row 1. The third pair (cc) goes into rows 1 and 5, and so on. (The columns are immaterial, but this layout helps disguise that fact.) The vital detail is that *every card pair is associated with just one row pair*, so that identifying the row pair identifies the card pair.

Now, the players are not likely to have the concept of a row-pair in their conceptual model, and the information display (the viewport) gives no indication of it: in fact, as the magician lays out the tableau, the cards go into 'random' positions in just such a way as to destroy any hint of a system and to suggest instead that the magician is choosing where to put each card at the instant of laying it on the table. So the act appears baffling.

Figure 4.10 shows the ERMIA. Notice that in this case we have included an explicit natural language constraint with the diagram because there is no easy way of showing it diagrammatically. Also, the degree of the relationship can be made explicit in this case, instead of using the usual indeterminate 'm' symbol, since the actual numbers are known – e.g. each Column defines 4 Cards. The trick works because of the 1:1 relationship between the conceptual entities Card Pair and Row Pair. Combining the two levels of ERMIA, perceptual and conceptual, reveals whether the information display supplies a good cognitive map of the conceptual model.

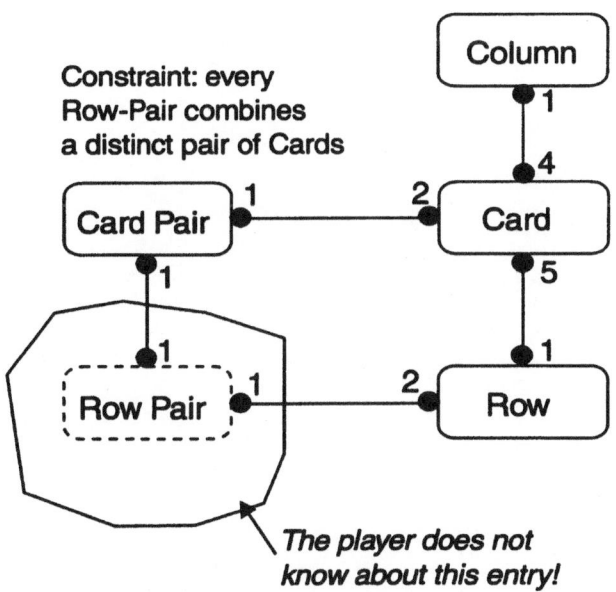

Fig 4.10 ERMIA for the card trick.

The ability of ERMIA to represent conceptual information – which resides in someone's head or in some information artefact – is extremely useful. Designers can quickly see whether the perceptual display accurately reflects the designer's model or whether a particular design imposes an excessive load on the user's memory, by failing to reveal certain information. This is not to say that a viewport that reveals all of the conceptual structure is always a good thing; this depends on the purpose of the display. What ERMIA provides is a way of making the relationship between conceptual structures and perceptual displays explicit. Designers, users and choosers of information artefacts can then see how effective the viewport is for particular tasks.

Summary

- *ERMIAs can be constructed of both perceptual and conceptual aspects of devices.*
- *Comparing ERMIAs of the viewport and ERMIAs of the conceptual structure can help to identify poor or restrictive designs. Designs which are good reflections of the conceptual structure also show up.*
- *Developing ERMIAs of the conceptual structure of a work system can highlight where information is stored – what does the user have to remember?*
- *ERMIAs can also be used to highlight the different 'mental models' – the different conceptual structures – which different users have.*

5. *Searching for Information*

![decorative divider]

Aims and Objectives

This chapter introduces the problem of searching for information in an artefact. The aim of this chapter is to show how ERMIAs describe how the user can locate interesting individual entities, or groups of individuals with relevant properties, in an entity class. It presents ERMIA notation for how the entities in a class are stored and accessed.

After reading this chapter, you should be able to

- understand the processes involved in finding information
- produce ERMIAs that describe the way that entities are stored
- interpret the effects on search of how entities are stored
- describe how a complex information artefact can be searched.

![decorative divider]

5.1 Information Can Be Hard to Find

Storing, finding, and changing information – those are the reasons for building information artefacts. A telephone directory exists so that people can find telephone numbers. If you know the name of your target person, finding the number is pretty easy.

Question: When is a telephone number hard to find?

Comment: When you know someone's address but not their name, when the number is ex-directory and so on.

In the ERMIA notation as we have developed it so far, a very simplified version of the telephone directory would look like this (Fig 5.1).

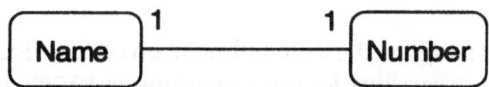

Fig 5.1 A simplistic version of a telephone directory.

In Figure 5.1 the relationship between Name and Number is entirely symmetric; there is nothing to show that getting from Name to Number is easy, but getting from Number to Name is hard. What is the key difference? The answer is that names are stored in alphabetic order in a telephone directory, while numbers are stored in essentially random order. So finding one name among many is easy, but finding one number among many is difficult. In Section 5.2 we introduce some additional notation so that we can represent such details on our models. The important idea is that a manifest entity class is a store of entities which is internally structured. The Name entity is different from the Number entity in that its internal structure is a *sorted list*. There are several types of internal structure detailed below; the structure of the Number entity is one we call a *chain*.

We are not suggesting here that the entities are always physically stored according to this internal structure (though in the case of a printed telephone book the entity occurrences are physically stored in alphabetic order). Rather, a manifest entity always *presents* the entities using some internal structure.

5.1.1 Search Time

The different types of internal structure impose differences in how long it takes to find something (the search time) and how many things have to be remembered while searching (memory needed). We can estimate the search time from the number of search operations needed, and as we shall see the search time for a sorted list is quite different from the search time for a chain. To find a name in the telephone directory, we would make a guess at where to start in the telephone directory and open a page accordingly. Then we turn further on or turn back, depending on the names we find on that page. That method, sometimes called the "binary search" method, is one of many intensively analysed search algorithms for computers; humans are less systematic, but we could say that the time taken to find a name is roughly proportional to log(#Name), the logarithm of the number of names.

Finding the name that goes with a given number is harder, because the numbers are not sorted alphabetically. One way to do it is to inspect each number in turn until we find the number we are looking for, then read off the name. On average we shall have to inspect half the numbers, so the number of search operations is (#Number)/2, that is the number of numbers divided by 2.

These "search times" are purely notional – they give us no indication of actual time. They can still be very useful, as long as we have an approximate idea of how many entities have to be searched. In the telephone directory for a major city, there might be several hundred thousand entries; in the directory of extensions for a small network, there might be only half a dozen numbers. These are quite different cases!

In case you have no feeling for the differences involved, consider searching for one name among 10, versus searching for one name among 10,000. If the search process takes advantage of the alphabetic ordering of a sorted list, it will take just four times as long to search 10,000 names as it does to search 10 names. Pushing the number up to 100,000 names means the search will now take five times as long, instead of four times. Big deal. Searching through an unordered list, a chain, is a complete contrast. Finding one number among 10 is a reasonable task. On average you will have to look at five numbers before you find the right one. Finding one number among 10,000 will take on average 5,000 inspections; and if there are 100,000 numbers, it will take 50,000 inspections. Not a task to be taken on lightly. Even without any good idea of the actual times involved, it is obvious that this is non-starter.

(Incidentally, it is possible to make rough estimates of actual times involved, if that is important. Several researchers, starting with Card *et al.* (1983), have presented tables of estimated times for simple user operations such as reading a name or a number and deciding whether it is the target. These time estimates, together with help in applying them, can be found in the books and papers dealing with the GOMS methodology; see the Resources section for details. Card, Pirolli and Mackinlay (1994) call the search time the *cost-of-knowledge*, and they analyze an interesting artefact called a spiral calendar. Their analysis nicely demonstrates the difference between GOMS and ERMIA; GOMS gives estimates of real time but can only be used when a prototype design is available, while ERMIA can be used much earlier in design, as soon as the information structure has been designed, but only gives symbolic time estimates.)

5.1.2 Memory Needed

Search time is not the only aspect in which information structures can be different. The other important aspect is the number of things to be remembered during a search. Searching through the names is easy enough: you put your finger beside the first name to be tried, read it, check it, and if necessary move your finger to the next name, read that, and so on. The 'finger' might only be in your mind, but it is still there – some kind of record of where you are in the search. The list of numbers takes more time to search, but you still only need one finger.

Now consider an 'untidy desktop' windowing system, where the window is full of icons arranged higgledy-piggledy all over the screen (Fig 5.2).

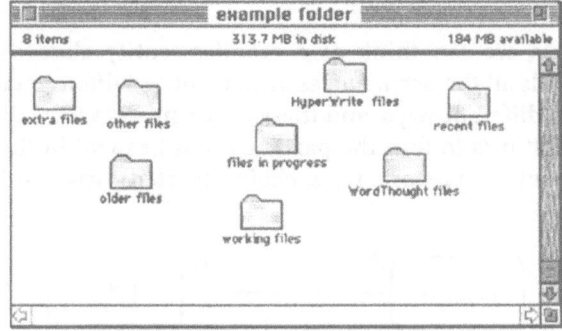

Fig 5.2 A pile of folders.

Somewhere among all those folders is the file you want. You have to search them one by one to find the file, and you have to keep track of which folders you have searched. Because there is no logical spatial arrangement, you simply have to remember.

The structure of this information artefact is not so very different from the structure of the telephone directory (Fig 5.1), except that it is 1:m rather than 1:1. Every folder contains some files, every file must be in a folder (Fig 5.3). (In fact this problem turns out to be rather more complex than this as we demonstrate later). The search will require you to inspect, on average, half the folders. But there is an important difference in the amount of memory needed; you now have to remember all the folders so far searched (unless you can devise some kind of visual strategy, like starting at the top left corner). We describe this part of the overall structure as a "pile" of folders.

In general, the memory needed to search a pile is equal to the number of items searched, whereas the memory needed to search a chain or a list structure is only one item, because the internal structure is such that one entity leads you to the next (like books along a shelf, lines on a page, etc.)

Remembering a large number of items is difficult, and very few effective information artefacts force the user to search through entity stores that are piles, unless there are very few items involved. When more than a few items are involved, most people convert pile structures into chain structures by writing out a list – or put the entity store onto a computer and get the computer to do the searching.

Question: How do you change a pile structure into a chain? How do you change a pile into a sorted list?

Comment: In both cases you impose some better structure on it. To turn a pile into a chain, provide some physical sequence. In the case of a sorted list, you arrange the pile in some physical *and* logical sequence, based on one of its attributes.

5.2 The Five Types of Entity Store

As explained above, we can think of a manifest entity class as an entity *store*, something that holds all the occurrences of that entity. Different entity classes store the occurrences in different ways, and these different ways have different effects on how easy or difficult it is to find the particular entities within the store. There are five different types of entity store: piles, chains, (sorted) lists and hashes. There are

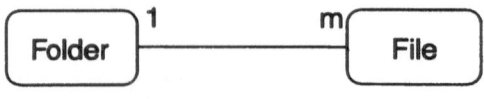

Fig 5.3 Files and folders.

also *unsearchable* entity stores that cannot be accessed for search at all. (In some cases although a store might theoretically be searchable if you have the right tools, it is unsearchable in practice if you do not have the right tools.)

Only manifest entity stores are searchable; conceptual entities outside people's heads are always unsearchable. Indeed the reason we have manifest entities is so that people can access conceptual information. The entities stored in a manifest entity class are always arranged in just one structure at any one time. This is why we often need a number of viewports onto the same underlying conceptual entity (as we illustrated in Section 2.3) in order to get at the manifest entities in different ways.

We shall illustrate the different structures in terms of what can be done with books: they can be left in a heap, placed along a shelf neatly but in random order, placed on a shelf in alphabetic or numerical order, or placed each in a particular position identified by a class mark. Sometimes you cannot look at the books at all.

The notation is simple, we just include an appropriate symbol positioned over the entity store. However, modelers must take care to think hard about which entity store should be marked in which way. In a telephone directory it is the Name entity store which is ordered by Name, not the directory which is ordered by name. Certainly the directory is in alphabetical order, but in ERMIA we need to concentrate on the internal structure of some artefact.

Question: What would it mean if we said that a manifest entity, Telephone Directory, was a sorted list?

Comment: It would mean that we are describing an entity class called Telephone Directory and how the various instances of the telephone directories which made up the class were ordered. In a large city the (conceptual) Telephone Directory is actually manifested as a number of directories, names A–C, D–F and so on. We would be describing these – the internal structure of Telephone Directory.

5.2.1 Pile

Some entity stores can be accessed but they offer the seeker no help at all with the search. A heap of books, lying around in confusion on a table, is one such store. Given N such entities (books) in an entity store, we would need N/2 inspections on average to find a particular entity, and we would need to remember that we had already looked at N/2 entities. This kind of entity store is called a *pile*, marked in Figure 5.4 with the symbol ∅.

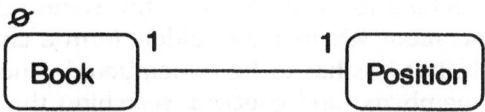

Fig 5.4 ERMIA for books lying on a table.

Question: Figure 5.2 shows a pile of folders. Where would you put a "pile" symbol in Figure 5.3 to show this structure?

Comment: The figure should look like this (Fig 5.5): it is the Folder entity (class) that is a pile, because the folders are arranged haphazardly over the screen.

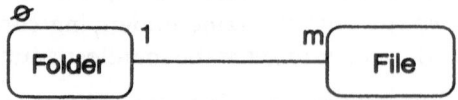

Fig 5.5 Marking the Folder entity as a pile.

5.2.2 Chain

Putting the books on a shelf gives the seeker far more help than a pile on a table – even if it is haphazardly arranged. Like the numbers in a telephone directory, this is an example of a *chain* structure. A chain structure consists of entity occurrences which follow one another, so that it is possible to go from the current entity occurrence to the "next" entity. The search will need N/2 inspections on average (like a pile), but the seeker only has to remember one position during the search, the current position. A chain is represented with a single arrow ↓.

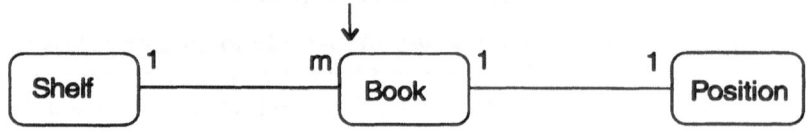

Fig 5.6 Books at random on the shelf.

Question: Look back at Figure 5.2. Can it be rearranged so that the folders form a chain instead of a pile? What would the ERMIA diagram be?

Comment: Arranging the folders in a row is one way to make a chain structure (Fig 5.7): another way would be to view the folders as a list of names instead of a set of icons. Notice that although the ERMIA diagram (Fig 5.8) indicates that the structure is a chain, it does not show which of those ways was used, because they are structurally identical.

Question: How does the new structure help searching for a file?

Comment: Searching for a file involves the same number of search operations whether the folders form a chain instead of a pile, but less has to be remembered. Since less has to be remembered and checked, searching the chain will probably be quicker.

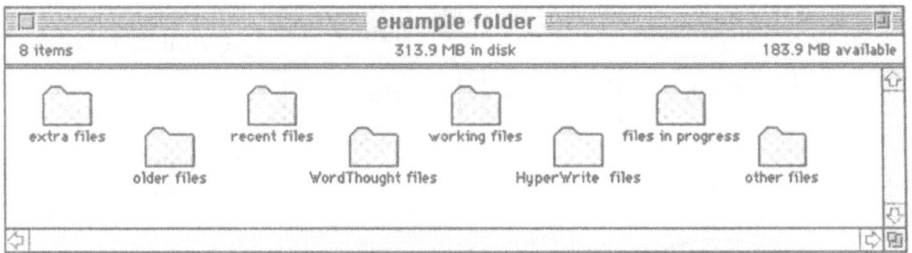

Fig 5.7 A chain of folders – this can be searched from left to right.

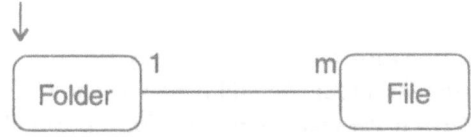

Fig 5.8 ERMIA of Fig 5.7 (compare Fig 5.5).

5.2.3 Sorted List

If the books on the shelf are arranged in alphabetical order by author, search can be still faster. The seeker can make a guess whether to start in the middle of the shelf or at one end, depending on whether the author of the book sought starts with an early letter or a late letter. If there are enough books it might be worth trying the binary search method described above (Section 5.1.1). This type of entity store is called a *sorted list*, represented ⇓. We also include the name of the attribute(s) by which the store is sorted (see Fig 5.9).

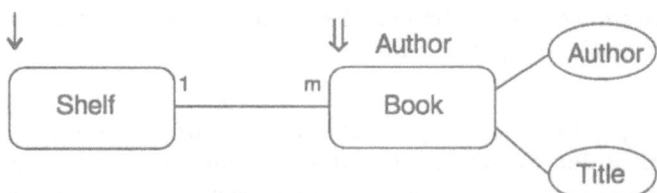

Fig 5.9 Books on the shelf in alphabetic order by Author; shelves are a chain.

Sorted lists can contain further sorted lists. The shelves might be arranged in numerical order of subject, perhaps. That would mean that the Shelf entity had an attribute of 'shelf-number' (Shelf-Num) and the ERMIA diagram would look like Figure 5.10.

Question: Figure 5.7 showed how searching through the folders could be improved if they were arranged as a chain instead of a pile. Would the search for a given file be improved still more if the folders were arranged in alphabetical order, as a sorted list?

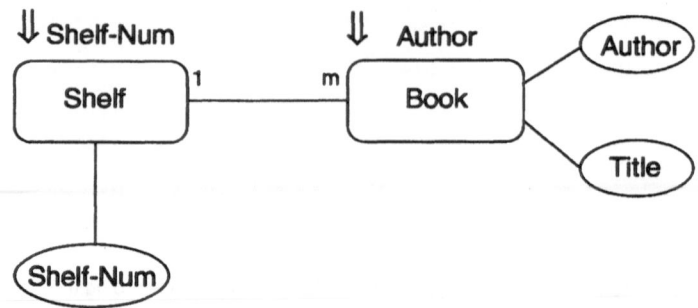

Fig 5.10 A sorted list of shelves, each holding a sorted list of books.

Comment: No, because we are searching for a particular *file*, not a particular folder. We still have to search on average half the folders. If we were searching for a particular folder (and we knew its name), alphabetical order would certainly be an improvement – but the effect would not be noticeable unless there were rather more folders than the eight shown in that figure.

5.2.4 Hash

A hash entity-store is not ordered, but there is a relationship between the value of the identifying attribute and the place where the occurrence of the entity is stored. Just knowing the value of the identifying attribute is enough to tell you where to find the corresponding entity in the store. In this kind of entity-store, the search time is always the same regardless of how large the store may be, and the only memory requirement is to remember the value of the identifying attribute. The symbol for a hashed store is #, together with the name of the attribute(s).

Yet another way of managing your book collection! Instead of using all those boring shelves, put the book by your favourite author under your pillow to keep your friends off it. Put the one by your second-favourite author on your desk. Put each of your other books somewhere precise. Now you have a hash entity-store. To find a book, you only need to know the value of the Author attribute, because you can immediately find the book you want. (Of course, you have to be more devious if you buy another book by the same author. Then you might invent some function that automatically mapped the author's name to the book's location)

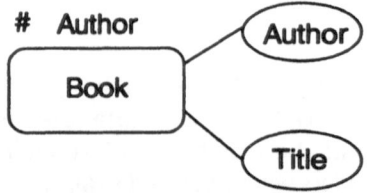

Fig 5.11 If the location of a book is specified absolutely by the author, then Book is a hash entity-store.

Question: Can files be arranged in a hash structure?

Comment: It would not be easy to put them all in a hash structure, but it is quite common to arrange a few special-purpose ones so that they can be accessed readily. For example, you might put some frequently used files on the desk top.

5.2.5 Unsearchable Entity Stores

The final kind of entity-store we consider is *unsearchable*. An unsearchable entity-store does not offer any way to identify its contents. We use the symbol X.

Many large libraries keep some of their books in a reserve store, sometimes called 'the stacks', from which they can be recalled by filling out a slip and waiting while a librarian fetches whatever is needed. There is no way for the average user to inspect the contents of the stacks; unless you know the details of a specific book, too bad.

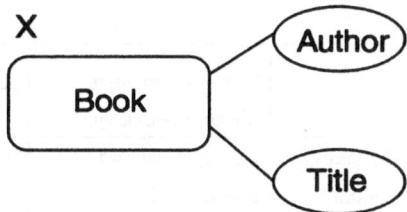

Fig 5.12 ERMIA diagram for unsearchable books. (The view shown is the average user's view; the librarians' view is probably the one in Fig 5.11.)

The books in the reserve are manifest entities. There are also conceptual entities to be considered. These are always unsearchable. One example is the plot of a book. Although Figure 5.13 shows the X symbol over the conceptual entity Plot, this is just for illustration in this case and it would not normally be shown, since conceptual entities are not searchable.

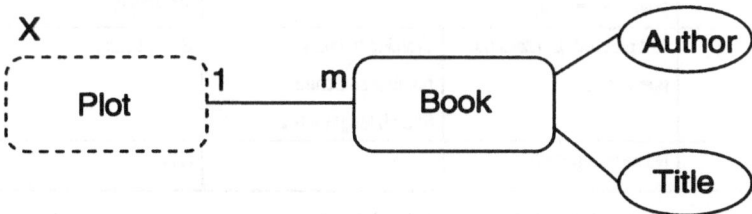

Fig 5.13 Every book has a plot (though several books might have the same plot!) but Plot is unsearchable, because it is a conceptual entity, not directly represented.

Unsearchable stores can also occur when a specific tool is needed to perform the search, and the tool is not available. A floppy disk is unsearchable if there is no computer available to read it!

Question: How would you make folders unsearchable? Would you ever want to do this?

Comment: One way would be to make them invisible (there is a specific way to do that in some operating systems). You may well want to do this in order to make some files secure from unauthorized access.

5.2.6 Summary

All entity stores (except for unsearchable ones) can be treated as a pile, and they often are. For example, if you miss the sign to a section in a library then you can wander round the library looking for that section. This will need on average N/2 searches (where N is the number of sections), plus remembering the places where you have looked so far. Walking round the library systematically might enable you to treat it as a chain instead. A summary of the different types of entity store is shown in Figure 5.14.

Entity-store type	Description	Memory requirements Average search length	Search strategies	Symbol
Hash	Not ordered, but there is relationship between attribute values and location	Working memory = 1 Search length = 1	Direct access	#
Sorted list	A collection of entities which are sequenced by an attribute	Working memory = 1 Search length = few	Sequential or binary search using the index attribute	⇓
Chain	Not ordered, but provides a pointer to the next item (usually the next in a physical sequence)	Working memory = 1 Search length = N/2	Sequential search using pointer (hence usually serial search using physical sequence)	↓
Pile	Not ordered, provides no pointers	Working memory = number searched Search length = N/2	Serial search	∅
Unsearchable	No search possible		N/A	X

Fig 5.14 A summary of the different types of entity store.

5.2.7 Perceptually-coded Attributes Speed Up Search

Perceptually-coded attributes can have a special role in speeding up search. If a perceptual attribute is a coding for a conceptual entity, then the search becomes, in effect, a hash search using the conceptual entity. That is, if we have marked all the detective stories with a blue label, then the search for a detective story becomes an at-a-glance search for a book with a blue label (instead of a one-by-one search through each book in turn). In effect, colour coding means that we have a hashed search for Plot. We can show this as illustrated in Figure 5.15.

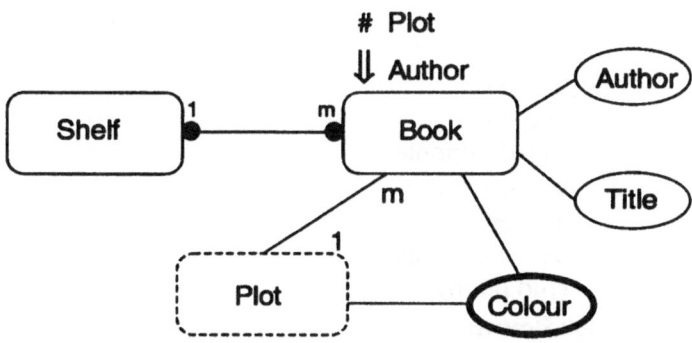

Fig 5.15 Colour-coding a book's plot assists search for that plot.

On many computers the 'label' attribute of a folder can be colour coded. If a user uses red for urgent items, searching for an urgent item becomes identifying the red folders.

5.3 Example: The List of Flowers Revisited

✳ We have presented an ERMIA for a list of flowers, grouped together according to their colour. Given a particular colour, if we then want to choose a flower with a given height, we would still have to search through all the items under that heading looking for the right height. We could improve on that by ordering the items into a list by height (Fig 5.16). The ERMIA for this arrangement is shown in Figure 5.17.

This layout makes it more difficult to answer some other botanical questions, such as "what possible colours can begonias have?" In order to answer this question, it would be necessary to look through all the items to find the name "begonia" and then look at the heading to see which colours it can have.

Question: Garden designers often want to choose plants of a particular height. Given this design, how easy would it be to find all the tall flowers?

Comment: The search would have to be through all the flowers, looking through all the colours.

Question: Draw an ERMIA for an alternative design that makes it easy to find all the tall flowers.

Yellow flowers
 Rose of Sharon   60 cm
 Buttercup   15 cm
 Dandelion   25 cm

Blue flowers
 Bluebell   40 cm
 Hebe   60 cm

Pink flowers
 Begonia   20 cm
 Dwarf begonia   10 cm

Red flowers
 Begonia   20 cm
 Dwarf begonia   10 cm
 Wild poppy   20 cm

Black flowers
 none

Fig 5.16 A list of flowers with headings, sorted by height.

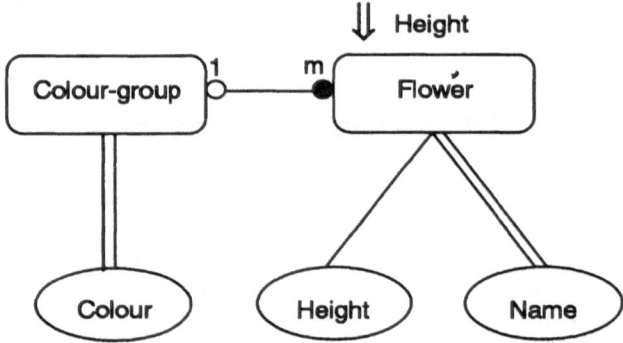

Fig 5.17 A conceptual ERMIA for the colour organized flowers list, sorted by height.

Comment: Instead of grouping the flowers by colour, group them by height (Fig 5.8). The perceptual ERMIA, on the left, would look the same as when they were grouped by colour, but the conceptual ERMIA, on the right, shows that the headings now group the flowers together by height, not by colour.

Question: What would be needed to make it equally easy to identify appropriate flowers by colour and by height?

Comment: One way to do this would be to have a main list which contains all the information about flowers, plus an index. The main list could be ordered by colour, and the index by height, or vice versa.

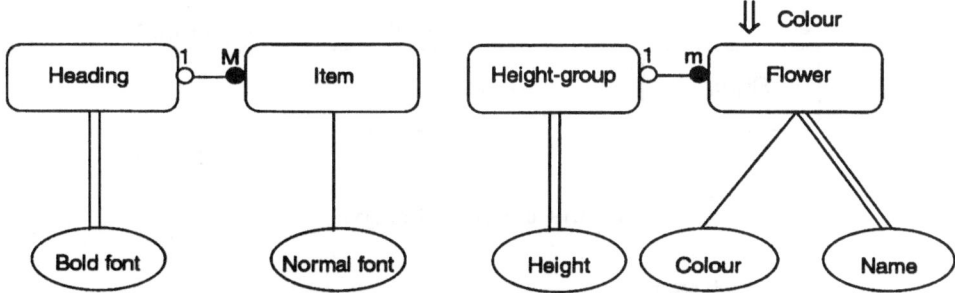

Fig 5.18 ERMIAs for a height organized flower list sorted by colour.

5.4 Searching More Complex Structures

All the examples we have given so far have been very small structures, possibly only a single step search. What happens when we search larger structures? What about other types of structure?

Consider making a list of all the books on all the shelves, where Shelf:Book is 1:m. That means searching through instances of Shelf, and then for each shelf, searching through the instances of Book that are associated with that shelf. The number of steps required to list *all* the books will be equal to the total number of books. If we do not know this, then we would estimate it as the product

number of shelves * average number of books per shelf[1]

Because we want to list *all* the books, the search length is not affected by the entity structure – that is, it makes no difference whether the shelves and books are in order or not. A pseudo-program could be written:

```
for each shelf S
    for each book B on shelf S
        add B to the list of books.
```

If we want to find a given book, the number of search steps will depend on how the shelves and books are organized. We shall need to know the target attribute of the book, say its title, in order to know when to stop the search; and when we have found the target entity (i.e. the instance of Book that has the required value for Title), we shall make a note of whatever output attribute is required, say the author.

Consider searching the typical books-and-shelves structure where the books are arranged on shelves in order of author, but the shelves themselves have no organization other than a chain (Fig 5.19). Suppose the question is, Who wrote *Robinson Crusoe*? We will assume there is only one book called that, so the target attribute is Title, and the output attribute is to be Author. Although the books are organized in a sorted list by Author, that is no use to us on this occasion, because we do not know the author; we have to regard the structure as no better than a chain.

---

[1]Below we use the abbreviation '#Shelf' for 'number of shelves' and '# Book/Shelf' for 'average number of books per shelf'. This use of # is not to be confused with the hash entity store.

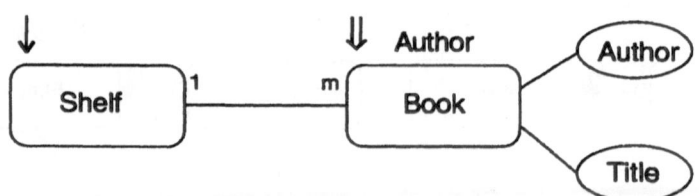

Fig 5.19 Books on shelves again.

```
for each shelf S
      for each book B on shelf S
            if Title (book B) = target
            then
                   note Author (book B) and stop searching.
            [if not found, search the next shelf].
```

The number of steps required is

$$1/2 \ (\#Shelf * \# Book/Shelf)$$

The memory required is two items: current shelf, and current book.

The search process is rather different if we reverse the question to, What did Daniel Defoe write? Again we will assume he only wrote one book, so the target attribute is Author and the output attribute is to be Title. Because the books are ordered by Author on the shelves, we can do a binary search for that part of the process:

```
for each shelf S
      do binary search for book B on shelf S using Author
            if Author found
            then
                   note Title (book B) and stop searching
            [if not found, search the next shelf].
```

The average number of steps required is:

$$1/2 \ (\#Shelf * \log(\# Book/Shelf))$$

As before, two memory items are required.

Search processes can be extended indefinitely. If we enlarge the model to include pages and words (Fig 5.20), we can search for the title of the first book found for which one of the words on page 41 is 'ship'.

The search program will now be something like this:

```
for each shelf S
      for each book B on shelf S
            do binary search for page P in book B using Number
                  for each word W on page P
                  if word W = 'ship'
                  then
                         note Title (book B) and stop searching.
```

The average number of search steps will be

$$1/2 \ (\#Shelf * \#Book/Shelf * \log (\#Page/Book) * \#Word/Page)$$

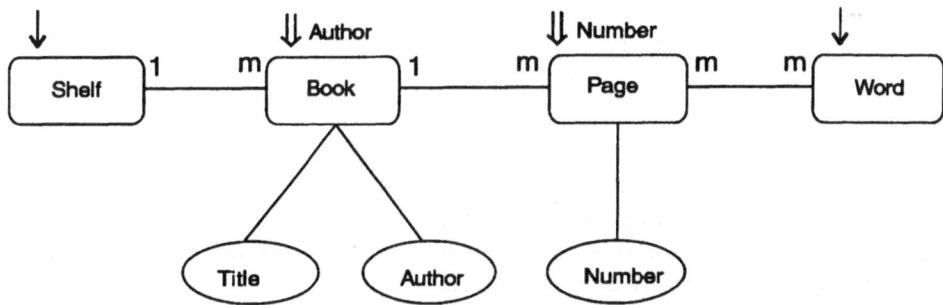

Fig 5.20 Extended model of books on shelves.

The number of memory items will be 4, one each for Shelf, Book, Page and Word.

So far we have looked at searches which only seek one target, going down a sequence of 1:m structures as deep as need be. There are also some other types of searches. First we look at multiple searches, where we search for one entity and then having found it we start another search inside it. The extended book model of Figure 5.20 will serve as an example. Suppose we search for *Robinson Crusoe* (that is the first search), and then when we find it we do another search for the first page on which the word 'ship' occurs.

The search program will now be something like this:

```
1) for each shelf S
        for each book B on shelf S
            if Title (book B) is 'Robinson Crusoe'
            then stop searching shelves.
2) for each page P in book B
        for each word W on page P
            if word W = 'ship'
            then
                    note Page (book B) and stop searching.
```

The number of search steps for the first search will be

$$1/2 \ (\#Shelf * \#Book/Shelf)$$

The number of search steps for the second search will be

$$1/2 \ (\#Page * \#Word/Page)$$

Thus the total number of search steps will be the sum of those two:

$$1/2 \ (\#Shelf * \#Book/Shelf) + 1/2 \ (\#Page * \#Word/Page)$$

The number of memory items will be 2 in each part of the search.

Next, what about searches over relationships that are 1:1? These will depend solely on the internal structure of the entity stores. At last we can return to the simplistic version of a telephone directory shown in Figure 5.1! Finding the telephone number that goes with a name, and finding the name that goes with a number, are different because of the different structure of the Name and Number entities.

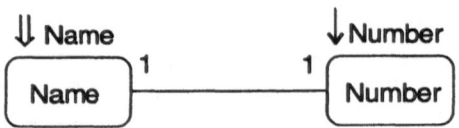

Fig 5.21 Structure of a name-number list.

Because Name is a sorted list, we can find the number for a given name very fast, using binary search. Conversely, because Number is only a chain, finding the Name that goes with a number will be very tedious.

Exercise 5

Now try this example. Spend 10 to 15 minutes developing your ERMIA before looking at our solution. Show all relationships on your ERMIA and also show how the manifest entities are structured. Don't worry about participation conditions.

> **✳ Example** You have remembered reading an interesting piece of text about human-computer interaction in a book called The Art of Human-Computer Interface Design by Brenda Laurel, so you set out to find it. You know that a book will have an index and a contents list, that it will have lots of pages each of which will have a page number and some text. The book will be in a library (though whether it is in your public library or a university library, you don't know). When you have found which library it is in you will be able to go directly to the non-fiction section and from the class mark, you will be able to find the appropriate group of shelves, the specific shelf and finally locate the book itself. You can then find the text which you want.

As you will see in the solution, if you are fed up with books and libraries, the problems easily map onto modern computer-based information artefacts; using these everyday examples helps to explain otherwise complex concepts.

The problems of searching for information in a complex information artefact are one of the main causes of frustration with computer-based and paper-based artefacts alike. Although computers can speed up the search by treating every structure as a chain and searching for some target value of an attribute, the original entities must possess that attribute in the first place. If the value is too broad, then too many instances will be retrieved (try doing a search of a large bibliographic database using the author name 'Smith') and the user still has a large task ahead.

It is up to the designers of information artefacts to consider how the structure which they have created will impact the tasks which people want to do. Drawing ERMIAs of the artefacts makes that structure explicit.

Summary

- *Frequently users will want to retrieve one or several specific instances of a manifest entity.*
- *The ease of locating a specific instance of an entity depends on the number of instances that have to be searched and on the amount of memory required by the user.*
- *Manifest entities have to be stored in some sequence, or structure.*
- *There are four possible structures – pile, chain, sorted list and hash.*
- *Some manifest entity classes are not searchable.*
- *Searching complex information artefacts can be extremely time consuming.*

6. *Dealing with Complex Relationships*

Aims and Objectives

This chapter continues the theme of searching for information. It describes the importance of searching for many-to-many relationships between entities.

After reading this chapter you should be able to:

- decompose many-to-many relationships to reveal the way that the information artefact deals with them
- understand the effect of many-to-many relationships on search
- use an ERMIA to identify how easy it is to find information about many-to-many relationships in an artefact
- be aware of how information in many-to-many relationships can be made fully accessible.

6.1 Decomposing Many-to-Many Relationships

The treatment of many-to-many relationships can make it harder or easier to find information. Many-to-many relationships conceal the potential for a new conceptual entity, one that deals with the relationship itself. By looking more closely at many-to-many relationships we can see the difference between artefacts that let us use the relationship to retrieve information and artefacts that do not. We explore the problem of traversing relationships in different directions.

To explore this last point, we first consider two different ERMIAs and the information that they represent. Both are simplified versions of the standard "parts-inventory" problem used in data modeling: we want to describe two information artefacts that maintain information about parts and their suppliers.

In the first case, we suppose we have two card indexes. The cards in one index each represent a Part. Each Part has a unique inventory number, each Part is stored in a numbered bin (noted on the card) and each Part may be ordered from one or more suppliers (whose name is also noted on the card). The cards may also include other information about the Part, such as its name and size. The cards in the other index each represent a Supplier. Each Supplier has a unique name, and an address, telephone and fax number (all noted on the card). Example cards are shown in Figure 6.1.

Inventory Number A10060
Name: Flange   Size 14 mm
Bin Number H5

         Suppliers:
     Smith and Co
     NorthEastern Ltd
     Davies Industries

Davies Industries

         14 Hangar Lane
         Western Industrial Estate
         London N1 1XX

Tel 0171 123 4567

Fax. 0171 123 7654

Fig 6.1 Card index of Parts (left) and Suppliers (right).

Figure 6.2 presents the conceptual model of this database. Each part can be supplied by many suppliers and each supplier can supply many parts. Our system allows for suppliers who do not currently supply any parts, but each part must have at least one supplier. In a large enterprise it is essential to know how to identify a particular instance of a given entity, such as a Part, and indeed the system will probably collapse if there is no way to find the right part for the job! In our model, a part is uniquely identified by its inventory number (Inv. No), a supplier by Name. Other attributes such as the name of the part and the supplier's telephone and fax numbers could be included but have been left off the diagram for simplicity.

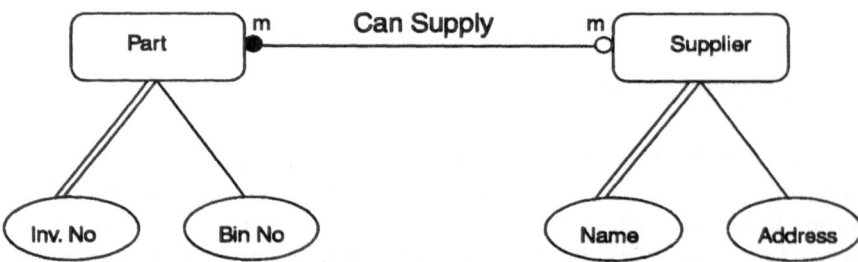

Fig 6.2 Conceptual ERMIA for a database of parts and their suppliers.

Suppose that a user of this card system needs to re-order a part. The user knows which part is needed and its inventory number, but each part is potentially supplied by many suppliers so we need to choose one. If we are happy to order a part from any supplier who can supply it, then this database is sufficient. The user just needs to look up the card for that Part, choose any supplier whose name is on the list for that card, and then look the supplier up in the other card index to find the address.

This card index can store information about parts and about suppliers, but it does not offer any space in which to store information about each part as ordered from each supplier. One supplier may offer better value on one part than the others. Delivery times may vary for the same part obtained from different suppliers and for different parts obtained from different suppliers. This card indexing system does not offer any space in which to store that information in an organized way, which could make it difficult to store and retrieve such information. Yet wherever there is a many-to-many relationship it is possible that such information will be needed.

Question: Think about our files and folders example again. How is a file identified? How is a folder identified?

Comment: File is identified by its name, Filename; Folder is identified by its name, Foldername.

Question: Given these identifiers for files and folders, what is the real relationship between files and folders?

Comment: It is many-to-many (and not many-to-one as we presented it in the previous chapter). The same Filename can occur in many folders and of course a folder can contain many files.

Question: So are two files with the same Filename always the same file?

Comment: No. Your operating system will not allow you to have two files with the same Filename in the same folder, but there is nothing to stop you having two quite different files with the same Filename as long as they are in different folders.

We now consider an ERMIA for a card index which does offer this kind of information (see Fig 6.3). As before, there is a card index for parts and a card index for suppliers. The card index for Supplier is the same as before. This time the card for Part contains not just the names of the suppliers, but for each supplier who offers that part, the card contains spaces where the Price and lead time (Delivery) are noted, for that part from that supplier.

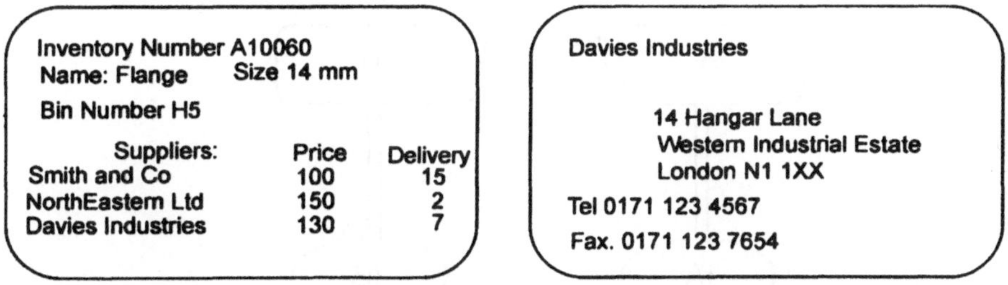

Inventory Number A10060			
Name: Flange	Size 14 mm		
Bin Number H5			
Suppliers:	Price	Delivery	
Smith and Co	100	15	
NorthEastern Ltd	150	2	
Davies Industries	130	7	

Davies Industries

14 Hangar Lane
Western Industrial Estate
London N1 1XX

Tel 0171 123 4567

Fax. 0171 123 7654

Fig 6.3 Card index of Parts and Suppliers, with supplier-part information on the Part card.

This analysis requires that we break down the many-to-many relationship between parts and suppliers and create an entity which represents the information that is stored about the parts and their suppliers. Each entity in the Part by Supplier class is identified by the inventory number and by the supplier name. Information about price and delivery time are attributes attached to the Part by Supplier entity class.

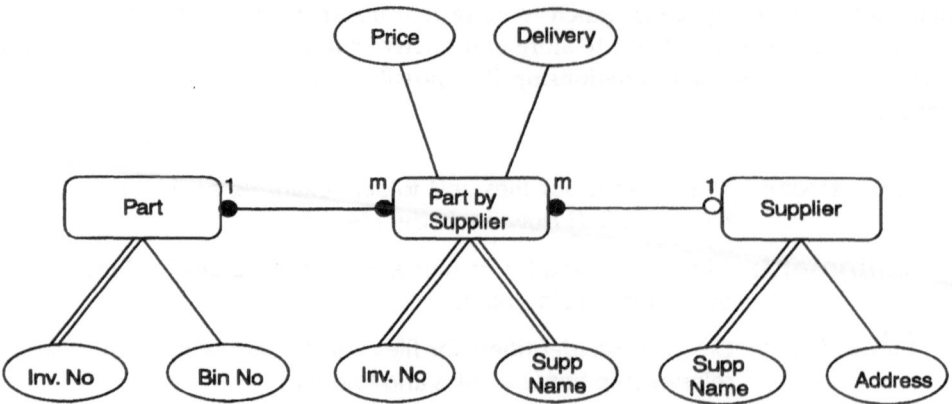

Fig 6.4 ERMIA for a database with information about parts by suppliers.

This card layout makes it much easier to find out about obtaining a specific part from a specific supplier.

6.1.1 Summary: Decomposing Many-to-Many Relationships

This kind of analysis of many-to-many relationships is very common. Whenever there is a many-to-many relationship in an ERMIA, the analysis should also consider whether information is being stored about the connection between items. A many-to-many relationship can always be broken down into a one-to-many relationship, followed by an entity that represents the connection, followed by a many-to-one relationship. The identifying attributes for the new entity will consist of the identifying attributes for entities on either side and the new entity will always have a mandatory relationship with both the original entities. (But you need to be careful that the entity which you uncover is the entity you think it is! Remember that it is the identifier of the entity that defines the meaning of the entity.)

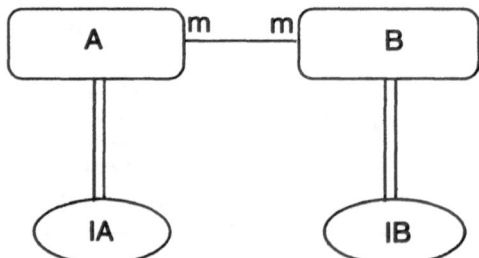

Fig 6.5 General many-to-many relationship between two entities.

Decomposing, or breaking down many-to-many relationships in this way enables us to see whether any conceptual attributes are attached to the connection between entities. And if these conceptual attributes exist, the breakdown enables us to see whether the information artefact allows us to store and to see those attributes.

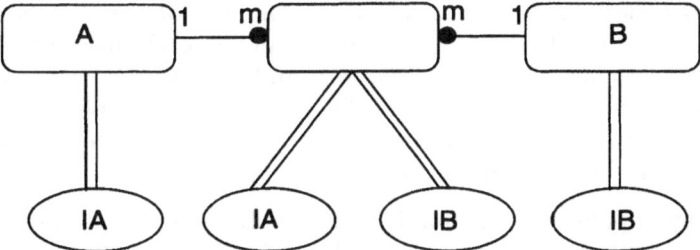

Fig 6.6 Breaking the relationship down (decomposing the relationship).

Exercise 6

Draw an ERMIA for the file and folder problem. Decompose the many-to-many relationship and find some other attributes for the new entity. Show all participation conditions on your diagram.

6.2 Different Manifest Structures Lead to Different Search

Information artefacts which look very similar may have quite different ERMIAs, with different consequences for search. The difference in the ERMIAs reflects the fact that in spite of their apparent similarity, there is a major difference in the structure of the information that can be stored in each card index and retrieved from it.

There are different card layouts that contain the same conceptual information. We have presented a card index which made the Part by Supplier relationship explicit on the Part card. We could have made the Part by Supplier relationship explicit in other ways. The Part by Supplier information could be noted on the Supplier card (Fig 6.7). A separate card could be used for each part obtained from a supplier. These alternative solutions would have similar conceptual ERMIAs because they hold the same conceptual information.

```
Inventory Number A10060
Name: Flange     Size 14 mm
Bin Number H5
```

```
Davies Industries
        14 Hangar Lane
        Western Industrial Estate
        London N1 1XX
Tel 0171 123 4567
Fax. 0171 123 7654

Parts      Price     Delivery
A10060     130          7
A10063     150          4
```

Fig 6.7 Part by Supplier on Supplier card.

So far we have described three card indexes. The first does not represent Part by Supplier information at all (Fig 6.1). The second two each make Part by Supplier information accessible (Fig 6.3 and Fig 6.7) and the ERMIA for both of these is similar (Fig 6.4), but they make it accessible in different ways. We now consider the effects of the different ways in which the information is accessible, and the way that we can represent this difference in an ERMIA.

If the Part by Supplier information is written on the Part cards and if we assume that the cards are in inventory number order, as in Figure 6.3, then it is easy to find out who supplies a particular part but more difficult to find out which parts are offered by a particular supplier. We would need to sort through all the part cards looking for that supplier. Conversely, if the Part by Supplier information is written on the supplier cards and if they are in alphabetic order by (supplier) Name, as in Figure 6.7, then it is easy to find out which parts a supplier offers, and more difficult to find out who supplies a particular part. Finally, if we have a separate card index with a card for each Part by Supplier entry, then the ease with which we can find out these two kinds of information will depend on how the cards are sorted – by part (Inv. No) or by supplier (Name). This is of course where computer databases win over card indexes – a properly designed database can quickly answer either query.

The difference in searching these otherwise identical conceptual structures can be added to the ERMIA by adding information about how the entity stores are organized. In both cases the part index is sorted by inventory number, the supplier is sorted by name. Then if Part by Supplier is written on the part cards, it is in effect sorted by inventory number (Fig 6.8). Conversely if Part by Supplier information is entered on the supplier cards, it is in effect sorted by supplier name (Fig 6.9). These ERMIAs show two different viewports onto the same conceptual structure.

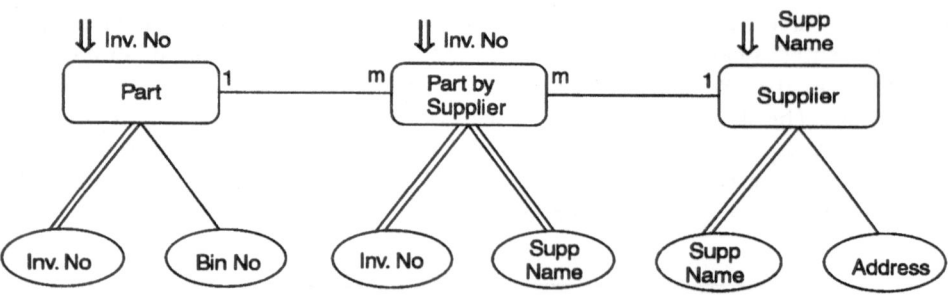

Fig 6.8 ERMIA for Part by Supplier information entered on the part cards.

6.3 Making Many-to-Many Relationships Easy to Explore

Whenever a many-to-many relationship exists, it is often only easy to obtain the information in one direction. To make information accessible in both directions, either an index or a search tool is needed. Indexes and search tools are easier to create in computerized systems than in card-based systems. Hierarchical structures

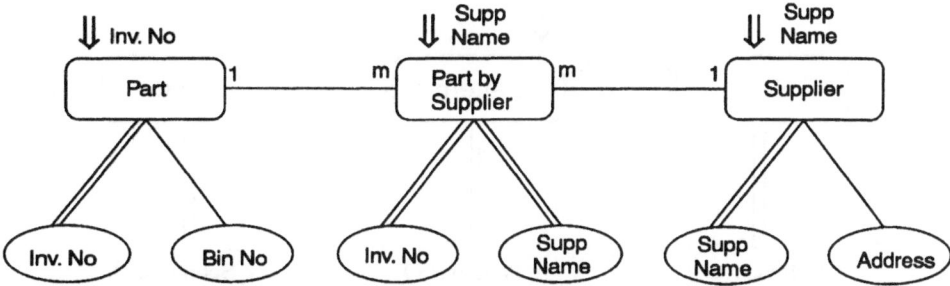

Fig 6.9 ERMIA for Part by Supplier information entered on the supplier cards.

are particularly troublesome in this respect as they only show one side of a many-to-many relationship, whereas networks and tables show both sides clearly (see Section 7.1 for more discussion of standard structures). The use of hierarchical structures, such as the Macintosh Finder, Windows Explorer, a Smalltalk browser and so on, result in these systems having to introduce search tools such as Find File in order to let the user access the structure in an alternative way.

It might be tempting to make both kinds of information equally easy to find by duplicating the information. In the Parts-Supplier card index example, this would mean entering it on both the Part cards and on the Supplier cards. This in itself causes further problems: a problem of duplication of effort in entering the information twice, a problem of space if there is a large amount of information attached to the Part by Supplier entity, and a problem of inconsistency if the information on the part's card is changed but the corresponding entry on the supplier's card is not.

6.4 Example: A Drum Machine Pattern Sequencer

✳   In this example, we consider the use of relationships to seek information and the need to represent many-to-many relationships as entities in the ERMIA. This analysis is based on a computer system which one of the authors uses; a synthesizer for drum music which can be attached to a personal computer.

The drum-pattern sequencer contains digital audio samples of different percussion sounds which can be sequenced together to form a rhythmic accompaniment to a song or tune. Percussion rhythms are normally highly repetitive – boom-tish-boom-tish boom boom, repeated ad lib. Rather than treat each "song" as a sequence of separate sounds, the user first defines patterns of sounds and then defines a song as so many instances of one pattern, so many instances of another, and so on. The user can switch between two viewports, one showing the songs and one showing the patterns.

Conceptually, the drum machine contains the information in Figure 6.10.

The design of the device allows each pattern to be re-used in as many

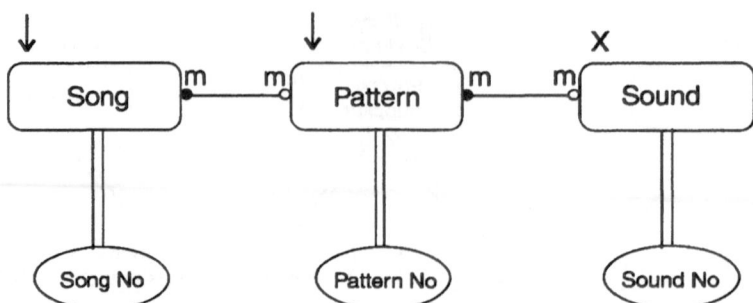

Fig 6.10 Conceptual ERMIA for drum machine.

songs as the user likes. The patterns are "masters", re-usable in as many songs as needed; if a pattern changes, then it changes in all the songs that use it. The problem here is that the device offers no way to look at a pattern and tell which songs it is used in: so there is no way to tell whether it is safe to change a pattern or whether changing the pattern will ruin another song.

The information display that is supported by the device allows the user to identify a song by its number, to display each song as a list of pattern numbers (together with the number of repetitions required) and to inspect each pattern (displayed as a sequence of sound samples). So to discover whether a particular pattern is being used by another song it is necessary to go through all the songs, one at a time, looking for that pattern number.

Only some of the information in the conceptual model of the sequencer is easily accessible. We can explain what information is accessible by exploring the many-to-many relationship between Song and Pattern. We replace this relationship with the entity Song has Patterns and two corresponding many-to-one relationships (as described in Section 6.1.1). We now consider how we access the Song has Patterns entity. The most likely access methods are to allow access by Song (allowing us to find out easily which patterns belong to a song) or by Pattern (allowing us to find out which songs use a pattern), and possibly by both. As described, this entity is only easily accessible by Song No. If we supply the song number, we can find out all the corresponding patterns (see Fig 6.11).

A similar problem exists with finding the sounds which appear in a particular Pattern, and we could expand the conceptual and perceptual ERMIAs to show this. We return to this example in Section 7.3. Also note that in this system the sounds are unsearchable.

6.5 Fossil Silt

One consequence of the display used in the drum sequencer is that when several songs have been removed or changed, it becomes difficult to tell whether a pattern

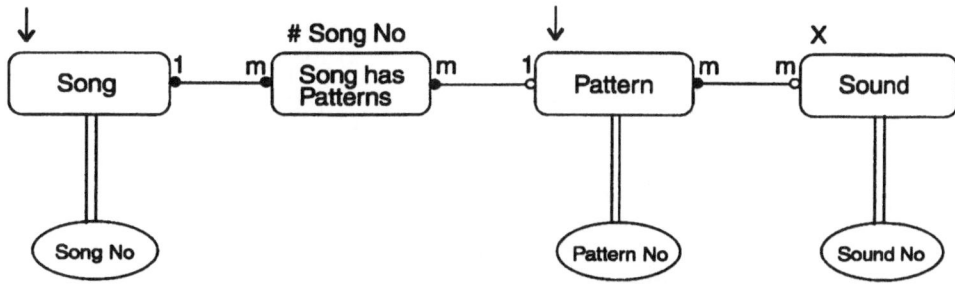

Fig 6.11 Decomposing the Song:Pattern relationship for the drum machine.

is still being used by some song or whether it is now obsolete and can be removed, leaving the user free to re-use the pattern number for a different pattern. In order to be sure that no song used the pattern, the user would have to look through every song in turn to see if it used that pattern, and remember which pattern numbers had been used. This is slow and prone to errors. As a result the users of the real device tend to leave old and possibly unused patterns where they are, and use a new pattern number for a new pattern instead of re-using an unused one. This results in an accumulation of old patterns that are never used and never thrown away. We call the accumulation of unused and useless data *fossil silt*. In a small device such as the drum machine which does not have much memory, the fossil silt soon becomes very tiresome.

Fossil silt arises when it is difficult to discover all the dependencies in an information artefact. "Dot" files in Unix suffer from this problem as do style sheets in word processors and the various .ini files in the DOS operating system. If it is hard to see all the dependencies, users will leave old information where it is rather than change it or throw it away. That is safer than throwing the old information away and then finding that there is still some process which depends on the old information and which now stops working or contains an error. The old, fossilized information accumulates, filling up the available storage with information that is probably useless until the storage is silted up altogether. It is a good idea to design interfaces that avoid fossil silt by making all the necessary dependencies clear.

In Figure 6.12 the Word 5.1 style sheet is shown. It tells the user what the currently selected style is based on, but it does not say which styles, if any, are based on it. If the user changes the characteristics of "fig caption" will this have consequences elsewhere? It is safer to leave it alone and define a new style. The document gradually silts up with fossilized styles.

Question: Try drawing perceptual and conceptual ERMIAs for the Word 5.1 style sheet, just showing the relationship between styles.

Comment: If you come up with something like the spreadsheet example (Fig 4.3) you will have found the problem!

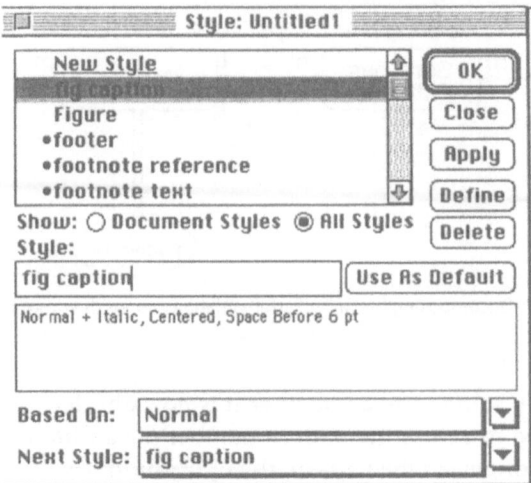

Fig 6.12 Word 5.1 style sheet. The interface encourages fossil silting.

Summary

- *Complex (i.e. many-to-many) relationships need careful consideration when designing information artefacts.*
- *ERMIA, as with standard ER modeling, provides a useful technique to decompose complex relationships – the relationship is represented as an entity which has a m:1 mandatory relationship with the two original entities.*
- *The identifier of the new entity is the concatenation of the identifiers of each of the original entities.*
- *Complex relationships should always be decomposed so that the "hidden" entity can be examined to see whether it is important or not with regards to obtaining information.*
- *Failure to provide information about both sides of a many-to-many relationship can cause problems and can result in fossil silt.*

7. Standard Structures and Safe Paths

Aims and Objectives

This chapter continues the theme of searching for information. It explores search that traverses many relationships. ERMIAs can be used to identify standard patterns which have standard characteristics for search.

After reading this chapter, you should be able to:

- identify standard patterns in the manifest structure of an artefact
- estimate the difficulty of finding information in ERMIAs with standard patterns
- use an ERMIA to identify connection traps – places in an artefact where information may be lost
- decide whether useful information will be lost as the result of a potential trap.

7.1 Standard Structures for Search

The purpose of ERMIA is to represent structure; so artefacts with similar underlying structure should have some similar properties. We have already noted that different artefacts can have similar conceptual structures. There are four very common topologies for conceptual structures:

- Trail: a linear chain of different entity types.
- Table: a structure usually consisting of three entity types, typified by a two-dimensional table.
- Tree: a single entity type and a single relationship type; their instances form a hierarchy (technically, a directed acyclic graph).
- Network: a single entity type and multiple relationship types; like a tree but forming a directed cyclic graph.

7.1.1 Trails

The fundamental structure of a trail is a linear chain of entity types connected by a succession of 1:m (or sometimes 1:1) relationships.

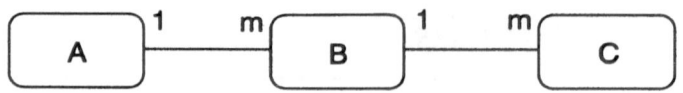

Fig 7.1 A simple linear trail.

Trails are particularly associated with complex information artefacts designed for looking up facts. At each step of the search process, a new entity type is encountered, and usually a completely new manifest representation. For instance, to locate a book in a large library requires finding the author and title, looking up the class mark in a card index or database from the author-title combination, then using a paper directory to look up the physical location of the book from the class mark (e.g. which section of the library), then finding the particular group of shelves (shelf group) by walking around the relevant room, then finding the place on the shelf by inspecting the class marks of other books.

7.1.2 Tables

A basic table structure represents an information artefact in which there are just three conceptual entity types, and in the manifest structure the instances of one entity type are represented by the rows, instances of another by the columns and instances of the third by the cells. Usually there are only two relationships – "cells on the same row" and "cells in same column". Furthermore, the only entity which holds real interest is the cell; the row and column entity types only serve to identify or describe the meaning of the data in the cells.

The structure of such a table is as follows (Fig 7.2):

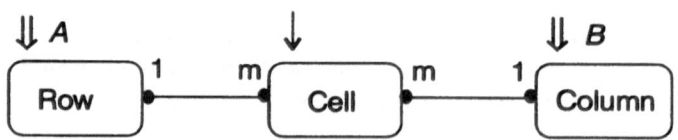

Fig 7.2 The basic table structure.

To determine a particular Cell we need to know both the Row and the Column. To obtain information users can scan the cells, but it is more common to scan the rows and columns, then to note the value contained in the cell at their intersection. Tables are generally easy to search, but they can become difficult if they are too large.

Question: Can you see what the identifier of Cell is in Figure 7.2? What relationship does it represent between Row and Column?

Comment: The identifier of Cell is {A,B} – the concatenation of the identifier of Row and the identifier of Column. It represents the m:m relationship between Row and Column.

7.1.3 Trees or Hierarchies

A simple tree structure has only one entity class, connected in a 1:m relationship with itself (that is, an entity in the class is connected with other entities in the same class). A tree structure is usually easy to search providing the user wants to go in the same direction as the tree, i.e. to follow the 1:m links. So structures that are conceptually trees are easy to search, but those that are not are difficult to search. Unfortunately most things are not "true" hierarchies. Even one exception to the strict hierarchical structure means that it should really be represented as a m:m relationship and not as a 1:m relationship. True hierarchies are not so well suited to an ERMIA analysis because they contain only one type of entity, referring to itself! Hierarchies tend to have a complex content rather than a complex structure. The conceptual tree, can be viewed as in Figure 7.3.

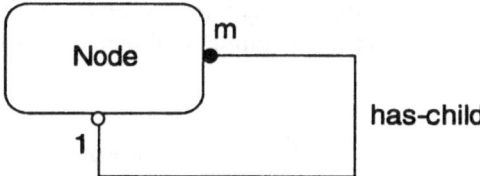

Fig 7.3 In a tree, every Node may possibly have a child; every Node is the child of some Node (thus, the root is left undefined).

Figure 7.3 does not mention the root of the tree. For many purposes the root would not need to be specially distinguished, so that would be alright. A more elaborate representation is needed if the root is to be distinguished (Fig 7.4).

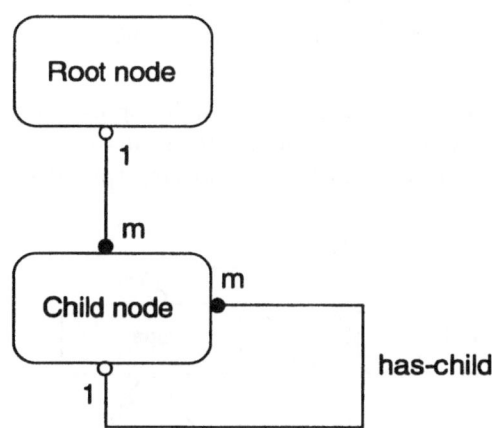

Fig 7.4 This version of a tree structure distinguishes the root.

Question: Describe the ERMIA of a tree structure shown in Figure 7.4 concentrating on the participation conditions of the entities in their relationships.

Comment: The root node of a hierarchy may have many child nodes (but does not have to have any). A child node must be related to just one root node and may itself have many (lower level) child nodes (but does not have to have any). (Lower level) child nodes must be related to just one (higher level) child node.

7.1.4 Networks

The network is a very common and general structure. It is typified by a many-to-many relationship between entities of the same type.

The classic example of a network-based information artefact is a hypertext, or hypermedia system, such as the World Wide Web (the Web). The information structure is very simple, consisting of pages, identified by their Web address, linked to as many other pages as desired. Our model is shown in Figure 7.5.

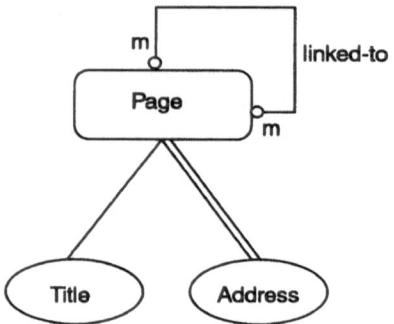

Fig 7.5 The basic network structure.

As we have seen the many-to-many relationship in Figure 7.5 can be replaced by an entity. Let's call this entity Link. If we do this the structure appears as in Figure 7.6. We have seen this structure before when considering spreadsheets (Fig 4.3).

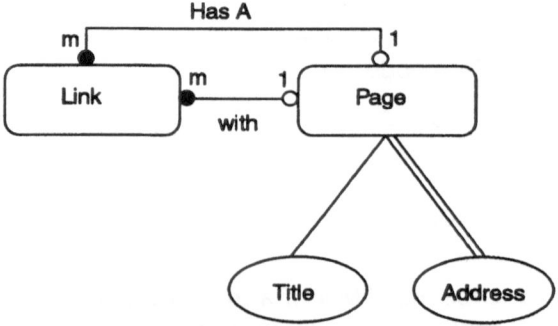

Fig 7.6 Decomposing the m:m relationship in Figure 7.5 to reveal a Link entity.

Exercise 7

At the time of writing, most browsers and servers for the Web have two important features missing which are common in other hypermedia systems. First, the Web only provides one type of link whereas other hypermedia systems provide any number. Secondly, while many hypermedia systems will ensure that links always link to another page, the Web does not do this – resulting in the "dangling link" syndrome.

Draw perceptual ERMIAs for a "good" hypermedia system and for the Web.

It is useful to identify these common structures because they have advantages and problems that we can recognize in a variety of situations such as:

- browsers for hierarchies;
- reverse links in tables;
- indexes and lists for trails;
- tracing paths through networks.

Browsers should allow users to traverse the hierarchical structure in the m:1 direction as well as in the 1:m direction. Moreover, browsers should enable users to locate multiple instances when searching and not just the next in a sequence. For example, the Macintosh Find File utility (prior to version 7.5) highlights a single instance of a matching file name whereas the Word Find File utility displays all instances (Fig 7.7).

Question: Recall the discussion of searching entity stores in Section 5.2. How do the two Find File utilities above treat the hierarchy?

Comment: The Macintosh Finder treats the hierarchy of files as a Pile; the user must remember all the instances previously found. Word treats it as a sorted list, displaying all instances found in alphabetical order, thus reducing the demands on the user's memory (see Fig 7.7).

We have also seen how important it is to reveal reverse links in table structures in order to avoid fossil silt for cautious users or unexpected results for the brave. Reverse links in network structures also need to be represented to avoid dangling links and to ensure consistent updating. Lengthy trails such as the library example (Exercise 5) need to provide various types of index in order to structure the search.

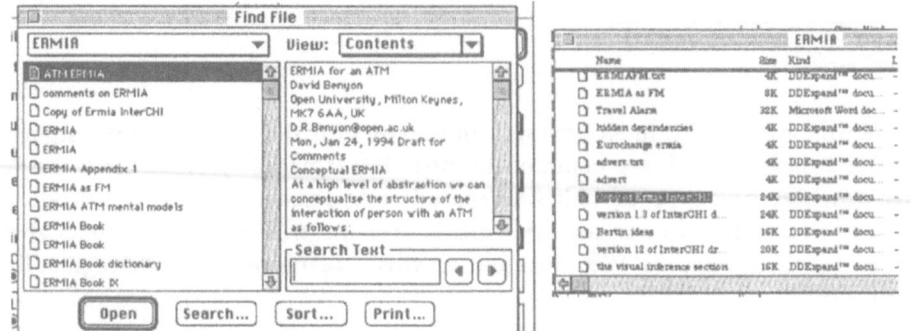

Fig 7.7 Word Find File (on the left) and Macintosh Finder Find File (on the right).

7.2 Safe Trails

ER diagrams can be thought of as a map of the information structure, in which the relationships provide a route through the entity terrain. In many cases there is a route through the information structure that gets us from the question we want to ask to an unambiguous answer. In other cases, there are "connection traps" along the path that mean that we may be unable to find an unambiguous answer to a query. ERMIAs can reveal both safe trails and the connection traps. In this section, we consider the elements to look out for in an ERMIA that reveal potential traps.

In many cases, trails are unambiguous; for example, mandatory 1:1 relationships between entities imply that if you know the value of one entity instance you can find the value of the associated one. Paths that follow successive 1:m relationships are also safe so long as participation is mandatory. Queries that cross other 1:m relationships are unambiguous so long as we know the values of the identifying attributes as are trails involving 1:m and m:1 relationships. In the part-supplier card index described by the ERMIA in Figure 6.4 if we know the inventory number of a part, then we can discover who supplies it, because the identifier Inv. No is the identifying attribute for a unique set of instances of Part By Supplier (which are each associated with a unique Supplier).

If we do not know the identifying attribute, then the search becomes more complicated. In the part-supplier card index if we know the price or the lead time of a particular part but not the inventory number, then we have to search sequentially to find the part and all the suppliers.

7.3 Connection Traps

The term *connection trap* is used to refer to ambiguous paths through a model (Howe, 1989; Benyon, 1997). A path that involves traversing an optional participation and that results in lost information is known as a *chasm trap*, while a path that passes through a many-to-one relationship and then a one-to-many relationship is known as a *fan trap*. A connection trap always involves a trail through three or more entity classes.

Designers often simplify information artefacts by removing relationships that seem to be redundant. The reasons for this are: to save space, since only one copy of the same information is stored; and to avoid inconsistency, since if the same information is stored in more than one place, then it is likely that one copy of the information will be altered and not the other. If an artefact has been designed carefully, it will be possible to reconstruct most of the important relationships by using search. But if the relationships have not been designed carefully, the result may be a connection trap.

For example, suppose we have a Products Division of a company that is divided into product groups. Each group makes several similar products, and each product is made within just one group. Each (product) group has members of staff, some of whom work on just one product and the rest of whom do not work on any particular product. Each member of staff belongs to just one group. We can summarize this in the conceptual ERMIA (Fig 7.8).

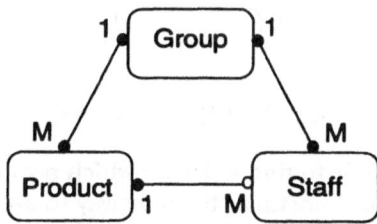

Fig 7.8 A cycle of relationships.

In Figure 7.8 we can find out which members of staff work in which group and which work on which products. We can find out which products belong to each group. This ER diagram shows a cycle of relationships. Generally, where there is a cycle of relationships, database designers will want to remove one of them to simplify things, as described above. We consider three different ways to do this. One way leads to a fan trap, the second to a chasm trap, and the third loses no information.

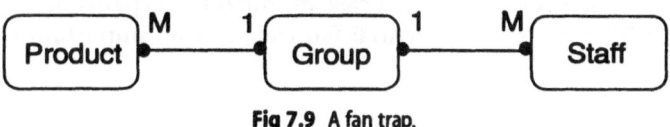

Fig 7.9 A fan trap.

Figure 7.9 contains a fan trap. There is a many-to-one relationship between Product and Group, and a one-to-many relationship between Group and Staff. In the database that this ERMIA describes, we can tell which members of staff are members of each group, and we can tell which products are in each group, but we cannot tell who is working on a particular product. (If you do not see that this is a problem, try writing out a few instances of the entities and you will soon see that there is no unambiguous path from Staff to Product, or from Product to Staff).

Figure 7.10 contains a chasm trap. The relationship between Staff and Product is optional because some staff are not assigned to any particular product. However, all staff should belong to a product Group even if they are not assigned to a product within that group. In this diagram we would only be able to find out which group staff belong to for those staff who are assigned to a specific product.

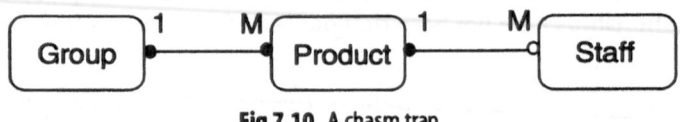

Fig 7.10 A chasm trap.

Figure 7.11 contains no connection traps. We can find out the group to which each staff member belongs, and which staff members are in each group. We can find out the products produced by each group, and we can find out which staff members work on each product. This describes all the necessary information.

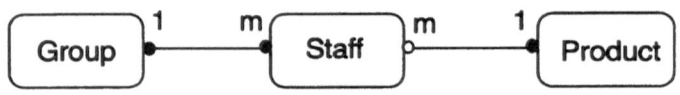

Fig 7.11 A diagram with no trap.

In this example we were able to find a design which avoids both a redundant relation and a connection trap. Sometimes the only way to avoid a connection trap is to keep the redundant relationship in place.

Connection traps can also result when we expand many-to-many relationships. As mentioned in Section 6.1 a many-to-many relationship can usefully be expanded into a one-to-many relationship, a new entity and a many-to-one relationship. This does not lead to a connection trap in itself, but if there are other many-to-one or one-to-many relationships already in the path, then the expansion may combine with these other relationships to reveal a fan trap.

It is important to realize that even if an ERMIA warns us that there is the potential for a connection trap, further analysis is needed to decide whether the connection trap is going to prevent the user from making the queries that the users will *need* to make. The following example shows a case in which the expansion of two many-to-many relationships leads to a potential fan trap, but no important information is lost.

✱ Example We return to the drum-machine pattern sequencer to show the way that this exposes a potential fan trap. To show this, we expand the conceptual ERMIA for the drum pattern sequencer so as to replace both of the many-to-many-relationships with entities (Fig 7.12).

If we look at the relationships around the Pattern entity, we can see that there is a many-to-one relationship from Song/Pattern to Pattern, followed by a one-to-many relationship from Pattern to Pattern/Sound. This is potentially a fan trap. We might have lost some information about the

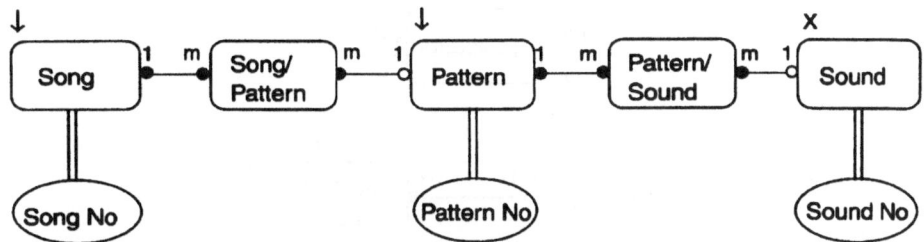

Fig 7.12 Drum machine highlighting potential connection trap.

connection between a particular Song and the Sounds it contains, and vice versa. However, in this particular case the fan trap is not important. The only important relationship between Song and Sound is whether a song contains a sound and whether a sound is contained in a song. If a song contains a pattern then that song also contains *all* of the sounds within that pattern. Similarly all the sounds within a pattern are used by every song that uses the pattern. So there is no special relationship between individual songs and individual sounds. In the drum pattern sequencer, no relevant information is lost due to the fan trap.

7.4 Short Cut Keys

We can further illustrate the power of ERMIA to reveal knotty problems by considering the use of short cut keys, or control keys which are used by most applications on computers. As you will see, the problem is not easy to solve and different software designers have come up with several different solutions. In this section you will work through a number of exercises in order to better understand the issues.

We can conceptualize the problem as follows.

    ✳   **Example** Each application has a number of functions (such as cut, copy, check spelling, italicize text, import text, etc.) and each application must have at least one function (mandatory participation). Every function must belong to some application. Each application also has a number of control keys (Ctrl X, Ctrl C, Ctrl L, Ctrl I and so on), but it does not have to have any (optional participation). A control key must belong to an application. In the general case there is a many-to-many relationship between the control key and the function. For example, one word processor may use Ctrl I to italicize text and another one may use Ctrl I to import a file. (The situation is exacerbated on many systems as the user can configure the control keys for different functions.) While a control key must perform some function, a function does not have to be associated with a control key. We will identify applications by App Name (e.g. Word or FrameMaker), control keys by Key Name (e.g. Ctrl X) and functions by Fn Name (e.g. Cut). This description results in the conceptual ERMIA in Figure 7.13.

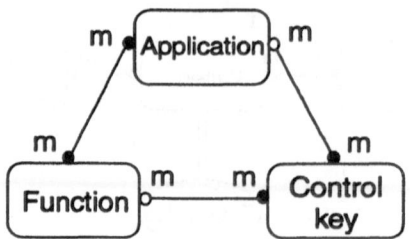

Fig 7.13 Applications, functions and control keys.

Exercise 8

Expand the m:m relationships in Figure 7.13.

You will see from our solution to Exercise 8 that we now have three newly "discovered" entities. Fn in App represents the functions in a particular application, Ctrl in App represents the control keys used in a particular application and Effect represents the function which a control key invokes.

Question: Exactly what is meant by the Effect entity? Is it very useful?

Comment: It is not particularly useful for us, but it may be useful for other people (e.g. Microsoft or Claris). The reason that it is not very useful for us is that it simply records all the possible combinations of control keys and the functions which they can perform. It does not tell us which control key does what in which application.

Exercise 9

Are there any connection traps in the solution to Exercise 8? Do they result in lost information? For example can you answer the questions:

'What is the control key in Word for importing a file?'

'What does Ctrl I do in FrameMaker?'

The solution to Exercise 9 shows how you can trace the paths through an ERMIA and see if particular questions can be answered using the structure. When they cannot, because the structure contains connection traps, we need to look for important relationships that are missing.

Exercise 10

Look at the solution to Exercise 8 and identify any missing relationships. Develop the ERMIA further by adding in the missing relationships.

The solution to Exercise 10 reveals the entity Effect in App. Effect in App is a more interesting entity than Effect (or indeed than Fn in App or Ctrl in App) for our purpose because it gives us more valuable information. Notice that it was only because we decomposed the m:m relationships in Figure 7.13 that we were able to discover the new entities, Effect, Fn in App and Ctrl in App. When we discovered the connection traps we had to look for other relationships and hence discovered the relationship between Fn in App and Ctrl in App which was subsequently decomposed to reveal the new entity, Effect in App.

Question: What is the identifier of Effect in App?

Comment: It is the concatenation of the identifiers of Fn in App and Ctrl key in App. The identifier of Fn in App is {Fn Name, App Name} and the identifier of Ctrl key in App is {Key Name, App Name} so the identifier of Effect in App is {Fn Name, Key Name, App Name}. An example of this might be {Cut, Ctrl X, Word}

Exercise 11

Now use the ERMIA in the solution to Exercise 10 to answer the questions:

'What is the control key in Word for importing a file?'

'What does Ctrl I do in FrameMaker?'

In this section ERMIA has been used to expose a problem with the use of control keys in applications. In fact Word, for example, does provide a display which corresponds to our entity Effect in App (Fig 7.14). In this figure the function Italic (italicize text) is highlighted. The short cut keys Ctrl I, Ctrl ⇧I and F11 are listed as performing this function.

It is exactly this sort of problem which has given rise to the development of standard control keys for certain functions. Users can learn standards and hence will know some of the entries in Effect in App without having to look them up.

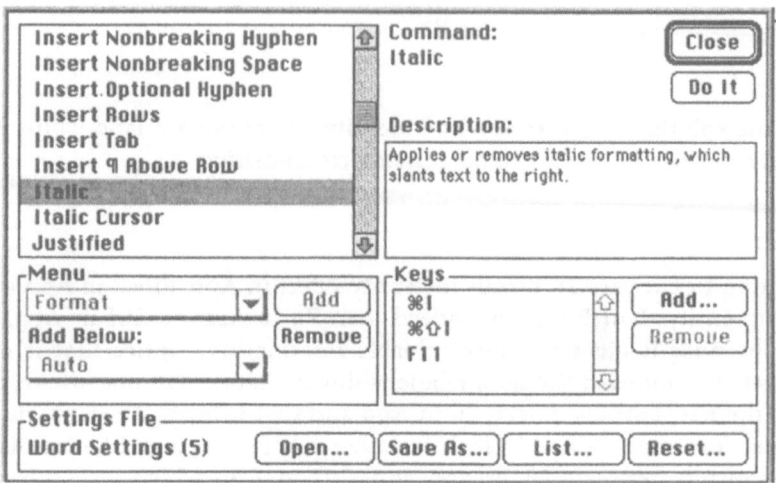

7.14 Display from Word showing instances of Effect in App.

Summary

- *There are a number of common recurring structures which can be modeled in ERMIA.*
- *ERMIA diagrams can be considered as "maps" of some underlying conceptual terrain.*
- *Some paths through this terrain are safe in that we know that we will always be able to retrieve certain information.*
- *Some paths, connection traps, may result in lost information.*

8.　*Representing Different Views*

Aims and Objectives

Information artefacts are built upon each other providing different levels of view onto the information and providing different types of view which reveal more or less of the underlying conceptual structure. In this chapter we examine the effect which these different views can have on helping or hindering users getting at the information they require.

After reading this chapter, you should be able to:

- describe hierarchies of views onto a structure
- understand the conceptualization of views
- understand the impact which views can have on user goals
- draw ERMIAs comparing different user views.

8.1 Levels of Information Artefacts

Up until now we have concentrated on developing ERMIAs in which the level of description of the conceptual and perceptual models has been given. What we have not done is to consider which level of description is appropriate.

We have seen that an information artefact consists of:

- a conceptualization of some object(s) in the experienced world which has the purpose of revealing some information about the underlying object(s) for some users;
- a viewport which provides access to that conceptualization and displays the actual data from which the user may derive information.

However, whenever we create a perceptual display it then becomes an object in the experienced world. Consequently it may have its own information artefact designed to reveal information about the display (recall the idea of hierarchical viewports mentioned briefly in Section 2.3). The fact that there can be multiple levels of information artefacts, each built upon the others is important. Figure 8.1 illustrates this idea and also shows how the software engineering concerns deal with the conceptualization of the artefact (at some level of abstraction) whereas the concerns

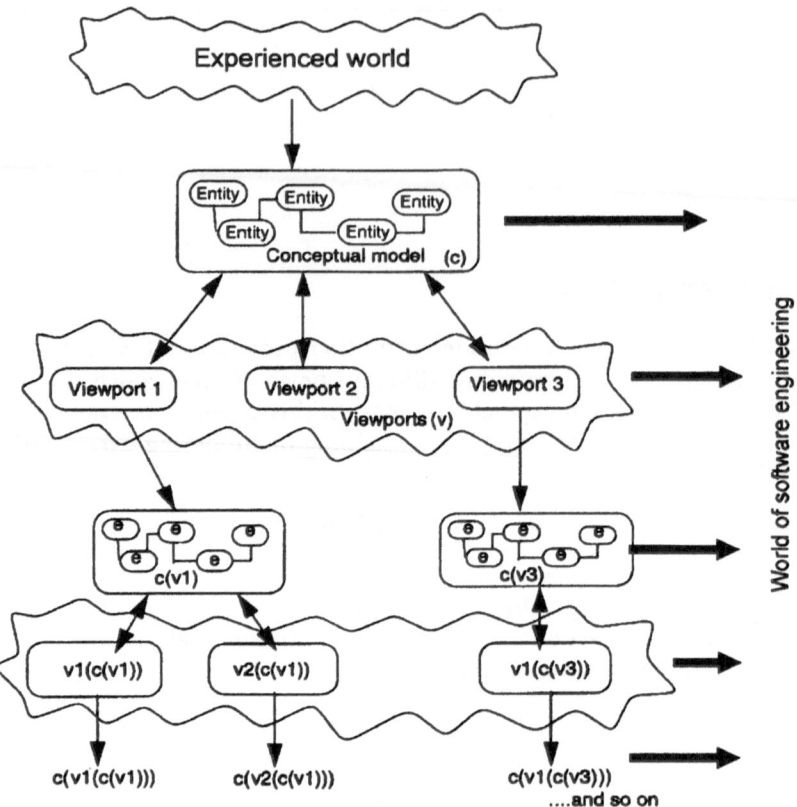

Fig 8.1 Structure of information artefacts.

of human-computer interaction (HCI) are with the different views and levels of abstraction in the user's world.

Figure 8.1 illustrates (from the top down) that some designers or choosers recognize something about the experienced world. They choose to conceptualize the structure of this in a particular way and develop a conceptual model. In order to access this conceptualization, various viewports are created. Each viewport reveals something about the underlying structure (and it is this combination of viewport and conceptual structure which we call an information artefact). As we move down the figure we see that the viewports can then be considered in a similar fashion – we recognize that the viewports are part of the experienced world. Accordingly we can conceptualize the viewport, represented as c(v), and provide a view onto that conceptual structure, v(c(v)) – a viewport of a conceptualization of a viewport. This produces another information artefact.

In theory this can continue indefinitely with information artefacts being created on top of one another revealing different aspects of the underlying experienced world. In practice, users tend to specialize in a particular level of discourse about information artefacts and lower levels effectively disappear from their experienced world.

✳ **Example** One view of the world of computers deals with the physical arrangement of files on discs, with the workings of disc access times and transfer rates, memory allocation and so on. For most of us such a view is not experienced, instead it is presented to us through information artefacts such as computer operating systems. The graphical user interfaces which are so ubiquitous provide another view onto the operating system and so the experienced world for us is one of dragging icons, double clicking and using menus to issue commands.

Occasionally we are forced to confront these lower level information artefacts, for example when we need to re-install an operating system. This can be quite a shock! The car mechanic experiences a different world from the driver. The surgeon experiences a different world from the patient.

Recognizing these different levels of information artefact is important in order to establish a shared level of abstraction within which we can discuss our needs and concerns. ERMIA can help to clarify the level of abstraction by making the conceptualizations and views of the experienced world explicit.

8.2 Example: Currency Exchange

✳ In order to see how this works in action, consider the following example. It is a feature of my experienced world that if I want to spend small amounts of money in another European country, I have to change currency.

This is conceptualized (from my perspective) as an exchange rate. A currency must have an exchange rate with another currency (Fig 8.2).*

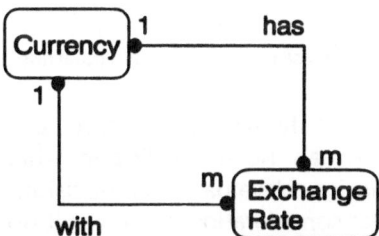

Fig 8.2 Conceptual model of exchange rates.

This abstraction may be revealed in several ways. One of which is a textual description (Fig 8.3 (a)) another is a tabular layout (Fig 8.3 (b)). Clearly these reveal different amounts of the underlying conceptual model (Fig 8.2).

We may conceptualize the displays of Figure 8.3 as illustrated in Figure 8.4. The ERMIA of the text layout (Fig 8.4 (a)) is not particularly useful, but the tabular layout (Fig 8.4 (b)) reveals the underlying structure well. This can be

---

*Of course this situation has changed with the introduction of the EURO!

The current exchange rate for £1 is 8 FF or 2.4 DM

(a)

	£	FF	DM
£	1	8	2.4
FF	0.125	1	0.3
DM	0.416	3.33	1

(b)

Fig 8.3 Two perceptual displays of the conceptual model of Figure 8.2.

seen by comparing the conceptual model of the perceptual artefact with the conceptual model of the underlying "experienced world". In this case, the relationships map 1:1 to the relationships in the conceptual model. The only difference between Figure 8.2 and Figure 8.4 (b) is that Currency maps onto both Row and Column.

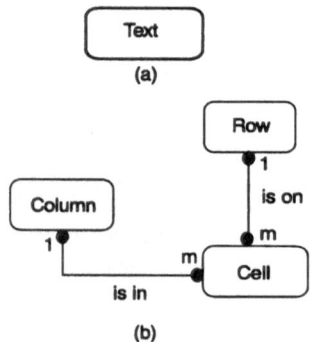

Fig 8.4 Conceptual representations of the perceptual displays in Figure 8.3.

A more detailed analysis of the tabular structure can be produced (Fig 8.5) which distinguishes between "header" cells and other cells. Whether this is more helpful for the designer/evaluator is a decision which must be taken based on the task under consideration. However, it does prove useful for us as we can now conceptualize two viewports onto the table structure conceptualized in Figure 8.5.

The analysis of the information artefacts can continue up another level of description. The tabular view of exchange rates may itself be displayed in a variety of ways. One viewport would be to display the whole table. Another would be to display just one row of the table. Another would be to display just one column of the table. Two viewports of the table structure are shown in Figure 8.6; (a) the row head view and (b) the column head view. These views might be implemented as different types of menu; (a) representing a walk-through menu or (b) a pull-down menu. Clearly the different viewports make some tasks easier than others. For example from the row head

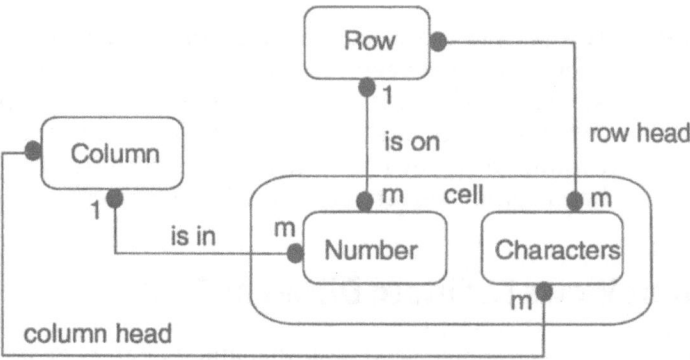

Fig 8.5 More detailed ERMIA of tabular display.

viewport you can find out how many French Francs (FF) or Deutschmarks (DM) you can get for a pound, but its difficult to work out how many pounds you can get for a Deutschmark or a French Franc. The reverse is true for the column-head view.

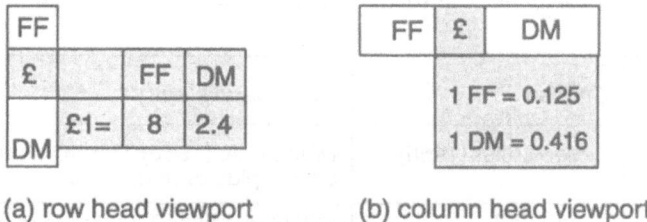

(a) row head viewport   (b) column head viewport

Fig 8.6 Two views of the table structure.

Although there may be multiple levels of information artefacts each built upon the others, conversations usually revolve around only one or two levels of abstraction and revelation. In a typical interface discussion the following levels are likely:

- the conceptual model of the underlying object;
- the abstract view of that structure;
- the display object.

Question: Identify the levels of discussion going on here when two people are discussing opening files in Word 6.0.

"Isn't it annoying that whenever you want to open a new file, and you do File New, Word asks you which template you want to use".

"I know. And I always use the Normal template. I don't really understand what templates are".

"I'm not sure either, but if you click on that little icon in the top left hand corner it gives you a new file without asking you about templates".

"Oh! That's what that icon is for!"

Comment: The people are discussing the conceptual model of the relationship between files and templates. Comments such as "open a new file", "which template", "Normal template", "what templates are" are abstract views of the structure. The comments about File New and the "little icon in the left hand corner" are references to display objects.

8.3 Different Views Facilitate Different Tasks

It is clear from the currency exchange example that different views facilitate different tasks. However, the currency exchange example does not show how important this can be. This section illustrates the trade-offs which exist when providing different viewports onto the same conceptual structure and how there is sometimes no ideal solution. The example concerns the notation for citing references in academic papers and the cost of updating a list of references to a paper-in-progress when a new citation is made. Two of the principal conventions for citing references are shown in Figure 8.7, which we shall call the "nominal" and the "numerical" styles.

Style	Citation	Bibliographic entry
Nominal	... see Miller (1956)	Miller, G.A. (1956) The magic number seven, plus or minus two.
Numerical	... see [23] ...	[23] G. A. Miller, The magic number seven, plus or minus two. (1956)

Fig 8.7 Two of the main typographic styles of citation.

Although the representation (viewport) is different for the two styles, they have the same conceptual structure, which is as follows (Fig 8.8):

- A citation occurs on at least one page and may occur on many pages.
- A page does not have to have any citations, but it may have many.
- A citation must have just one entry in the reference list (a bibliographic Entry).
- A bibliographic entry may relate to many citations. It must relate to at least one.

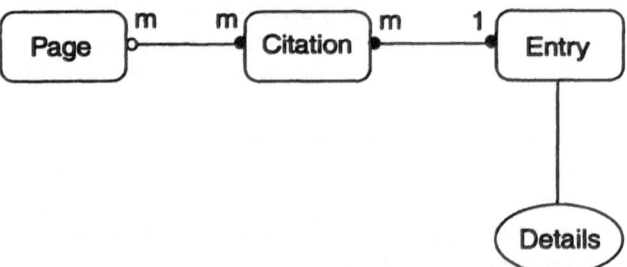

Fig 8.8 The conceptual structure of citations and a bibliography.

The differences between the nominal and numerical styles lie in the internal structure of the entity-store called Entry, and in the linkage between citations and entries. In the *nominal* style, the Details attribute is separated into Name, Date, and Other details, and the combination {Name,Date} is used as the link between a citation and an entry (Fig 8.9). As all academic authors know to their cost, the Name and Date mentioned in the text can sometimes fail to correspond to the Name and Date in the bibliography, so since they might be different things it is clearer to show two separate entities on the ERMIA (Fig 8.9); the name and date listed (called Listed Name & Date) and the name and date cited (called Cited Name & Date). In the *numerical* style, the entries are ordered by Name & Date but are then assigned a number. That number forms the link between citations and entries (Fig 8.10) – and here again, the cited numbers in the text may fail to correspond to the numbers in the bibliography. Notice the additional entity in Figure 8.10, Name & Date. This has been highlighted because the whole bibliography is ordered alphabetically by surname and by date and then numbered sequentially by Biblio Number.

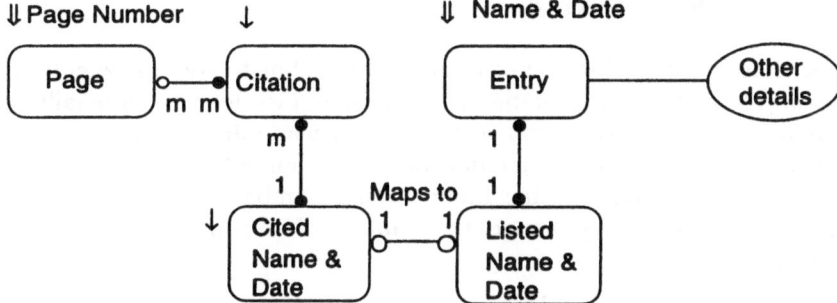

Fig 8.9 The structure of citations using the nominal style, as in "... Miller (1956) ...."

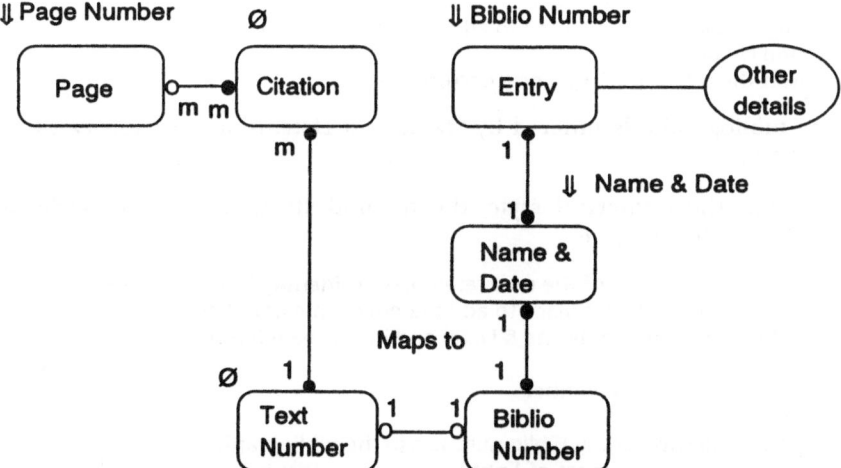

Fig 8.10 The structure of citations using the numerical style, as in "... see [23] ...."

Question: How well do the two viewports represent the underlying conceptual structure shown in Figure 8.8?

Comment: They both represent the conceptual structure well. Page maps to Page, Citation to Citation and Entry to Entry. The 1:1 relationships in the perceptual structures, together with the m:1 relationship from Citation map onto the Citation:Entry relationship in the conceptual model. They show the manifest entities which are used by the different viewports to reveal the conceptual Citation:Entry relationship.

Now we will consider two tasks which users commonly perform when developing an academic paper – correcting the name or date of a reference and adding a new reference – and one task that the reader of a paper has to do – deciding whether to look up the details of a reference.

8.3.1 Adding a New Reference

The task of adding a new reference requires the author to add a new entry to the bibliography, to link to a new citation in the text, and to clean up all details so that the structure is left consistent and correct. The crucial difference between the two structures is that the Name & Date information for an entry is unchanged by the addition of a new entry, but the bibliographic number is potentially changed (because adding a new entry changes the numbers of all entries that are below it in the bibliography).

Working with the nominal style, the method for adding a new reference (i.e. an occurrence of Entry) is:

> note the name and date of the new bibliographic entry
> (i.e. identify Cited Name & Date)
> search the bibliography for place to add the new name and date
> (i.e. Listed Name & Date)
> and insert the reference (add Entry occurrence).

Since the bibliography is ordered by Name and Date, binary search can be used (Section 5.1.1).

Working with the numerical style, the method starts straightforwardly but a "clean-up" stage is required:

> note the name and date of the new reference (i.e. identify Name & Date)
> search the bibliography for place to add the new name and date
> (i.e. identify occurrence of Name & Date) and insert the reference
> (add occurrence of Entry)
> compute the new Biblio number
> clean up:
> > update all succeeding Biblio numbers in the bibliography
> > (i.e. update occurrences of Entry)
> > update all references to those numbers in the text
> > (i.e. update all related occurrences of Citation).

The clean-up stage allows several methods. One is to turn the pages one by one (Page is a sorted-list entity, but it is sorted by Page Number which has no relationship to Citation, so Page has to be treated as chain (Section 5.2.2) and searched serially). As each citation is found, it is updated. This method requires each page to be searched once, and needs one memory item to keep track of the current page, plus a complete mapping from old Biblio Number to new Text Number. (Although the change is often no more than adding 1, it can be much more complex if several changes are to be made at once, involving deletions as well as insertions.) Another method is to consider each new citation, search the pages until it is found, and then update it; the pages will have to be searched more often, but fewer memory items are needed because only one mapping from old number to new needs to kept.

Question: Can you think of an automated tool which could help the author do this?

Comment: Yes. A Find and Replace utility is available on many computers which could change all occurrences of Citation to match the new occurrence of Text Number.

Question: If multiple changes have been made is there a problem using Find and Replace?

Comment: Yes. The author must remember to update them in reverse numerical order (i.e. change Text Number 29 to 30 before changing 28 to 29) otherwise our author will get in a complete mess.

Question: In both systems who has to maintain the "Maps to" relationship?

Comment: In most word processors the author has to do this.

8.3.2 Updating a Name or Date

Now consider what happens when the author has made an error and needs to change either the name of the cited author or the date of the citation. In the case of the numerical style (Fig 8.10), the author simply changes the occurrence in Name & Date.

Question: But what would happen if our author had spelt "Miller" as "Niller"?

Comment: The whole clean up operation would have to be performed again because the corresponding Biblio Number would probably need to be changed to maintain the required ordering of Name & Date.

Using the nominal style of citations, a change in the name or date of a citation causes more problems. In a similar fashion to the clean up operation described above, the author will have to search for and correct all occurrences of Citation which match the new Cited Name & Date.

8.3.3 A Reader's View

Now consider the reader of the finished article. Which is the more meaningful representation as far as the reader is concerned? In the numerical style, the reader comes across a citation such as [23]. In order to obtain the details of this reference the reader turns to the bibliography and searches the occurrences of Entry to locate the occurrence with Biblio Number [23] and can then read off the details. Using the nominal style the reader comes across a citation such as (Miller, 1956) and searches the occurrences of Entry to locate the occurrence with Listed Name & Date of Miller, 1956 and reads off the details. So there is very little difference between the two styles.

Question: What happens if the user simply wants to know the name and date of a reference and does not want to know any other details?

Comment: The nominal style is better since it makes fewer demands on the user's memory. This information is directly revealed by the nominal viewport, but must be looked up, or remembered, using the numerical style.

8.3.4 Comment

We have no particular desire, in this case, to comment on which of the two styles considered for citations is the better. Indeed it is quite clear that using the numerical style it is generally easier to change the name or date of a citation, but more difficult to add a new citation. From the reader's perspective it depends what information the reader wants to know as to which would be the preferred style.

Both viewports represent the conceptual structure well as there is a clear mapping between the conceptual ERMIA (Fig 8.8) and perceptual ERMIAs (Fig 8.9 and Fig 8.10); the perceptual ERMIAs may have more entities, but the 1:1 relationships effectively just split the conceptual relationship into the perceived entities. However, each viewport has an impact on the tasks which users can perform and on the type of information which can be retrieved or amended more easily. In many ways this example is similar to the smart phone example (Section 4.5) as there are important relationships (particularly the Maps to relationship) which exist but which are not supported by any feature in the device.

As problems like this are recognized so they are often rectified. For example, the word processor called FrameMaker does provide automatic updating of references (provided the user tells the device that two pieces of information should be related in a certain way) and more recent versions of Word have begun to include some cross-referencing. Other more generic functions such as Find and Replace facilitate the updating of 1:m relationships, that is, automatically changing all the 'm' occurrences when the '1' is changed.

Another solution sometimes employed is to provide the users with two (or more) viewports onto a structure so that different tasks can be undertaken. The only problem with this approach is that providing several viewports onto a structure usually involves constructing another information artefact to make the user aware of the different viewports. And so the information artefacts build once again on top of one another.

8.4 Representing Mental Models

In Section 4.6 we showed how ERMIA could be used to highlight conceptual entities which the user might not be aware of – either intentionally as in the case of the card trick, or unintentionally through poor design. The tasks which users can do, or believe that they can do with an information artefact are not simply dependent on the "actual" conceptualization of some device. They are equally dependent on what users *think* a device is like. We can use ERMIA to compare what different people think a device is like; the "mental models" which users have of devices. A mental model is the conceptualization which someone has of an information artefact. Mental models are developed as people interact with devices. People read about things, talk about things with others, observe the behaviour of a device and use their previous experience in order to develop a conceptualization of the structure of a device.

As we have seen the various viewports which are provided by an information artefact reveal more or less of the underlying information and they reveal it in different ways. The use which people make of the artefact depends on their conceptualization of the device, or "experienced world".

We will illustrate this using a real life example. Payne (1991) elicited models of the functioning of automatic teller machines (ATMs) from 16 subjects (numbered S1 to S16) and showed how they affected people's behaviour in using the machines. He reported:

> "A striking observation about the mental models of S14 and S15 . . . is how different they are. One subject [S14] believes that a great deal of information is stored on the plastic card, and that this information is updated when the machine is used. The other subject [S15] believes that the only information on the card is the user's PIN (Personal Identification Number). The first user believes that each bank machine is 'intelligent' . . . The second believes that each bank machine is a 'dumb' terminal to a central computer, where all the records are stored and all the computations are performed . . . Such variety is rampant in the data." (p. 12)

In ERMIA the structural aspects of these different beliefs can be represented as in Figure 8.11. We have omitted participation conditions on this ERMIA since we do not know what the users believed them to be.

Because ERMIA presents a clear view of the different models, it could be used as part of the process of reasoning about the revelation of models. If we have a designer's model that the designer wishes to reveal, he or she can look at the model of the interface and see to what extent the "intended" model shows up. Similarly

S 14: network of interconnected intelligent machines, everything stored on the card

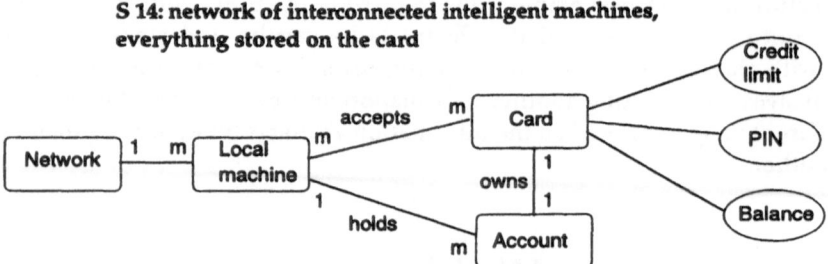

S 15: central machine with local "dumb" clients, nothing on the card except the PIN

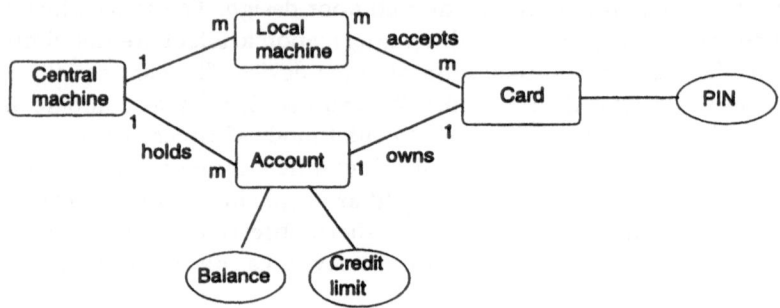

Fig 8.11 Comparison of two mental models of ATMs described by Payne (1991).

one can gather different user views, in the manner of Payne's work, and compare them to the designer's view, making the models and their possible differences explicit through ERMIA.

Summary

- *Information artefacts are built upon each other.*
- *Viewports reveal more or less of the underlying conceptual structure.*
- *Viewports are themselves part of the experienced world which can have information artefacts constructed to reveal information about them.*
- *Different viewports enable different tasks to be performed.*
- *Different users may have different conceptualizations (mental models) of how devices work.*
- *The mental models which users have influence the tasks which they think they can do with an information artefact.*

9.   *Developing ERMIAs*

Aims and objectives

Developing ERMIAs is something that takes practice. However, there are a number of useful "rules of thumb" which can help to guide the modeler. ERMIAs are also useful in focusing the discussions between different modelers. This chapter describes in detail the rules for building an ERMIA model.

After studying this chapter you should be able to:

- describe how ERMIA can be used as a language for design
- understand the main heuristics which apply to developing ERMIAs
- use ERMIA to reason about design problems.

9.1 ERMIA as a Language for Design

The components which define an ERMIA should be obtained by analysts in consultation with users or by users who have learnt ERMIA and have a good understanding of the domain. Depending on their perspectives, different modelers may make different decisions about how to represent a domain or an artefact. These decisions will often depend on the tasks that they think are important. This is not to say that there is no consistency between the way different modelers will choose to represent aspects of the artefact; different modelers with a similar perspective will choose similar constructs. However, it does mean that there is a degree of choice.

Because ERMIA provides a limited set of well-defined concepts, it provides a professional language in which designers and users and choosers of information artefacts can discuss various issues. In database design ER models have been used for many years for this purpose and in other areas of endeavour, such as choreography, music, engineering and so on, specialised professional notations (or languages) are used.

To be effective a professional language needs to provide a set of appropriate constructs and a set of rules and conventions for using those constructs. The constructs need to focus on important issues in the domain and need to be able to constrain the discussion so that the important aspects of some system stand out for the purpose at hand. For example, musical notation provides the staves, key signatures, timing and pitch of notes along with annotation to convey a set of concepts to the player of the music. The "designer" (the composer) is better able to express his or her ideas because of the constraints of the language and to convey these ideas more accurately to the user (the musician). Of course, sometimes a language will be too constraining for a particular person (e.g. jazz music often requires improvisation) and in such cases the notation has to be extended or bent in order to allow sufficient expression.

ERMIA can be seen in a similar way. It provides a limited set of constructs – conceptual and manifest entities, relationships and attributes – in which design ideas can be formulated and expressed. Different designers or evaluators can come together and compare their understandings, using the constraints imposed by the language to focus discussions on the key ideas.

In the next section we summarize the rules and methods of ERMIA modeling and in Section 9.4, we show how ERMIA worked in practice on one case study.

9.2 Heuristics for ERMIA

Throughout this book we have hinted at various features of ERMIAs which can be used to guide the modeler to find an effective representation for a particular problem. These can be presented as general-purpose "rules of thumb", or heuristics. Although there is not a definitive set of hard and fast rules involved in ERMIA modeling (and most modelers we know use ERMIA in slightly different ways), there are some general guidelines.

9.2.1 Rules for Entities

Entity classes should be chosen so that the entities in the class are similar. All the entities in a class should have similar attributes, and they should all be presented in the same way. Entity classes and their attributes should be chosen in such a way that it is clear what belongs in the entity class and what does not.

Each entity class can appear just once on the diagram. All relationships connect to that one class. This restriction is for semantic reasons, and it also has the useful consequence that changing the name of an entity or relationship when you think of a better one has no side-effects elsewhere in the diagram.

A manifest entity class in the model must represent a visible (or otherwise perceptible) entity class in the artefact. If the existence of an entity class is implicit in the artefact but this entity class is not distinctly visible anywhere in the artefact, then it should be shown only as a conceptual entity class.

Entities represent important things about the artefact. Each entity class in the artefact should be considered, but the modeler can choose to include only the entity classes that are relevant to the purpose of the model and to leave out any others.

The object that is being modeled does not usually appear on the ERMIA as an entity. This is because an ERMIA describes the structure of the object that is being modeled, and the object is not part of its own structure.

It is sometimes possible to simplify the diagram by merging entity classes. If there is a one-to-one and mandatory relationship between two entity classes, then they may be merged into a single entity class without losing any conceptual information. However, if the two entity classes are manifest entity classes that appear in different parts of the interface, it is a good idea to treat them as separate, as we did in the citations example, Section 8.3.

9.2.2 Rules for Attributes

All entities (except for clones, Section 3.2.2) have an identifying attribute. It is useful to highlight identifying attributes (by showing them with a double line of an ERMIA), as these suggest how easy it will be to identify particular entity instances.

Attributes may be treated as entities. There is no definitive test for whether to treat some feature of an information artefact as an entity or as an attribute (recall the discussion in Section 3.5). Representing something as an entity instead of an attribute is a way to focus attention on it, to express the importance of the element.

It is sometimes possible to replace an entity with an attribute. If there is a relationship between two entity classes (say classes A and B) that is mandatory and many-to-one, and if B does not have any attributes except for its identifier, then entity B can become an attribute of entity A without losing any information.

When we are modeling an existing artefact, think about how that artefact treats each feature. An entity may be conceptually important, but the particular information artefact may not treat it as important in its own right. Instead the information artefact may treat it as an attribute of some other entity. This may suggest that the interface is hiding some important information.

9.2.3 Rules for Relationships

Relationships are the paths between entities. When drawing an ERMIA it is important to discover whether it is necessary to traverse the relationships and if so, whether it is possible to do so easily and without ambiguity in the interface.

Relationships may contain some complex information in itself that we need to explore. In order to explore a relationship between two entities in more detail, it is often useful to replace the relationship by an intermediate entity that represents the relationship, connected to the two entities by simpler relationships.

In a conceptual ERMIA important relationships can be replaced by entities. A perceptual ERMIA conveys information about which entities are manifest and which are only conceptual. We may also want to use the ERMIA to find out which relationships are accessible and which are not.

Many-to-many relationships are potential sources of difficulty and ambiguity in finding information. It is therefore useful to break down a many-to-many relationship into an entity and two one-to-many relationships, as described in Section 6.1. It is also important to indicate the way in which the new entity is accessed, as that section describes.

9.3 Methodology for ERMIA

Having read through this book we hope that you will have developed a good understanding of the concepts in ERMIA and how to use them. However, many people find it difficult to get started on developing ERMIAs and are concerned that they are not doing it 'right'. By thinking about the rules described in the rest of this section and by following the simple methodology presented here, you will soon be producing useful and effective ERMIAs.

9.3.1 Where to Start?

Depending on the problem, you may start with a conceptual or perceptual ERMIA. For example, one of the authors was asked to use ERMIA to see what insight it could give into the problem of queues building up when people were using an ATM. In this case he started by developing a conceptual ERMIA of ATMs (shown in Section 10.3) and continued by using this ERMIA to examine whether users had a clear mental model of the operation of an ATM. On another occasion he was puzzling over why his alarm clock was difficult to use and used ERMIA to focus on the perceptual display of the device (this example is discussed in Section 10.2).

You always start an ERMIA analysis by identifying the main entities and their attributes. Often you will not be able to find any attributes, but don't worry. They will come later if necessary.

9.3.2 What to Represent?

The next issue is to consider what to represent. If you are considering a specific information artefact then look at the display and identify the main *types* of things that you can see. For example, looking at this word processor, I can see icons, menu headers, the text that I am writing, some windows which have scroll bars, size boxes, close boxes and so on. I can see a ruler with tab markers on it. I can see information about pages numbers and various other pieces of information (some of which I do not understand!). These immediately suggest some entities and attributes. The entities from the above description are Icon, Menu header, Text, Window and something we might call Document information. The attributes which are mentioned are Scroll bar, Size box, Close box (attributes of Window, since we have noticed that windows *have* scroll bars, etc.). Page number and Other bits are probably attributes of Document information.

Question: Look at the information artefact in front of you (this book) and describe the entities and attributes which you can see.

Comment: You can see some Text, an entity Page with an attribute Page number. You may want to distinguish Left page from Right page if you see that as important. You can see different headings and text styles.

If you are starting with an idea, or a generic information artefact such as a word processor, a calculator or an ATM, then you should start thinking about a conceptual ERMIA. This can be more difficult because you have to think in the abstract. For example, thinking about a word processor you might come up with entities such as Word, Paragraph, Page, File and then depending on the sort of documents which you want to produce you may think of Footnote, Chapter heading, Standard letter and so on.

Question: Now think about books in general and identify some entities of these information artefacts.

Comment: You probably thought of Page, Index, Chapter, Table of contents. Hopefully you did not consider Book to be an entity here as you were asked to think about books – i.e. about the structure of books.

Don't worry if you didn't think of the same things as we did. *At this stage you cannot be wrong!* The process of developing ERMIAs will take a bit longer if you start off with entities which turn out to be unimportant, but at this early stage you are really just making an educated guess.

9.3.3 Problems with Notions of Entity and Attribute

Everyone has trouble with the difference between attributes and entities – but there really is no need to worry about it. The golden rule here is *when in doubt consider it an entity.* If it turns out later that you are not interested in something which you initially considered to be an entity, then it can subsequently become an attribute. Distinguishing between entities and attributes just serves to keep the model more simple. When we said that, for example, Scroll bar is an attribute of Window we were stating that we were not particularly interested in scroll bars themselves, we were more interested in windows as they seemed to be at the same level of abstraction as icons and menu headers. If another modeler does represent Scroll bar as an entity then we can discuss what is interesting about the entity Scroll bar later.

One thing that is useful at this stage is to say what you mean by an entity. You might do this by writing a short description of it or you might do it by specifying its identifying attribute(s). A good test to distinguish between entities and attributes is to decide if you can find something which will distinguish between members of the class as this is how you specify the identifier of the entity.

9.3.4 Progressing the Analysis

Once you have identified a first choice of entities, you should begin to consider the relationships between them. If you cannot find any interesting relationships between some entity and the others then it suggests that that entity is inappropriate. For example, you may have one entity which is at a different level of abstraction from the others or you may have thought of an entity which really turns out not to be important.

As you consider relationships it is important to think about what the relationship means. Try to find a suitable name for the relationship as this can clarify what you mean by it, but you do not have to have names. For example looking at my word processor I can see that there is a relationship between Icon and Menu header. Clicking on an icon will often invoke a command which can also be found under a menu header.

Thinking about the relationship may help you to discover other entities. In the sentence above by thinking about the relationship between Icon and Menu header, I have discovered a possible entity Command.

9.3.5 The First Sketch

Once you have a few entities and relationships it is time to start sketching the model. Putting the entities on paper means that missing relationships are more easily seen. You should also start to add in more details such as the degree and participation conditions of the relationships. Once again you will not be able to fill in all the details, nor is it desirable to do so. You are using ERMIA to explore the ideas. For example, the relationship between Icon and Command is optional on both sides because I quickly discover that some icons do not relate to commands on menus and some commands do not have icons. Looking at the relationships also means that you think about the degree. Is the relationship always 1:1 or 1:m or are there cases when there is a m:m relationship?

9.3.6 Decompose Many-to-Many Relationships

It is very important at this early stage of modeling that you decompose all m:m relationships. This is necessary because these complex relationships are often hiding important entities. Of course as soon as you have decomposed a m:m relationship you have another entity to deal with and now have to consider what this new entity means and what relationships it has with the other entities.

9.3.7 Iterate

The process of developing an ERMIA now iterates around the processes of identify, sketch, check. Each entity is considered in terms of what it means and how it is defined. Each attribute is allocated to an entity and identifying attributes are speci-fied. Relationships are added and removed as the modeler thinks about what they mean and how important they are. New entities are discovered by decomposing m:m relationships and by checking the model with the perceptual display or by thinking about how accurate a model is of some conception of the experienced world. Entities are discarded as the overall purpose of the model becomes clearer or are combined as the modeler settles on a consistent level of abstraction. The sketches become more refined as relationships are clarified in terms of participa-tion conditions and their degree.

9.3.8 Completing the Model

As the model nears completion, the modeler can start using the model to think about user tasks, where information is located and what someone has to do to retrieve information. The modeler can check paths through the model being particularly careful about connection traps (Section 7.3) and whether they result in lost information.

The final, first draft, model can then be checked with other designers or with users to see how much agreement there is about how the problem or the physical artefact has been conceptualised. The model can be tidied up so that the paths through the model are more easily read. There is no fixed way of representing an ERMIA map. Modelers should try to avoid lines crossing over each other as this makes it more difficult to read, but sometimes this is unavoidable. The modeler might choose to provide fairly formal definitions of the entities in terms of their attributes. In addition, a modeler might choose to provide more informal definitions – of both entities and relationships – using textual descriptions, examples or pictures as appropriate.

The point of finishing the model at this point is to make sure that everything is clear. The purpose of a completed ERMIA is to communicate ideas to people. Previous to this stage the model was being used to help the designer think about a problem. The model can be annotated with comments and detailed constraints which cannot be easily represented using the notation.

9.4 Case Study: The Oven Hob Problem

In this section, we illustrate the way that ERMIAs help to reveal and explain the difficulties in using a simple everyday information artefact, the interface between an oven hob and its panel of control knobs. This section describes the ERMIAs that were created by the modelers and how they can be interpreted to suggest that some designs are better than others. This section also describes some of the problems and issues that arose for the modelers while they were building the ERMIA.

A group of modelers, variously knowledgeable about human interface design and about ERMIA modeling, were given the task of considering the structure of the display-control relationship for a typical oven hob. A typical oven hob is a set of four gas burners or electric rings, controlled by four knobs placed at the front of the oven in a single horizontal row. These hobs are designed (see Fig 9.1) like (a) or (b), rarely like (c). What is the problem with design (c)?

A possible explanation for why (a) or (b) is preferred to (c) is that the first two layouts of knobs – and especially the relationships between the positions of the knobs and the burners – are conceptually simpler and therefore easier for cooks to learn and use. (We are not suggesting that is especially difficult for cooks to learn any of the layouts! However some might seem more quickly learnt than others.) We were interested to see if this difference would be reflected in the ERMIAs for each

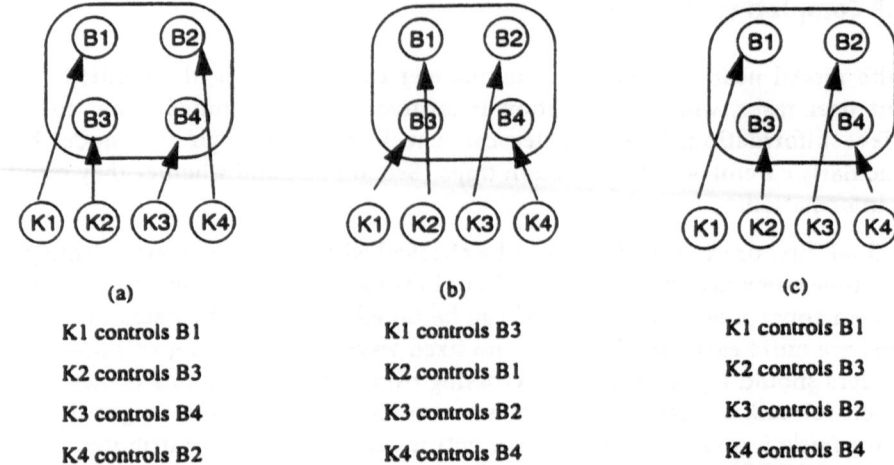

(a)	(b)	(c)
K1 controls B1	K1 controls B3	K1 controls B1
K2 controls B3	K2 controls B1	K2 controls B3
K3 controls B4	K3 controls B2	K3 controls B2
K4 controls B2	K4 controls B4	K4 controls B4

Fig 9.1 Three arrangements of knobs (K1–K4) and burners (B1–B4) on a typical oven hob.

hob. To test this theory, the modelers were asked to construct ERMIA representations of these three hobs.

Question: Look at Figure 9.1. What manifest entities would you choose?

Comment: The main manifest entities are Knob and Burner.

9.4.1 An ERMIA Analysis of the Oven Controls

The simplest way to view the relationship between knobs and burners is shown in Figure 9.2. We know the relationship is 4:4 in this case and we are being non-committal about the relationships other than to say that knobs relate to burners.

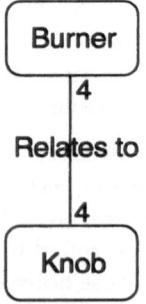

Fig 9.2 Initial ERMIA for oven hob problem.

In this simplistic analysis, there is no difference between the different layouts. The only way to map between knobs and burners is to remember which knob corresponds to which burner. This requires people to remember all four relationships. However, it seems likely that people take advantage of the physical aspects of the layout and the relationships between them so that there is less to remember.

The modelers suggested that the interesting aspects of the problem were the side that the knobs and burners were on and the position that they had. These features could be represented by attributes of Knob (Side, Position) and Burner (Side, Distance). In fact these features could also be represented by relationships or by entities (recall the discussion in Section 3.5). Since they wanted to focus attention on these issues the modelers decided to represent these characteristics as entities. The following entity definitions were formulated.

> Knob-Side (i.e. a knob could be on the left or on the right)
> Burner-Side (i.e. a burner could be on the left or on the right)
> Knob-Position (i.e. a knob could be on the inside or on the outside of the controls)
> Burner-Distance (i.e. a burner could be at the front or the back of the hob)

The relationships between these entities could then be considered. Some of the relationships were the same for all three control layouts. In all the hobs, the knobs on the left-hand side of the control panel correspond to burners on the left-hand side of the hob, and vice versa. Other relationships varied between the different layouts. In hob (a), the knobs on the inside correspond to the burners at the front, and the knobs on the outside to the burners at the back. In hob (b), the knobs on the outside correspond to the burners at the front, and the knobs on the inside to the burners at the back.

Hobs (a) and (b) can be treated together since it is the values, or occurrences, of the entities which differ and not the structure (illustrated in Fig 9.3). Hob (c) has a different ERMIA (Fig 9.4) since the structure is different. Participation in all relationships is mandatory, so these conditions have been left off the diagrams.

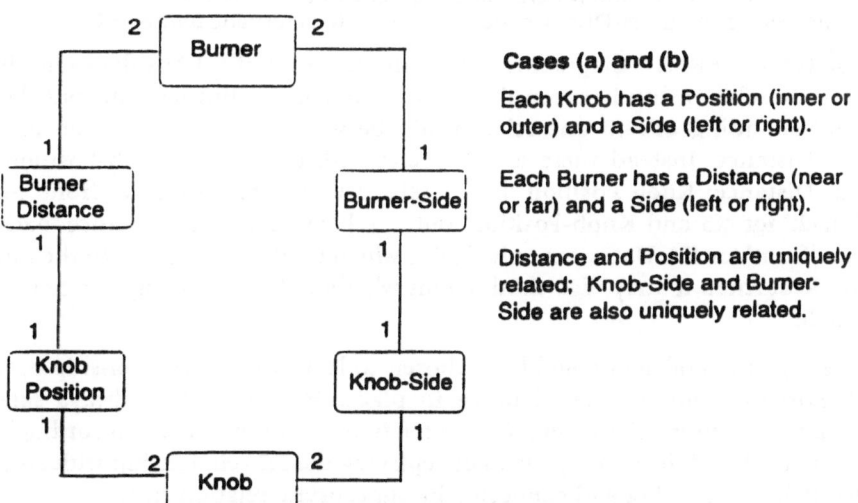

Cases (a) and (b)

Each Knob has a Position (inner or outer) and a Side (left or right).

Each Burner has a Distance (near or far) and a Side (left or right).

Distance and Position are uniquely related; Knob-Side and Burner-Side are also uniquely related.

Fig 9.3 ERMIA for oven hob layouts (a) and (b).

For layouts (a) and (b), the modelers derived the same ERMIA, which is shown in Figure 9.3. There is a simple one-to-one relationship between Knob-Side and Burner-Side, and between Knob-Position and Burner-Distance. The trail of relationships

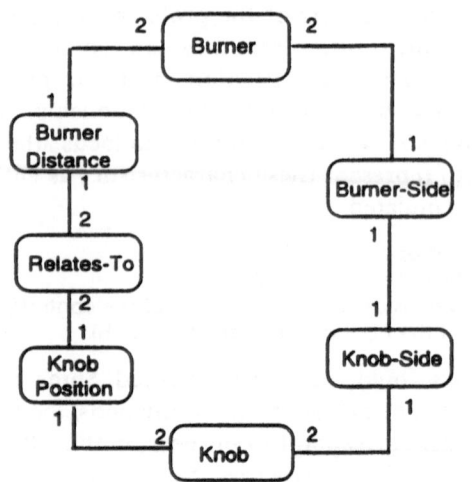

Case (c)

Distance and Position are not uniquely related. Each of the two Knob Positions relates to two Burner Distances, giving a 2:2 relationship.

To resolve this ambiguity, a further entity has to be introduced.

This leads to fan traps around Burner Distance and Knob Position.

Fig 9.4 ERMIA for oven hob layout (c).

on each side is 2:1, 1:1, 1:2, which suggests the potential for a fan trap (Section 7.3), but the combination of Knob-Side and Knob-Position is enough to determine the Burner unambiguously. To associate knobs with burners, or vice versa, there is a simple search path through the diagram for (a) and (b).

> For example, to find the burner associated with a given knob for layout (a):
> Start at the knob, say K2. Note Knob-Side (=left) and Knob-Position (=inner).
>   Knob-Side uniquely determines Burner-Side (=left).
>   Knob-Position uniquely determines Burner-Distance (=front).
> Burner-Side and Burner-Distance together uniquely determine Burner (=B3).

In case (c), the ERMIA diagram is more complex. Layout (c) has the same simple one-to-one relationship between the Knob-Side and the Burner-Side, but there is no corresponding one-to-one relationship between the Knob-Position and the Burner-Distance. Instead there is a 2:2 relationship between Knob-Position and Burner-Distance; Knob-Position 'inner' relates to Burner-Distance 'front' for K2 and 'back' for K3 and Knob-Position 'outer' relates to Burner-Distance 'back' for K1 and 'front' for K4. Users can only decide which knobs correspond to the front or the back burners if they also think about whether they are using the left or the right side.

In case (c), the modelers could have chosen to leave the 2:2 relationship between Knob-Position and Burner-Distance in place. However, it is always safer to decompose any m:m relationship (or 2:2 relationship in this case). Accordingly, the modelers explored the consequences of replacing the 2:2 relationship with an entity (called Relates-To in Fig 9.4) connected by appropriate relationships.

Question: What is the identifier of Relates-To?

Comment: It is the concatenation of the identifiers of Burner-Distance (which can take the value 'front' or 'back') and Knob-Position (which can take the value 'inner' or 'outer').

Introducing the Relates-To entity leads to fan traps around Knob-Position and Burner-Distance, and in this case information is lost. For example starting from K2, say, the user notices that it has the attribute value 'inner', but that is associated with two values of Relates-To (namely {inner, front} and {inner, back}). The same problem arises when starting from a particular burner. These traps can still only be resolved by taking side into account. This extra complexity suggests that the third layout is likely to be more difficult to remember and to use than either of the first two.

Given this particular way of analysing the oven hobs and the kinds of cues that people use to understand and remember control layouts, we can see a potential problem with layout (c). Constructing an ERMIA has enabled the modelers to explain why hob (c) is more complex than (a) or (b). Indeed it is precisely this problem which has been recognized by designers and why arrangement (c) is rarely used.

9.5 Building the ERMIA

In this section we provide transcripts of the actual conversations which took place between two modelers working on the oven hob problem. We hope that this provides an insight into the modeling process. The transcripts show how first of all the main entities and relationships were discovered. The subsequent discussion enciphered some further relationships leading finally to the recognition of the fan trap which caused all the problems with layout (c).

The discussion started off with one modeler describing the purpose of the model. The modeler introduced an ERMIA of the oven hob problem by describing its purpose and proposing a description of the burners and knobs.

Modeler: Take your typical oven. The question is which knob do you turn to put on each burner. There are two standard arrangements, where this (back burner) is connected to the outside here, let's number these burners 1, 2, 3, 4. The standard arrangement (a) is that, knob 1 controls burner 1 (the back left), knob 2 controls burner 3, knob 3 controls 4, and knob 4 controls burner 2. So the standard arrangement is 1, 3, 4, 2 and then there is of course the possibility of having something like 1, 3, 2, 4 or correspondents.

The modeler created the initial representation and had to explain his decisions to the group so that the group could understand. Colleagues continually asked the modeler to define his terms and relationships more fully. For example:

Modeler 1.   There is also a control switch which is 1 to 1.

Modeler 2.   Oh yes. Do you have a distance relationship between the knobs, or is distance mainly to do with the ring?

Modeler 1.   No, it is a characteristic of the ring and of the knob.

Several times, the modelers discussed whether a particular representation was appropriate and allowable, as illustrated by the following discussion. This piece of dialogue highlights the problem of choosing whether to represent certain variables as entities or as attributes.

Modeler 1.   OK, so do I need that as representative of an entity, oh let us leave it at the moment.

Modeler 2.   OK.

Modeler 1.   It could be an attribute of the ring.

Modeler 2.   Yes exactly, it is an attribute of the ring but I wasn't happy about whether or not I could tie attributes together and say it was an entity. So I change it to entity. And,

Modeler 1.   If in doubt make it an entity.

Modeler 2.   Always make it an entity?

Modeler 1.   Yes.

In order to jointly construct the diagrams in Figure 9.3 and Figure 9.4, the group recognized that the ERMIAs for cases (a) and (b) are symmetrical while (c) is not. At first, the group wanted to represent symmetry in the ERMIA, but the notation does not support it. A first draft of an ERMIA was created (not shown) and the following discussion ensued:

Modeler: What the demonstration (ERMIA diagram) shows us is what the mappings are, and it shows us that quite clearly, but the fact that the symmetry principle works there (a and b) but a repetition principle works here (c) is something you need to know from the structure. If I knew how to represent symmetry directly in the ERMIA then we would be in a strong position, but I could not quite seem to do that.

The analysis that the modelers developed did not use the concept of symmetry directly. However, the greater complexity of the asymmetrical arrangement (c) was expressed through a many-to-many relationship, an extra entity and two fan traps, none of which exist in the symmetrical arrangements (a) and (b).

This subsequent diagram (Fig 9.4) revealed more clearly that the paths connecting the entities in case (c) were not straightforward. Case (c) contains a connection trap between Knob-Side and Burner-Distance which reveals a potential ambiguity. One of the modelers identified the connection trap as soon as it was drawn. He explains:

Modeler: So here is your connection trap. It is classic. Whenever you have many-to-one and one-to-many (on this occasion one-to-two), you have ambiguity. You cannot map directly from Knob-Position to Burner-Distance because you have got this sort of fan shape. Which is the asymmetry. Whereas if you do not have that interfering, if you have a direct relationship between Knob-Position and Burner-Distance or if you have a one-to-many relationship, then you are OK. Now you have got this additional entity Relates-To coming in there, with a many-to-one then one-to-many relationship. That causes fan traps. How about that as a possibility?

In fact the whole of this discussion took about one and a half hours. Both modelers had prepared for the discussion session by thinking about the problem and drawing their own ERMIAs before coming together. When ERMIAs are presented to people, they often forget the amount of time which goes into creating them, and the amount of discussion that is needed in order to arrive at a useful set of entities and relationships. For example to produce the ATM example in the next chapter (Section 10.3) the first draft was completed in about five hours which consisted of three hours sketching and exploring the problem space and two hours to produce a semi-formal ERMIA suitable for circulating to the other modelers. This first draft was discussed in a session lasting about four hours and it took another four hours to produce the second draft shown in Figure 10.18. So, although ERMIA is relatively quick to do, modelers cannot be expected to understand problems without putting in some time!

Summary

- *ERMIA provides a professional language for thinking about, and communicating design issues.*
- *There are a number of 'rules of thumb' which can be used to develop ERMIAs.*
- *The approach to developing ERMIAs is highly iterative, starting with identifying potential entities, looking at relationships and revising the model.*
- *There is usually a need for discussion between modelers and this discussion helps to clarify ideas.*
- *Modelers must expect to put time and effort into developing ERMIAs.*

10. *Practical ERMIA Modeling*

Aims and Objectives

The main aim of this chapter is to give you experience in developing ERMIAs. We look at three examples. In the first you will do most of the work. The second provides a detailed example of developing a perceptual ERMIA and the third of developing a large scale model of a conceptual ERMIA. As discussed in Chapter 9 ERMIAs take time to develop and need to be discussed with others. If you have the opportunity work through the examples in this chapter with other people.

After reading this chapter you should be able to:

- develop an ERMIA of a medium-sized problem
- use higher level ERMIA constructs to develop perceptual ERMIAs
- understand the development of a large scale ERMIA

10.1 The Appointments Diary

In this section we ask you to undertake a number of exercises to provide practice in ERMIA analysis. We do not provide a complete and exhaustive analysis, but rather use the problems to highlight how developing ERMIAs can help you think about a problem. In particular you will find that the ERMIA models which you develop in this section include both conceptual and manifest entities.

A diary can be defined as a daily record kept of events. Consider an appointments diary similar to the one shown here (Fig 10.1). Spend ten or fifteen minutes on each of the exercises below. After each one you can look at our solution if you like, but do not be tempted to look ahead at the solutions to subsequent exercises. Alternatively you can use the exercises to guide your thinking and spend about an hour on developing an ERMIA for the diary before looking at the solutions.

Exercise 12

Thinking of the uses of a structure can be a useful way into compiling a list of likely entities for a (conceptual model of a) particular artefact. To what sorts of uses are the diary put? Think of the sorts of queries that can be discovered by using a diary.

Exercise 13

Compile a list of possible entities for a diary. Include a one line description of the meaning for each entity. What attributes does each entity have? Are any entities conceptual? If so, do they correspond to any other entities? Are any entities manifest? Are any of the entities ordered?

Exercise 14

Draw an ERMIA diagram linking your entities which you identified from the previous exercise.

Exercise 15

Compare these two queries:

Who am I going to meet today?

When am I next going to meet Jane Smith?

Which query is easier to answer? In the ERMIA, what does the trail (Section 7.1.1) for these queries look like?

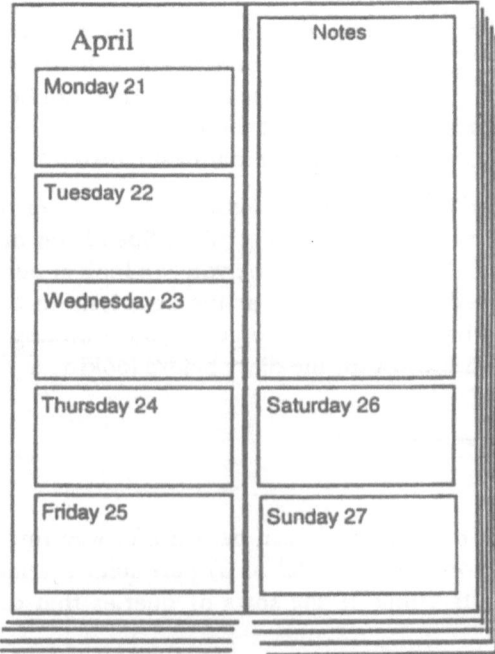

Fig 10.1 A typical diary information artefact.

10.2 The Alarm Clock

This example shows how a perceptual ERMIA was constructed and how building that model brought a number of issues to the fore which helped to explain why one particular information artefact was difficult to use. The case here is a typical small travelling alarm. The layout of this device and the instructions for using it are shown in Figure 10.2.

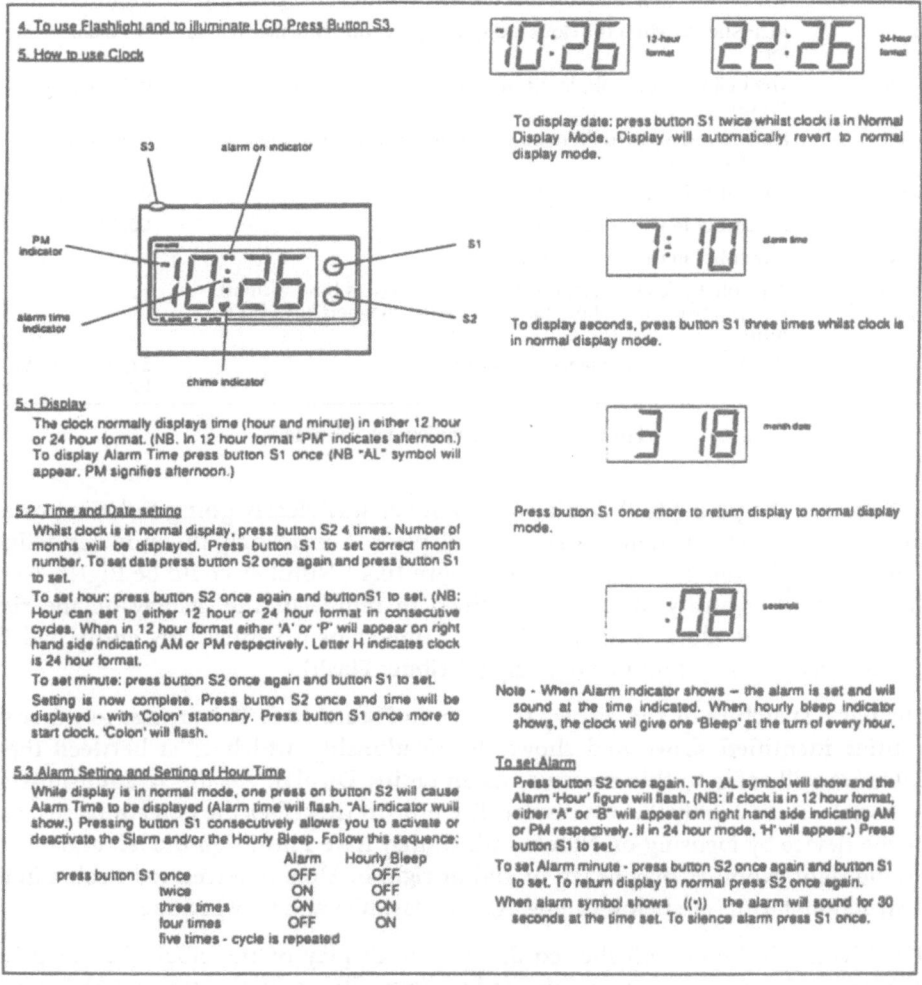

Fig 10.2 Layout of alarm clock.

The first thing which the modeler did in this case was to identify the perceptual entities involved in the device. These are shown in the table below (Fig 10.3). In order to clarify the meaning of the entities it can be useful to specify the values which occurrences of the entities can take; for example the AlarmOn entity can take the values of ((●)) or it can be blank. Several of the perceptual entities could only take one or two values, but numbers could take many values and the buttons could be pressed (denoted by ^) or pressed and held (denoted by *).

Name	Description	Values
PMInd	The PM indicator, used to indicate afternoon when clock is in 12 hour format	PM. Blank
AlarmOn	The symbol ((●)) indicates that the alarm function has been set on	((●)), blank
AL	AL is shown when the clock is displaying the time the alarm is set for	AL, blank
Chime	The bell symbol is displayed when the chime function has been set on	Bell, blank
Dots	Dots separate the right hand side of the display from the left hand side	:, :Flash, blank
BigNo	A number in the range 00 to 59	00...59
No	A number in the range 00 to 31	00..31
SmNo	A number in the range 1 to 12	1..12
Letter	An alphabetic character taking the value H (=24 hour format), P (= pm when in 12 hour format) or A (= am when in 12 hour format)	H, P, A
Button	Two buttons are available, S1 and S2.	S1, S1^, S1*, S2, S2^,

Fig 10.3 Entity descriptions for alarm clock.

In this case the perceptual display of a number was clearly going to be important since it forms the substance of so many displays. Accordingly the modeler defined a new entity, Number, as illustrated in Figure 10.4.[1] Number could be BigNo, No or SmNo. Another entity, Right, was defined to represent the display on the right hand side of the clock. This could be a Number or a Letter. This entity had the characteristic that it could be flashing (attribute Flash).

The basic structure of the display is shown in Figure 10.5. This brings together the entities identified above and shows the relationship which exist between them. Later we will refer to this structure as an entity, Display. All the relationships are optional – it is a highly flexible display. The ERMIA describes the perceptual structure of the device by focusing on Number which may have PmInd on the left and a letter on the right. Number may be left of and/or right of Dots (referred to as colon in the instructions). Dots are below Chime, Above AlarmOn and may include AL.

The ERMIA in Figure 3.5 showed the normal display of the clock (i.e. when it is displaying the time of day) and defined a composite entity (Section 3.2.3), Normal. This figure shows that the normal display has a number on the left of some flashing dots and a number on the right of the flashing dots. The alarm on indicator (AlarmOn) and chime indicator (Chime) were shown as attributes of this composite entity.

[1]This figure shows exclusive relationships mentioned briefly in Section 3.3.1; Number can only participate in one of the relationships with BigNo, No or SmNo.

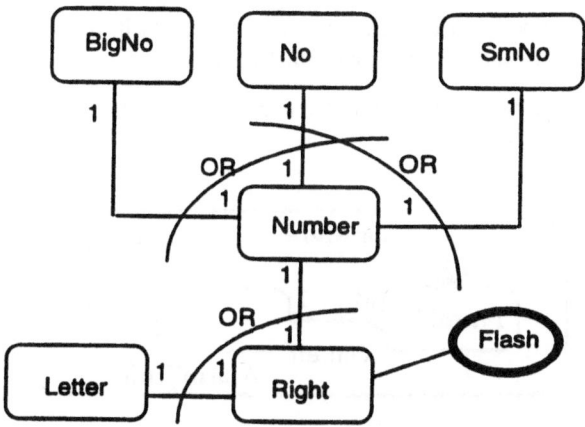

Fig 10.4 Defining the Number and Right entities using exclusive relationships.

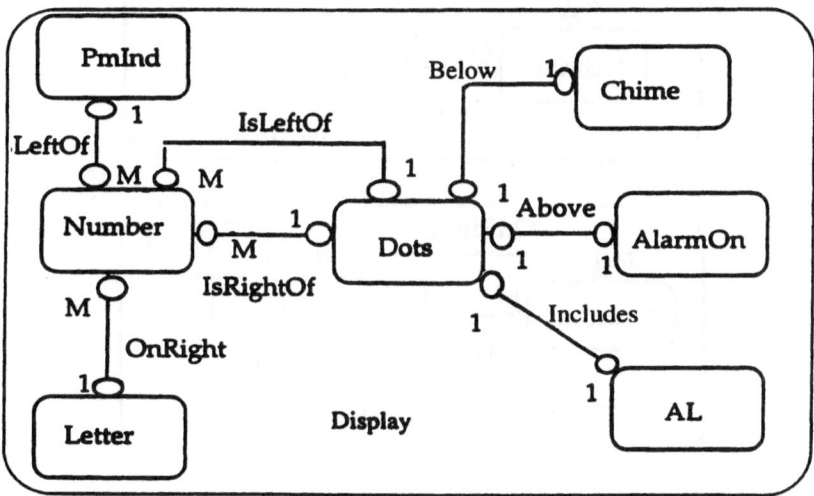

Fig 10.5 ERMIA of basic display.

One of the features of ERMIAs is that similar displays will have similar ERMIAs and so displays which were considered by the designer to be quite different can appear quite similar. For example, Figure 10.6 presents an ERMIA for each of three possible displays: the alarm time display (for changing/viewing the alarm time), the normal display and the Alarm/Chime display (for setting the combination of when the alarm and the hourly beep will sound). The only difference between the alarm time display and Normal is that the dots are not flashing and the AL entity is present. On the Alarm/Chime display the number is flashing, otherwise the displays have an identical structure.

The designer can consider whether the displays are sufficiently different by looking at the structure of the displays. In this case, we feel that the displays are not sufficiently different and that the user of the clock has to remember what the small differences mean.

Question: Can you remember what it means if the display has an AL indicator and is not flashing?

Comment: It means that you are looking at the time at which the alarm will sound.

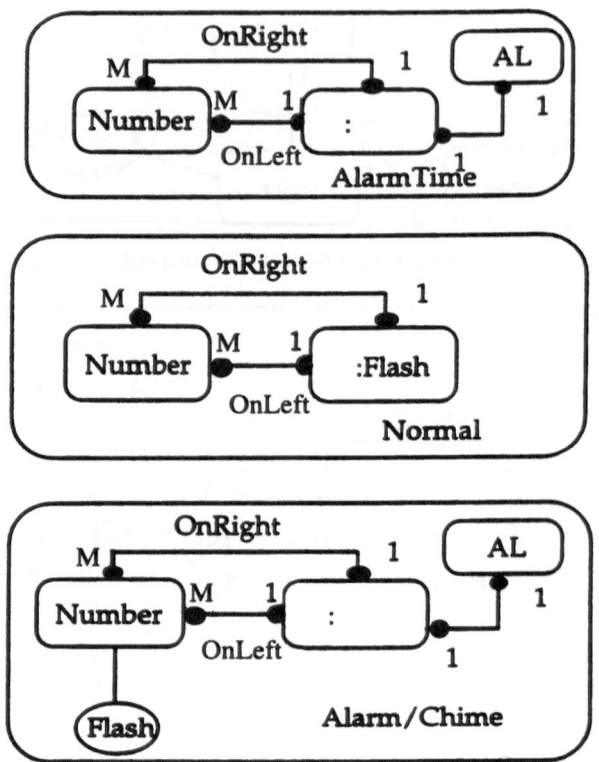

Fig 10.6 Comparing Alarm time, Normal and Alarm/Chime displays.

Another problem with the alarm clock is that there are only two buttons, S1 and S2 (the third button is irrelevant for this discussion as it operates a small torch and does not affect the functioning of the clock). The relationship between the display and the buttons is very complex. Initially one might be tempted to represent this relationship as shown in Figure 10.7 because there is only one top button and one bottom button.

Question: Think carefully about what the ERMIA in Figure 10.7 might mean. Is it a useful ERMIA?

Comment: All that Figure 10.7 is saying is that the display relates to the top button and the bottom button, but this is not what is important. The more interesting relationships are those that relate to when the various buttons are pressed.

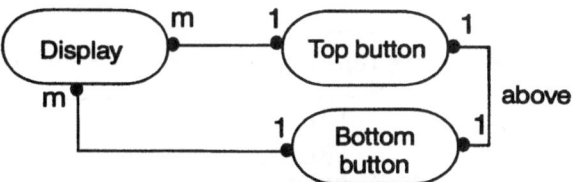

Fig 10.7 First try at ERMIA of display and buttons.

Question: What impact does the comment above have on the degree of the relationships between Display and the buttons.

Comment: They will be many-to-many relationships and not many-to-one.

An occurrence of Display is a particular time, a display of the date, a time with the chime indicator on and so on. So the buttons must relate to many displays. If we are interested in what happens when the buttons are pressed then clearly each display can relate to many button presses. As you can see from the descriptions in Figure 10.2, a display such as 10:26 can relate to one press of the top button (button S1), two presses, three presses and so on. Similarly each display can relate to many presses of button S2 (the Bottom button). Introducing the concept of a button press gives the ERMIA in Figure 10.8.

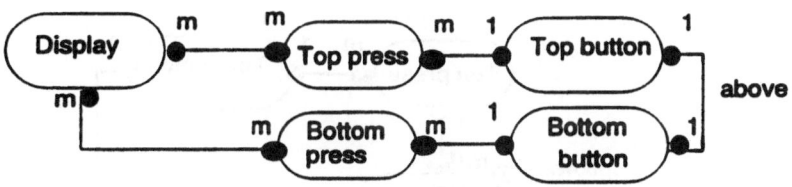

Fig 10.8 Refining the ERMIA of Display and buttons.

Question: Can you see a relationship which is missing from Figure 10.8?

Comment: There is a m:m relationship between Top press and Bottom press since an occurrence of Top press can be followed by one or more occurrences of Bottom press, and vice-versa.

Question: How should the modeler proceed from here?

Comment: Decompose the m:m relationships and think about what the new entities mean (see Fig 10.9).

Figure 10.9 is quite interesting because at first sight it is not clear what the entities X and Y are. We need to think about their identifiers to help us understand them. X is identified by a value of Display (which could, for example, be Normal with alarm on) and a value of Top press (which could be press twice, for example). This will result in a new display (perhaps). Similarly with the entity Y.

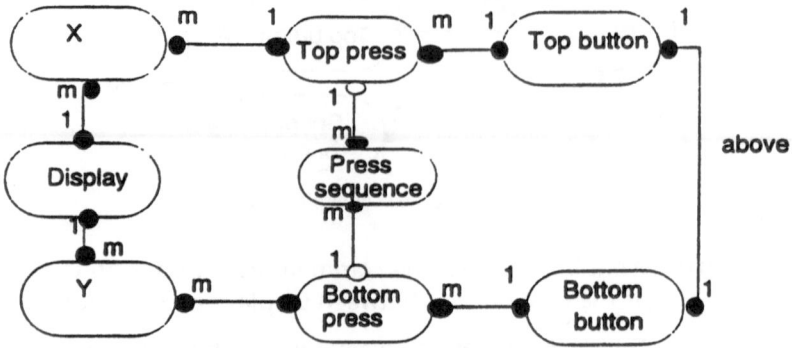

Fig 10.9 Decomposing the m:m relationships from Figure 10.8.

The sequence of top and bottom button presses is also important (for example, see section 5.2 in Fig 10.2). At present, the entity Press sequence is identified by {Number of top button presses, Number of bottom button presses}. Since this might result in a new display, Press sequence should have a relationship with Display. If we introduce this relationship we can remove entities X and Y since the information which they represent is covered in Press sequence. The final ERMIA for this along with some examples of the Press sequence entity are shown in Figure 10.10. The identifier of Press sequence is the (rather daunting) {Display, Number of top presses, Number of bottom presses, Display}.

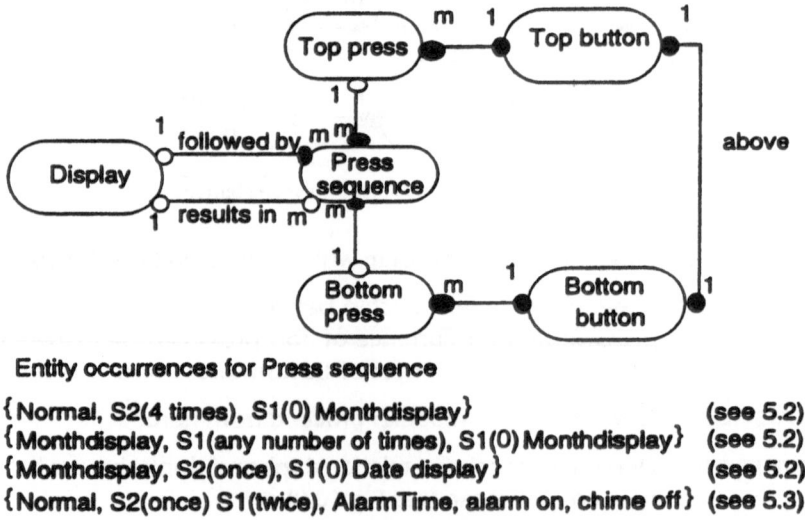

Entity occurrences for Press sequence

{ Normal, S2(4 times), S1(0) Monthdisplay }	(see 5.2)
{ Monthdisplay, S1(any number of times), S1(0) Monthdisplay }	(see 5.2)
{ Monthdisplay, S2(once), S1(0) Date display }	(see 5.2)
{ Normal, S2(once) S1(twice), AlarmTime, alarm on, chime off }	(see 5.3)

Fig 10.10 Final ERMIA for Display and Buttons (section numbers refer to Figure 10.2).

This discussion and the development of the ERMIAs concerned with button presses and the effect they have on the display highlights several important problems with the design. Clearly the relationships between displays and button presses is complex. *The user has to remember all these sequences.* The amount of information provided by the display is extremely limited. Whilst the user might recognize that the bell icon indicates that the chime function has been set to on, the ((●)) icon is less clear and the symbol AL similarly does not obviously reveal that the user is looking at the alarm time. An accidental, or ill-informed button push at this point can alter the alarm setting or turn it off.

The similarity of many of the displays has also been clearly revealed by the ERMIAs above. Some of the displays provide even less information. This combination of lack of information on the displays and complex combinations of key presses makes the device difficult to use.

10.3 The ATM

Although we have developed some quite complex ERMIAs during the course of this book, we have not yet seen ERMIA applied to a really large problem. Of course, scale is relative and ERMIA would be quite inappropriate to use at the level of a whole application such as a word processor or spreadsheet application. However, this section does illustrate that it could be applied to a part of such an application, such as spell checking, paragraph formatting or the graph producing part of a spreadsheet. In the next chapter we provide an example of ERMIA being applied to a real, large complex piece of software.

The problem here is to look at the design of one sort of ATM (Automated Teller Machine) and try to discover why queues are building up when people wish to use the machine at busy periods.

10.3.1 ATM Conceptual ERMIA

The modeler commenced this problem by considering the conceptual ERMIA for an ATM. As it is quite a complex system, it is a good idea to start with high level entities. These can be investigated in detail later.

At a high level of abstraction we can conceptualize the structure of the interaction of person with an ATM as illustrated in Figure 10.11. This shows that a user undertakes some transaction using the machine and that the transaction is for some service (such as 'Withdraw Cash' or 'Obtain Balance'). The transaction results in some Delivery (such as Cash, or a display of the user's balance).

When we consider the details of the user, we need to consider other things (see Fig 10.12). Most importantly, a little thought reveals that a user in this context is not simply a person. All the ATM is concerned about is having a valid card placed in its slot – the 'user' can then undertake a transaction. Since a card can be put into many slots (since there are many ATMs which will accept the card) and of course a slot will accept many cards, there is a m:m relationship between Card and Slot. When this is decomposed a Card in slot entity is identified.

However, this is not sufficient to make a transaction with the machine. A PIN (personal identification number) is also needed before the 'user' can be allowed to

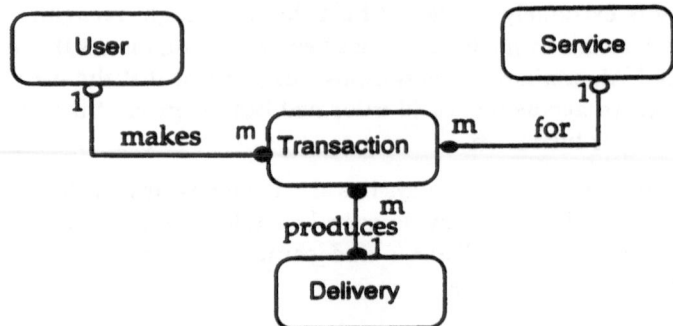

Fig 10.11 High level ERMIA of ATM.

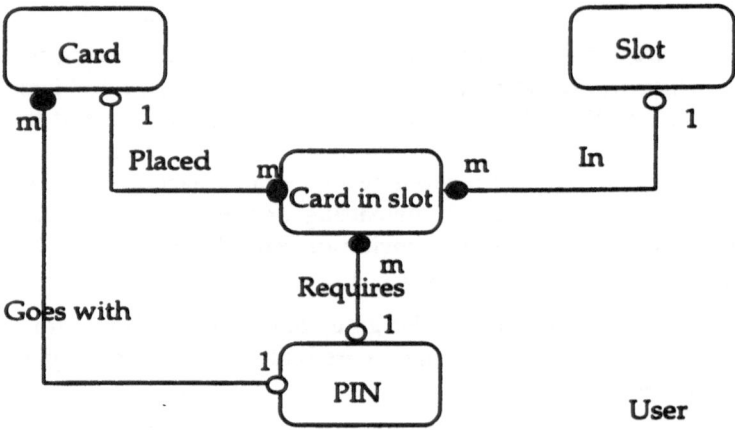

Fig 10.12 More detail about users.

get some service. A PIN is related to a card and of course each card has only one (valid) PIN associated with it.

The service is represented as shown in Figure 10.13. The service is displayed in the form of a message which requires some actions to be taken. An action may cause effects to the service message. An action will have some effect on the service offered. Notice the need for both the requires and the causes relationships here. The Service message requires some actions, but the user might take some other action (e.g. they might press the wrong button). The actual effect of the action is covered by the Effect entity.

The delivery consists of cash and/or a receipt and/or the card (see Fig 10.14).

These three models can be brought together and the whole ERMIA explored to see if it accurately represents the situation (Fig 10.16). In addition to looking at the user, service and delivery it is necessary to consider the layout of the key pad and other perceptual aspects of the interface. At this point, then, the modeler turned to look at an actual example of the ATM in order to see what the display looked like. An impression of this display is shown (Fig 10.15).

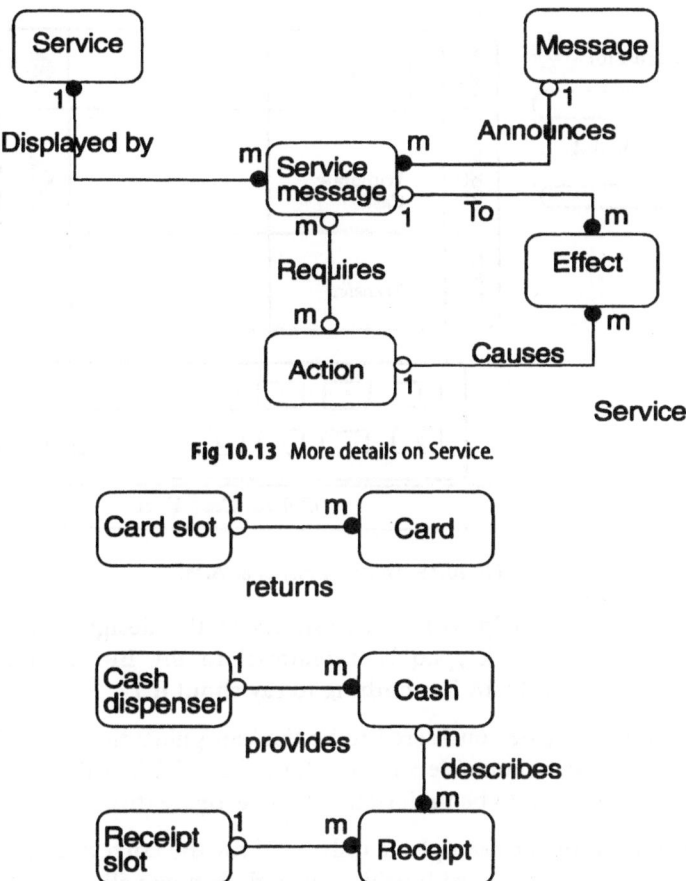

Fig 10.13 More details on Service.

Fig 10.14 More details of the delivery.

The key pad consists of an enter key, a cancel key and ten number keys. The touch sensitive arrows were used to select the various services available. The ERMIA in Figure 10.16 shows these aspects and also shows the different sub-types of the transaction. This is necessary because different transactions have different relationships. The audible 'beep' is another aspect of the perceptual ERMIA.

10.3.2 Analysis

ERMIA provides only an analysis of structure. It does not deal with the sequencing of processes.[2] Nor does it deal with the aesthetics of layout, etc. Other forms of

---

[2]Though we can use ERMIA to describe the structure of events and the relationships that exist between events and aspects of the artefact's structure such as button presses and displays as in Section 10.2.

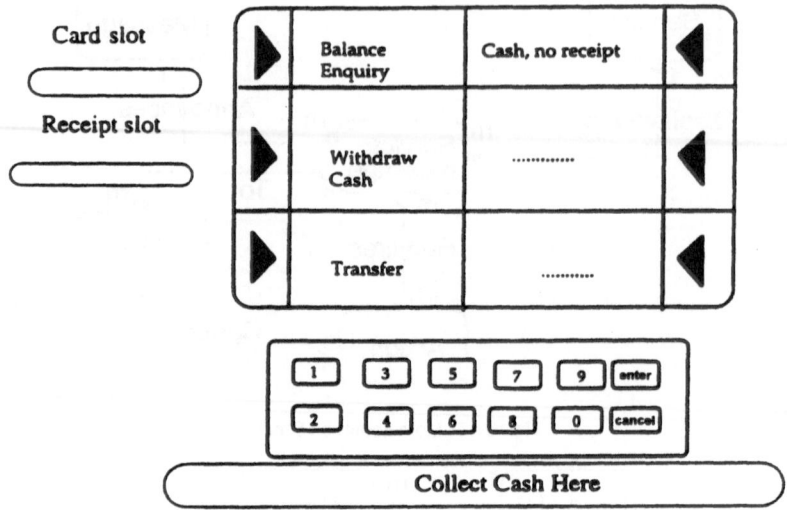

Fig 10.15 Typical display of an ATM.

analysis are required to help with these aspects of the design. Hence the actual layout of the display and keypad is immaterial to the ERMIA analysis. (It is important in itself, but ERMIA has nothing to say about it.)

The ERMIAs above may be considered to be the 'designer's model' of the interface and may not necessarily coincide with the 'users' models'. A detailed analysis of users' models would need to be undertaken to investigate this.

The Card in slot entity, for example, is only valid for the correct orientation of the card. If the user inserts the card 'upside down' then how will the ATM react? The

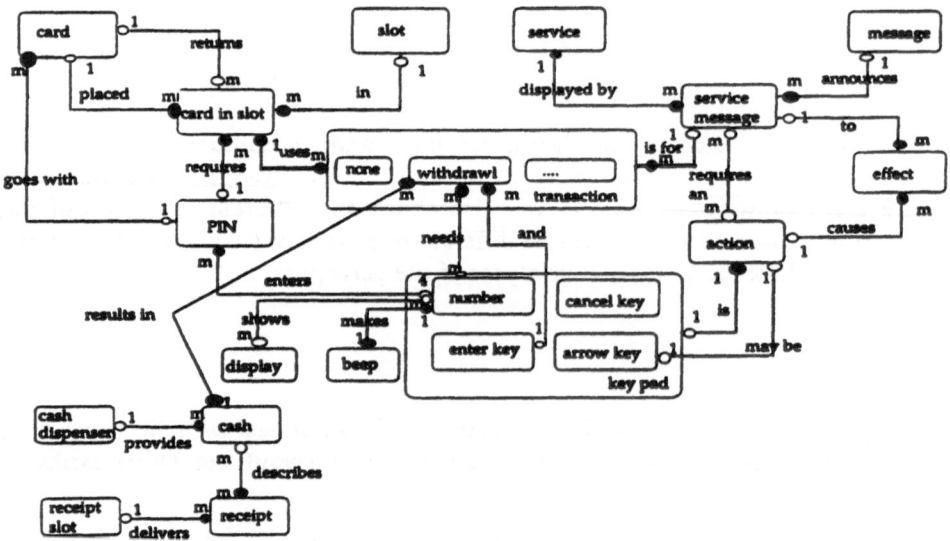

Fig 10.16 First full try at ERMIA of an ATM.

card itself is only one or more of some specific card types – is this knowledge clear to the users? The PIN currently requires four key presses. Is this physical arrangement necessary? Are there alternatives to typing in the PIN? Are there alternatives to having a PIN? The ERMIA shows that only numbers on the key pad result in a 'beep' (the principal form of feedback). Do users press other keys without knowing it? Arrow keys are related to some service messages. Is it clear which arrow key is meant to be pressed?

A Withdrawal requires both the typing of numbers and the pressing of the enter key. Is this necessary? For example, default options could be provided which required only a single key press.

The relationship between a transaction and the effect of an action is overly complex and potentially ambiguous owing to the m:1, 1:m relationships between the entities Transaction, Service message, Action and Effect (traversing the relationships 'is for' and 'requires an' or 'is for', 'to' and 'causes').

10.3.3 Re-design

The design could certainly be simplified by removing some of the m:m relationships – at the cost of some lost flexibility. For example, if a message always related to a single service and if each service message was associated with a single action; the Message:Action relationship would be 1:1. The ERMIA below (Fig 10.17) describes a simpler design as demonstrated by the number of 1:1 relationships. A 1:1 relationship is inherently simpler, particularly with mandatory participation. For example, a service now has just a single message and each message relates to one service. A withdrawal is now for a fixed amount of cash which corresponds, 1:1 with a labelled key. A sketch of the new layout is shown in Figure 10.18.

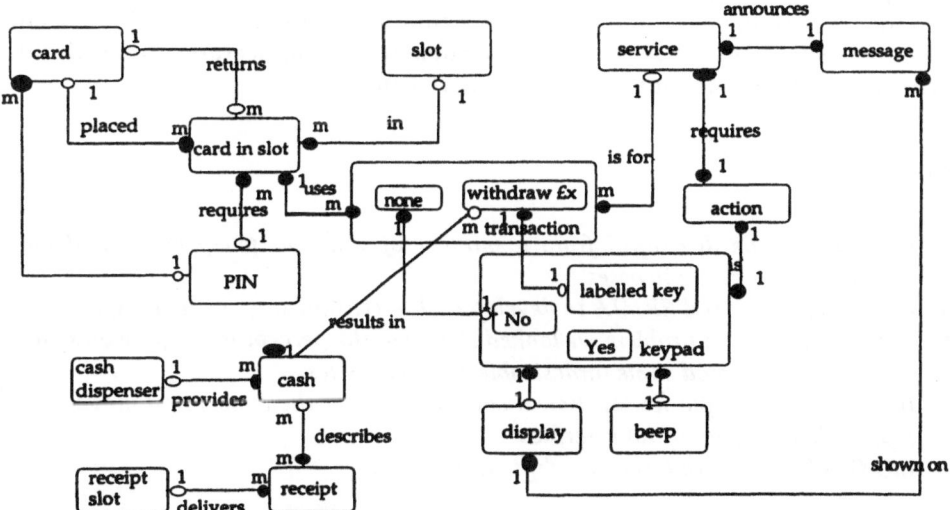

Fig 10.17 Simplifying the conceptual design of the ATM.

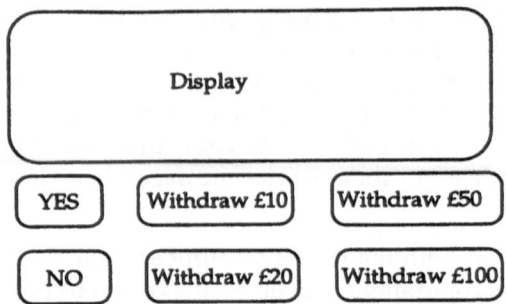

Fig 10.18 Sketch of new layout of ATM.

The issue of PIN numbers has not been addressed here and of course there may be restrictions which force us, as designers, to have the user enter a 4-digit PIN through a numeric keypad. If this is the case, then some of the advantage of having labelled keys is lost since a keypad is required in order to enter the PIN. However, it would be possible to use the same keys for entering a PIN, or for changing the way in which PINs are entered – e.g. having the system ask a number of questions which required a yes or no answer, using finger print recognition or using a touch screen for selecting the PIN digits.

Other aspects of the analysis above should also be taken into consideration – e.g. the card slot should accept a card inserted any way round.

10.3.4 Evaluation

The evaluation of this new design must now continue. In this case the modeler discussed his ideas with colleagues and it soon became clear that there were a number of other features about the whole ATM which needed to be considered. For example, how closely did users conceptions correspond with the designer's view and indeed with the Bank's view? There are complex interrelationships between the accounts which a user has and there are some interesting features to do with the order in which user actions have to be undertaken.

Summary

- *ERMIAs can be developed from a number of different perspectives and for a number of different purposes.*
- *In the diary we used ERMIA to develop and to critique a possible design.*
- *In the travel alarm problem we looked closely at the perceptual display and found that it demonstrated some undesirable characteristics.*
- *In the ATM example we saw how a consideration of the conceptual model led to a possible re-design of an interface.*
- *ERMIAs 'scale up' to large and difficult problems.*

11.   *Case Study*

Aims and Objectives

We have seen ERMIA in operation in a number of situations, mostly quite small systems. In this chapter we present a case study of ERMIA being used to evaluate a real and complex piece of software. Although the software is complex, and the domain will not be familiar to many readers, it is worth studying this chapter to get a feel for what ERMIA is like applied to a real software design problem. In particular, when discussing the conceptual ERMIA (11.2), it is necessary to delve deep into the details of the domain.

After studying this chapter you should be able to:

- understand a conceptual ERMIA of a complex piece of software
- see how a comparison of conceptual and perceptual ERMIAs can lead to useful insights into potential interface problems
- understand how using ERMIA leads to useful interface design ideas.

11.1 The Domain

There are many occasions in life when we want to demonstrate that some conjecture that we have is, in fact, true. For example, a software engineer developing a safety-critical system such as a program to control the signalling on a railway may need to demonstrate that a particular requirement of the system is correctly and completely implemented. A user interface designer may need to demonstrate that the interface will always display the correct data. A manufacturer of hydraulic pumps may want to demonstrate that a particular configuration of components will deliver the required performance.

In all these cases the system developer is concerned with establishing the truth of some statement in a formal manner. In software engineering, for example, it is very difficult to show that the test data used to test a program has covered all eventualities. Particularly in safety-critical systems it is sometimes necessary to prove, completely and theoretically, that the program is correct. The developer must show that the implementation of some software that has been specified using a formal notation such as 'Z' (discussed briefly in Section 12.1.3) meets the specification.

The way that the truth of some statement is demonstrated is by applying rules, simpler statements that have already been proven and logical methods to the statement. Together these can be used to determine if the statement is valid. Mathematicians have long been interested in this area. For example, one conjecture from Mathematics is called 'the associativity of plus' (abbreviated to assp). It says that

$$X + (Y + Z) = (X + Y) + Z$$

This may seem pretty obvious, but how can we prove that it is true – in all cases, no matter what the circumstances are? By applying common mathematical laws, and using the method of induction, associativity of plus it can be shown to be true. Once a conjecture has been shown to be true it is known as a theorem.

It is not surprising that people have developed software to help them with this rather time consuming task. These systems are called theorem provers. Theorem provers automate (to a greater or lesser extent) the process of proving theorems. They contain knowledge about the theorem proving process, details of previously proven theorems and rules and heuristics to select suitable methods for proving theorems.

CLaM is an automated theorem prover. The interface to CLaM, XBarnacle, allows users to interact with CLaM while it is performing a proof. XBarnacle is designed to allow users to step in and use their domain knowledge to guide CLaM in the search for a proof. This might be appropriate if they conclude that CLaM is pursuing an unproductive search strategy or if CLaM performs a proof step the user knows to be unproductive. XBarnacle allows users to stop CLaM in a proof, redo proof steps, direct the progress of the proof and override CLaM's choices of proof rules applied during a proof. XBarnacle also provides a more natural visualization of proof plans and allows menu-based and iconic access to many CLaM functions. The main XBarnacle interface is shown in Figure 11.1 and an example of the information users may retrieve about the underlying proof state is shown in Figure 11.2.

CLaM with its XBarnacle interface is known as XBarnacle/CLaM. Details of what the various parts of the interface mean are elaborated in Section 11.3, but basically the example shown in Figure 11.1 illustrates a proof of the associativity of plus conjecture. CLaM has chosen to use the induction method of proving this conjecture. This method requires two sub-methods, called *evaldef* (on the left of the display) and a *wave* method on the right. Various highlighting is used to help the user see what is going on. The menus at the top of the screen allow the user to choose different methods, plans, etc.

Mike Jackson was working on improving the XBarnacle/CLaM system. In particular he was interested in the interaction between the users and the existing XBarnacle and at how the current interface presented details of the proof planning process. He wanted to make it easier for users to interact with the underlying CLaM system, so that they could intervene during the automated part of the process.

In order to see where possible usability problems lay in the existing system, Mike developed ERMIAs of both the conceptual and perceptual aspects of XBarnacle. These were discussed with colleagues and refined over a period of several weeks. As a result of developing the ERMIAs, Mike identified a number of potential

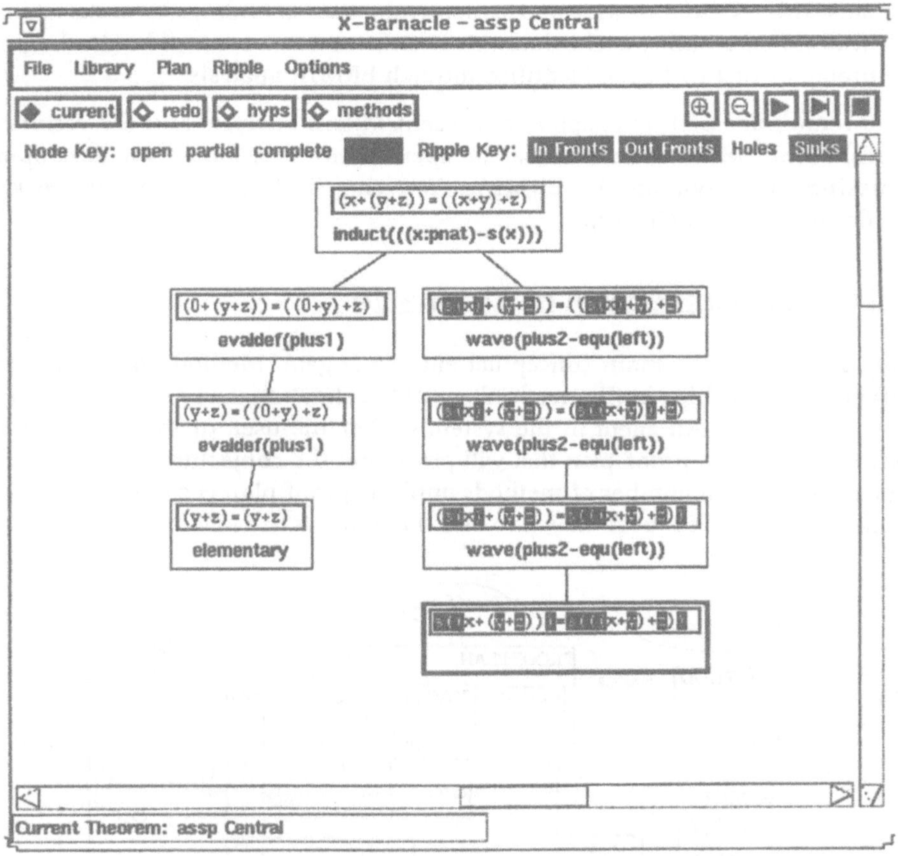

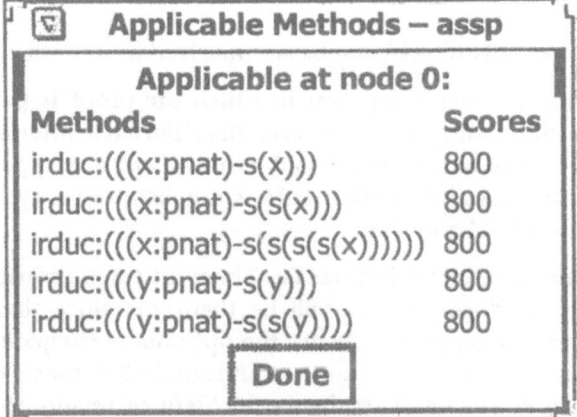

Fig 11.1 The XBarnacle Interface to CLaM.

Fig 11.2 Information from the XBarnacle interface.

problems with the existing system. He then evaluated his findings by undertaking a more traditional usability evaluation which confirmed that users did indeed experience problems that had been identified through ERMIA analysis.

In the remainder of this chapter we present Mike's analysis and the results of his evaluation. Mike estimates that he spent some fifty hours on developing, discussing and revising the ERMIAs. You can find details of his work at www.dcs.napier.ac.uk/~mikej.

11.2 Conceptual ERMIA of XBarnacle

Figure 11.3 shows the main conceptual entities (Agent, Method, Proof Plan and Goal) and relationships in XBarnacle. The ERMIA shows that a user defines (one or more) conjectures. An agent in the system (either the user, or the CLaM system itself) tries to find a proof plan that will prove that the conjecture is a theorem. A proof plan applies a number of methods until the proof plan is complete, in which case the conjecture has been shown to be a theorem, or has failed.

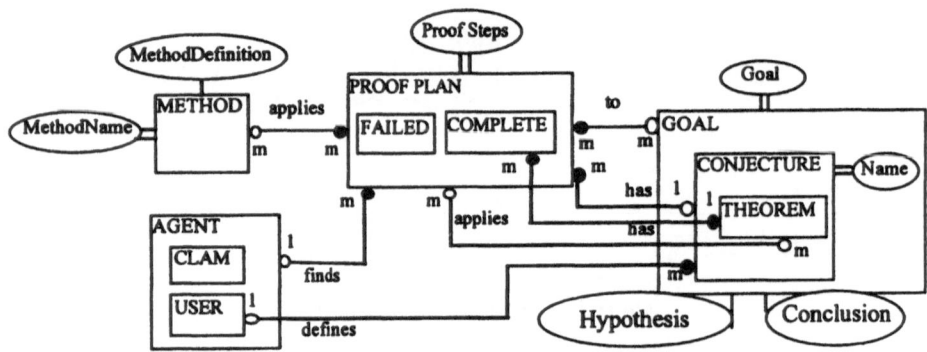

Fig 11.3 High level conceptual ERMIA of XBarnacle.

The main features of this ERMIA can be summarized as follows.

CLaM is an automated theorem prover in which the proof is performed (i.e. the proof plan is found) by the system. However, the XBarnacle interface supports user interaction to allow the user to guide and assist CLaM in the performance of its theorem proving task. As XBarnacle/CLaM is a collaborative system we have two sub-types of agent: CLaM and User.

While all theorems must be conjectures (so Theorem can be considered a sub type of Conjecture), not all conjectures will be theorems since there will be many conjectures that cannot be proven (hence the optional participation of Conjecture in the has relationship with Proof Plan). At present, in XBarnacle conjectures must be defined by the user, not by CLaM, hence the 'defines' relationship.

Conjectures (and theorems) are a type of goal. A goal has one or more hypotheses and a conclusion. The user tries to prove the conjecture by showing that the conclusion follows from the hypotheses. During this process other (sub-)goals may arise.

We distinguish our conjectures (and theorems) from other goals by giving them a unique name, for example assp (for associativity of plus).

An agent performs a proof through the use of methods. Methods are applied to a goal and either solve the goal trivially or break up a goal into sub-goals each of which is then solved recursively by the application of further methods. Methods have a unique name and a definition which determines to what goals the method may be applied and the results of applying the method.

The application of a method to a goal is termed a proof step. A proof plan is defined as a collection of such proof steps. Thus there are m:m relationships between Proof Plan and Method and between Proof Plan and Goal: each method may be applied in a number of proofs and each proof will apply a number of methods, and each proof will have a number of goals and a goal may arise in a number of proofs.

Figure 11.4 shows an example proof plan; the application of the *induction* method to the associativity of plus conjecture. This proof plan consists of eight proof steps using four methods (called *eval_def,wave, elementary* and *fertilize*). This proof plan results in two (sub-) goals. The sub-goal on the left consists of the three proof steps *eval_def(plus1)*, *eval_def(plus1)* and *elementary* and the sub-goal on the right consists of five proof steps *wave(plus2)*, *wave(plus2)*, *wave(plus2)*, *wave(cnc_s)* and *fertilize(strong)*. Note that due to the fact that methods applied to goals may give rise to other goals the proof plan has a tree-like structure. If the agent has success-fully applied methods to all the goals associated with a proof plan then the proof plan is said to be complete and the conjecture may then be said to be a theorem. The proof plan in Figure 11.4 is an example of a complete proof plan.

$$X + (Y + Z) = (X + Y) + Z$$

$$induction(s(x),x)$$

$$0 + (Y + Z) = (0 + Y) + Z \qquad X + (Y + Z) = (X + Y) + Z \quad s(X) + (Y + Z) = (s(X) + Y) + Z$$

$$eval\_def(plus1) \qquad\qquad\qquad wave(plus2)$$

$$(Y + Z) = (0 + Y) + Z \qquad X + (Y + Z) = (X + Y) + Z \quad s(X) + (Y + Z) = s(X + Y) + Z$$

$$eval\_def(plus1) \qquad\qquad\qquad wave(plus2)$$

$$(Y + Z) = (Y + Z) \qquad\qquad X + (Y + Z) = (X + Y) + Z \quad s(X) + (Y + Z) = s((X + Y) + Z)$$

$$elementary \qquad\qquad\qquad wave(plus2)$$

$$X + (Y + Z) = (X + Y) + Z \quad s(X + (Y + Z)) = s((X + Y) + Z)$$

$$wave(cnc\_s)$$

$$X + (Y + Z) = (X + Y) + Z \quad s(X + (Y + Z)) = s((X + Y) + Z)$$

$$fertilize(strong)$$

An example proof plan for the theorem *associativity of plus*. Induction, eval_def, elementary, wave and fertilize are all the names of methods. The conjecture is shown at the top of the figure, methods applied to goals are shown immediately beneath the goal and resulting sub-goals beneath those. So, for example, the application of the *induction* method to the conjecture leads to two sub-goals.

Fig 11.4 An example proof plan.

As there may be a number of ways in which a method may be applied to a goal and further a number of methods applicable at a goal we may have a number of ways of proving that a conjecture is a theorem. Therefore we have a 1:m relationship between Theorem and Complete – each theorem may have a number of complete proof plans (and must have at least one) but each complete proof will define only one theorem (since each complete proof will have only one related conjecture). Similarly a conjecture may have a number of proofs associated with it, including partially completed proofs, failed proofs and (if it is a theorem) completed proofs.

11.2.1 Finding a Proof Plan

In the ERMIA of Figure 11.5 we show the entities and relationships of XBarnacle/ CLaM in more detail and we use this to highlight the main aspects of theorem proving in XBarnacle/CLaM. In particular the many-to-many relationships between goals and proof plans and methods and proof plans have been expanded. This shows how methods are tested to see if they are applicable to the conjecture that we are trying to prove and how there are then applied to the goals and sub-goals that arise in the proof plan. The associativity of plus example (as used in Fig 11.1 and Fig 11.2) is shown in full in Figure 11.4.

Applying Methods

We described how a proof plan is formed by applying methods to goals and recursing on the sub-goals produced (if any). Determining whether a method is applicable to a goal involves retrieving a method and then evaluating the preconditions of the method with respect to the goal to determine whether the method is applicable to the goal.

If both these operations succeed then the method is applicable to the chosen goal and the method's effects are then executed. It is the execution of a method's effects that may cause the creation of sub-goals. The result of testing a method's preconditions with respect to a certain goal breaks up the m:m relationship between Method and Goal (as each method may be applied to many differing goals and each goal may have many methods applied to it). Tested Methods may be of two types: methods whose preconditions failed when evaluated with respect to the goal and methods whose preconditions succeeded with respect to the goal.

For tested methods we have key attributes Goal whose value is the name of the goal to which the method was applied; MethodName, storing the name of the method applied to the goal; and InstantiatedPrecs which stores the state of the preconditions of the method after their evaluation on the goal. We require InstantiatedPrecs as a key attribute since the preconditions of a method may be satisfied (or fail) in more than one way when evaluated using information from a goal. For example the *wave* method may be viewed as a method for transforming certain forms of sub-terms of a goal (as seen in Fig 11.4) and in a goal there may be a number of such sub-terms that the wave method could transform – a number of differing values of InstantiatedPrecs would then arise, one for each of the sub-terms.

Aside from the key attributes we also have attribute InstantiatedEffects which is the Effects attribute of the method instantiated with goal-specific information (this

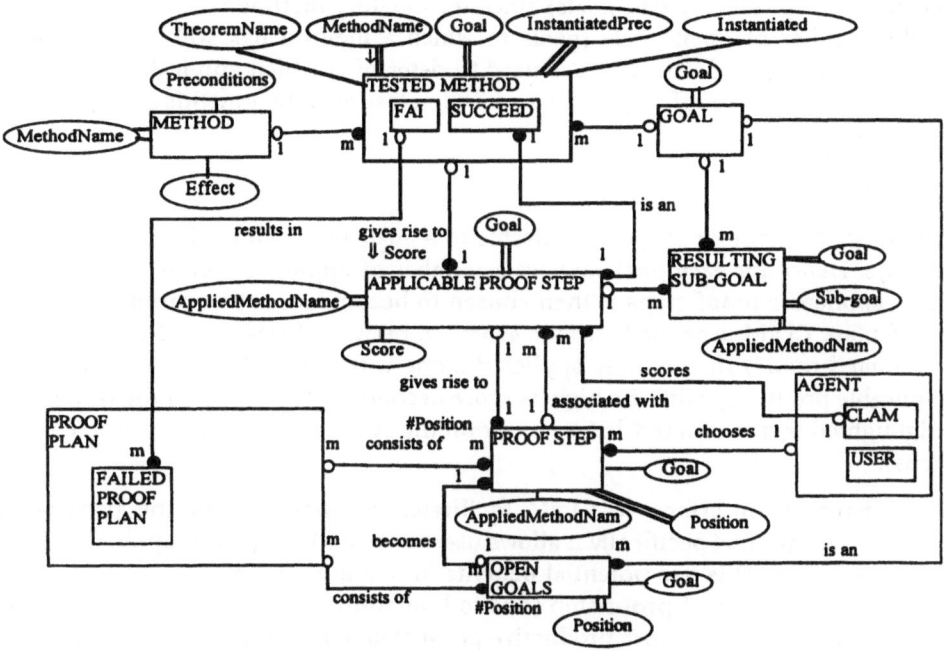

Fig 11.5 Detailed conceptual ERMIA of XBarnacle/CLaM.

arises as a side effect of evaluating the method's preconditions using goal-specific information); and attribute TheoremNames, since methods may apply theorems when being applied to a goal. For example the *wave* method makes use of existing theorems to transform sub-terms of a goal.

Applicable Proof Steps

If the preconditions of a method execute successfully with respect to a goal then we have an applicable proof step which, if chosen to be part of the proof plan, will advance the proof. It advances the proof if it either trivially solves the goal or gives rise to sub-goals which must then be proven similarly. Applicable proof steps have key attributes Goal and AppliedMethodName.

There is a 1:1 relationship between successfully tested methods and applicable proof steps since each applicable proof step must have arisen from a successfully tested method (i.e. one that can be applied to a goal) and each successfully tested method must give rise to an applicable proof step. There is a 1:1 optional relationship between Tested Method and Applicable Proof Step as a tested method may give rise to an applicable proof step (for successfully tested methods) but then again may not (for methods whose preconditions fail i.e. are not applicable to the goal).

CLaM uses a simple heuristic to score each applicable proof step in terms of some measure of goodness reflecting the possible benefits that applying that proof step may have on the proof as a whole. For example methods that result in no sub-goals (so-called terminating methods) are to be preferred to non-terminating methods (i.e. methods producing sub-goals) since terminating methods lead to no increase in the number of open goals (goals to which a method has still to be applied) remaining in a proof. This score is used to determine which applicable proof step becomes an actual proof step in the proof plan (see also the way this is displayed as in Fig 11.2).

Proof Steps

A number of methods may be applicable to a goal, and each of these in a number of ways. Hence for each goal we have a number of applicable proof steps. One of these applicable proof steps is then chosen to become an actual proof step in the proof plan. CLaM uses the heuristic scores to rank applicable proof steps and (in automated mode) then simply applies the one with the highest score, that is the applicable proof step with the highest score becomes a proof step in the proof plan (highlighted by the ordered-list operator on the Score attribute of applicable proof steps).

The XBarnacle interface to CLaM facilitates co-operation in the process of performing a proof. Specifically it allows users to redo the methods applied to goals in a proof plan. This has potential benefits in that a user may detect when CLaM makes a poor choice of proof step (due to limitations in its scoring heuristic) and can step in and apply a more productive proof step, for example a proof step which leads to a shorter search for the rest of the proof plan. The user may therefore apply a method that was not the one that was scored highest by CLaM. This introduces a chooses relationship between Agent and Proof Step reflecting the fact that either CLaM or the user may choose the proof steps that arise in a proof plan. This relationship is 1:m reflecting the fact that an agent may choose a number of proof steps and that each proof step must have been chosen by some agent.

There is a 1:1 optional relationship between Applicable Proof Step and Proof Step as each applicable proof step may give rise to a proof step (but may not since only one applicable proof step may be chosen for a goal) and each proof step must have resulted from an applicable proof step. Further each proof step will have associated with it a number of applicable proof steps, all the applicable proof steps that could have become actual proof steps at that point in the proof.

There is also a m:m relationship between a Proof Plan and Proof Step – a proof plan consists of a number of proof steps, each proof step having a unique position in the proof plan which provides immediate access to the proof step, and a proof step may belong to a number of proof plans. This relationship is left undecomposed as it is not of direct interest in this analysis.

Sub-goals

For methods that give rise to sub-goals the effects of these methods will determine what the resulting sub-goals are. The Resulting Sub-goal entity represents the relationship between applicable proof steps and the sub-goals each applicable proof step will give rise to. This entity relates a goal to the sub-goals produced when a method is applied to it, that is, it relates applicable proof steps to the sub-goals it gives rise to, and relates goals to the applicable proof steps they may arise from.

Note that it is not mandatory for a goal to have a related Resulting Sub-goal entity since some goals will not have arisen from any method applications, a prime example being goals that are also conjectures – these having arisen from the user. Similarly the relationship between proof steps and resulting sub-goals is not mandatory since some applicable proof steps will not give rise to any sub-goals.

Open Goals

As well as consisting of proof steps a proof plan may also consist of some open goals, that is, goals in the proof plan to which a method has still to be applied. Each of these goals will also have a specific position in the proof plan. When a goal that is an open goal has a method applied to it then it will become a proof step (and each proof step must have come from a goal that was open).

Failed Proofs

A sub-type of a proof plan is a failed proof plan. A failed proof plan is just a proof plan that has some sub-goal to which we cannot apply any method. There is a 1:m relationship between failed tested methods and failed proof plans as failure to find an applicable proof step (i.e. failure to find a successfully tested method) may result in a number of failed proof plans (as the instance of the tested method entity may arise in a number of proof plans).

11.3 A Perceptual ERMIA of the XBarnacle Interface

XBarnacle is the interface, or viewport, for the XBarnacle/CLaM system (Figs 11.1 and 11.2). By developing a perceptual ERMIA of the interface we can see how the interface maps onto the conceptual ERMIAs developed in the previous section. In the next section we show how comparing conceptual ERMIAs of an application domain with both conceptual ERMIAs of the software and the perceptual ERMIAs of the viewport(s) onto that software highlights potential usability problems.

Figure 11.1 shows the XBarnacle interface with a proof in progress and Figure 11.6 shows the perceptual ERMIA for the main body of this viewport (i.e. the various components such as menus and buttons have been ignored). While XBarnacle allows three views of the proof tree differing in the amount of detail shown the one that is of interest to us is the default view as shown in Figure 11.1.

In the following description we concentrate on presenting an ERMIA of what is perceived at the interface, presenting the mappings between conceptual and perceptual ERMIAs later. So, for example, we refer to an attribute of the entries in the list box (Fig 11.2) as 'number' and only subsequently recognize that this maps onto the conceptual attribute of Score.

The XBarnacle interface presents the user with a collection of nodes where each node is either a parent of some other nodes or is childless. Each node has a position in the interface and a formula. Colour (shown as shading in Figure 11.1) is used to distinguish parts of the node display. One of these nodes will also be a root

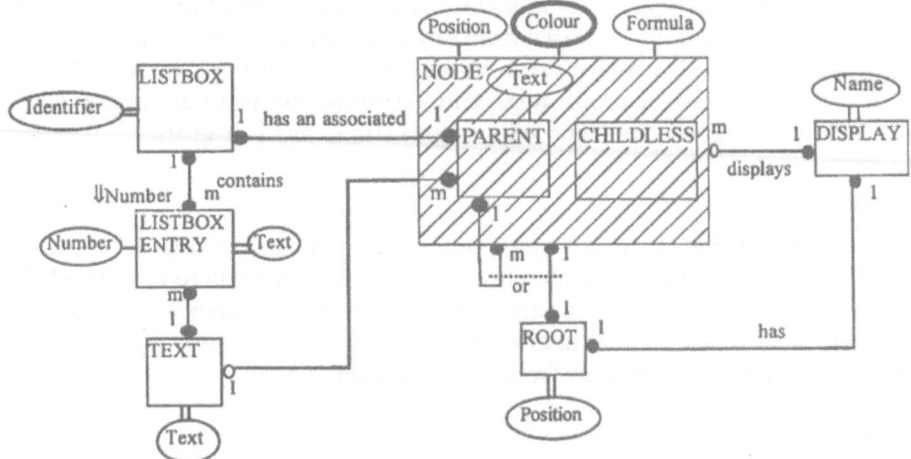

Fig 11.6 Perceptual ERMIA of XBarnacle.

node which has a distinguishable position. As the proof progresses this tree will update with more nodes being added to the interface. Not all nodes will be display-able on screen at once, therefore many nodes may end up occupying the same posi-tion on screen at differing times. Therefore Position does not act as an identifying attribute. Position does however act as an identifying attribute for the root since this node has no parents. Also notice that Node is shaded, indicating that nodes are clones; there is no way of distinguishing, perceptually, between occurrences of nodes.

XBarnacle allows the user to click on the nodes of this tree to gain information about them. If users click on a node they may access a listbox (Fig 11.2) associated with the node, the listbox having a unique identifier. This display is only applicable to parent nodes. This listbox consists of a number of entries each of which has a number and a piece of text, the entries being ordered by number. The text displayed in listboxes is the same type of entity as the text that occurs in parent nodes.

Table 11.1 shows the relationship between entities and attributes in our conceptual ERMIAs to those in the perceptual ERMIA of our viewport (i.e. the XBarnacle interface).

11.4 Using ERMIA to Identify Potential Usability Problems

The construction of the conceptual and perceptual ERMIAs has provided important insights both into the nature of the domain and into design of the interface. The fact that the conceptual ERMIA in Figure 11.5 is a lot more complex than the perceptual ERMIA in Figure 11.6 immediately suggests that there are some things not revealed by the interface. The comparison in Table 11.1 shows where there are direct representations and where there are not.

The Proof Step and Open Goal entities in the conceptual ERMIA are represented at the interface by the Node entity and the ListBox perceptual entity allows the user to

Table 11.1

Perceptual ERMIA	Conceptual ERMIA
DISPLAY	PROOF PLAN
Name	Name
NODE	PROOF STEP or OPEN GOAL
Position	This refers to the position of the NODE on screen and is not analogous to any conceptual entity or attribute
Formula	Goal
Colour	Denotes whether NODE is PARENT or CHILDLESS i.e. Whether it represents a PROOF STEP or an OPEN GOAL
PARENT	PROOF STEP
Text	AppliedMethodName
CHILDLESS	OPEN GOAL
ROOT	PROOF STEP / OPEN GOAL whose Goal value is that of the conjecture/theorem with name Name
LISTBOX	No analogue – but may be viewed as denoting the associated with relation between applicable proof steps and proof steps
Identifier	Position
LISTBOX ENTRY	APPLICABLE PROOF STEP (but see Section 11.4)
Number	Score
TEXT	Entity for applied method names

see occurrences of the applicable steps and resulting sub-goal entities. We can see how the Goal conceptual entity appears as the Formula attribute of Node and how the methods button (not modeled in Fig 11.6, but visible in Fig 11.1) does allow the user access to details of the methods that CLaM has at its disposal. By working carefully through the diagrams, comparing conceptual and perceptual and comparing conceptual models with the data held in CLaM we see where other problems might arise.

11.4.1 A Problem Due to the Collaborative Nature of the Interface

In Section 11.2 we described how the XBarnacle/CLaM system allows the user to collaborate with CLaM when finding a proof plan. While either users or CLaM may determine which of the applicable proof steps to apply neither the Proof Step nor Applicable Proof Step entities contain any attribute to record who actually applied each proof step. Thus there is no means of determining the division of labour (if any) between CLaM and a human user when performing a proof. This is important since users and other interested parties may overestimate or underestimate the power of CLaM or may gain a false impression of the reasoning strategies used by CLaM if this information is not available to them.

Constructing a conceptual ERMIA has revealed the existence of a relationship, 'chooses' that is not represented as an attribute of any entity in the system. In this example this problem can be solved through the addition of an attribute to Proof Step to identify who executed each step in the proof and the provision at the interface of a suitable presentation of this new attribute.

11.4.2 A Problem with Proof Steps

We see in Figure 11.6 that each node has an associated listbox which has a number of listbox entries each of these being the viewport onto the applicable proof steps. We can also access the goal to which each of these applicable methods applies since this is just the goal related to the node upon which we clicked to get the listbox in the first place. However, Figure 11.5 shows that each applicable proof step is related to its resulting sub-goals which denotes the sub-goals (if any) that result from the applicable proof step. Yet there is no visual representation of this entity at the interface.

At the interface we may access the sub-goals of a proof step by following the 1:m relationship between Parent and Node and viewing the formula associated with these child nodes. This in effect allows us to follow the relationship between proof steps and resulting sub-goals (via applicable proof steps). Hence we can view the resulting sub-goal entity but only for those applicable proof steps that were actually applied i.e. those applicable proof steps that became actual proof steps in the proof plan.

However, it can be useful for users when intervening in a proof to see what sub-goals each applicable proof step produce. This is because the user may deem that the sub-goals produced by an applicable proof step that was not actually applied may have more chance of being proven than the sub-goals resulting from the proof step that was applied. The user can access the sub-goals associated with each applicable proof step but only if they apply each applicable proof step in turn and see the results as displayed at the interface. Not only does this require interaction from the user but it also puts a burden on the user's memory since they would have to remember the sub-goals produced by each applied method so they could compare between the applicable proof steps to determine which to apply.

While the resulting sub-goals of an applicable method are generated by CLaM they exist only for a short time and disappear when one of the applicable proof steps is chosen to be the next proof step in the proof plan. To address this problem would require retaining these resulting sub-goals, perhaps as an attribute of applicable proof steps. Then an extra attribute could be added to the listbox entry at the interface which would provide a rendition on the display of the sub-goals that result from each applicable proof step.

Where sub-trees of the proof tree are the same, i.e. the proof contains two distinct but identical subproofs, the user may be unable to distinguish between them. This happens because the nodes (Fig 11.6) are clones and therefore are perceptually indistinguishable.

11.4.3 Preconditions of Methods

As well as knowing what methods are applicable to a given goal it can be informative to know why each method was applicable to the goal. This information can be provided by the preconditions of a method which encode the situations in which the method is applicable. Combined with information from a given goal the preconditions can therefore provide a means to explain why the method was applicable to the given goal.

While the instantiated preconditions do exist as an attribute of a tested method they exist only for a short while. When a tested method is found to be successful (i.e. is an applicable proof step) then the instantiated preconditions are discarded. It might be useful to retain the instantiated preconditions by keeping them as an attribute of applicable methods. Then they could be rendered in some suitable manner at the interface. Similar comments refer to the explaining the effects of methods which is also related to the display of the resulting sub-goals already described.

Thus we can again see that the whole of the conceptual model of the domain is not captured by CLaM and not revealed at the interface.

11.4.4 Failed Proof Steps

Figure 11.5 shows how failed tested methods may lead to a failed proof plan. Again, however, there is no entity in the structure of the interface to present such failed proof steps to the user (nor are there any commands to enable users to access these). As well as knowing what methods are applicable (and why they were applicable) it can also be informative to know why a method was not applicable to a given goal. This can be useful for learners to learn the sorts of goals to which certain methods can and cannot be applied as well as highlighting to experts limits in the definitions and knowledge that CLaM uses when theorem proving. This may allow the deduction of why a proof failed and how the proof may be 'patched' to enable its success.

This is a problem with the underlying conceptual structure as well as with the interface. While methods that failed to be applied do exist they do so for a short time only and are then discarded. Again what may be required is a more permanent entity for these methods which can be visualized at the interface so the user may see what methods were not applied at each node.

As methods fail to apply to goals due to failure of their preconditions examining exactly how the preconditions failed can be informative to the user. Therefore any entity representing failed method/goal combinations should have as an attribute these failed preconditions also. This again gives rise to the possibility of rendering these into English language explanations for the user.

11.5 Did the Problems Materialize?

Mike Jackson subsequently undertook a more traditional evaluation of the XBarnacle/CLaM system. In undertaking this evaluation he was interested in both the usability problems that ERMIA had identified and in adding additional functionality to the system in the form of interactive critics (more about this in

Section 11.6). He used a co-operative evaluation technique in which Mike, as the system designer, worked with users as they performed a number of pre-determined tasks using the system. Six users, three expert in theorem proving and three less expert, used the system and their comments and criticisms were recorded. Details of the evaluation can be found in at www.dcs.napier.ac.uk/~mikej.

The problem of the collaborative nature of the interface (Section 11.4.1) was commented upon by two of the expert users. They both commented on how a particular choice of method was 'clever', but were unable to access details about how the system had selected that method. Similarly the problem of the nodes being clones (Section 11.4.2) did prove to be a problem highlighted by the users. In the conceptual ERMIA discussion (Section 11.2) the point was made that both proof steps and open goals have a unique position in a proof plan. However, there is no representation of this position explicitly at the interface. The proof plan is visualized in a tree-like structure but for some large trees finding a position in the proof plan may take some effort on the part of the user as the user has to count through the nodes in order to determine where a change to the proof could be made. Five of the users commented upon this problem. A related problem was knowing where a critic had been invoked (see Section 11.6).

The other issues identified through the ERMIA analysis were not specifically tested for in this evaluation, but it is clear from this piece of empirical work that an ERMIA analysis can be used to identify usability problems. As we have stated several times in this book, developing ERMIAs is *relatively* quick to do. Relative, that is, to other ways of evaluating interfaces. Of course ERMIA will not pick up all usability problems and Mike found many detailed areas of the interface that users found confusing or did not like, such as, the labelling of buttons, inconsistencies in the use of symbols and so on.

11.6 Introducing Critics: XBarnacle 3.2

To complete the story, we will mention briefly the latest version of XBarnacle and the ideas of interactive proof 'critics'. Proof critics provide functionality to CLaM to allow the 'patching' of failed proof steps allowing then to succeed. A patch facilitates the conversion of failed tested methods into successful tested methods. Interactive proof critics provide interaction to these proof critics to allow user-CLaM collaboration in the patching of a proof. Part of the functionality of the interactive proof critics is an explanation facility which describes why a method failed in terms of its preconditions. One aspect of the evaluation was to see whether such explanations of failed proof steps are of use to the user. If this is the case then this will confirm the points raised by ERMIA as to the importance of rendering major conceptual entities (in this case failed proof steps) at the interface as well as showing how addressing a problem highlighted by ERMIA analysis results in benefits for the user.

Another aspect of proof critics is that they allow CLaM to form its own conjectures (with the motivation that these conjectures, once proven, be used as rules to transform goals in the user's proof). Thus the relationship between User and Conjecture (see Fig 11.3) would become a relationship between Agent and Conjecture.

This in turn gives rise to a new potential usability problem. As both CLaM and the user can define conjectures there should be some way of distinguishing which agent defined which conjecture. If this is not done then outside observers may not appreciate the power of CLaM as they will be unaware of the conjectures that CLaM generated automatically as a means to prove the user's conjecture. Thus we can see how ERMIA can highlight potential sources of problems due to the addition of new functionality in an underlying conceptual system.

Mike implemented and evaluated the interactive critics. He found that interacting with proof critics led to reduced times in proving theorems that were beyond the power of the fully automated version of CLaM because users were able to use their own knowledge when the 'knowledge' of CLaM ran out. He also found that users viewed the suggestions provided by the critics as credible and relevant. The explanation part of the interactive proof critics also proved useful and informative.

Interactive proof critics are an example of more general critics – software systems that have a (limited) amount of knowledge about some other system and that can advise the user on how to accomplish things. One of the things that Mike's work has highlighted is the importance of users being able to *interact* with the critics. Users may have domain knowledge where a critic does not and no matter how 'intelligent' a critic may be, users need to be able to intervene when the critic's intelligence runs out.

Summary

- *ERMIA can be used to model complex and large pieces of software.*
- *Constructing and analysing the conceptual ERMIAs both individually and in conjunction with the perceptual ERMIA can highlight potential usability problems.*
- *ERMIA can certainly be effective in identifying usability problems.*
- *ERMIA highlights the distribution of knowledge through the whole human-computer system.*
- *ERMIA highlights the memory load imposed on the user by the interface.*
- *ERMIA can be used to identify usability problems when software is being extended.*

12. *Conclusions*

Aims and Objectives

In this chapter we look briefly at a number of other techniques which can be useful in HCI and compare them to ERMIA. We present some features of ERMIA which we feel are its strengths and discuss some of the wider issues which ERMIA raises.

After reading this chapter you should be able to:

- recognize that ERMIA cannot do everything in HCI design and evaluation
- describe the strengths of ERMIA
- describe the weaknesses of ERMIA
- select a modeling method appropriate to your purpose.

12.1 ERMIA and Other Techniques

ERMIA is an approach to modeling the structure of information artefacts and we have shown that this can bring a number of useful analyses to bear. However, as we saw in Chapter 1, structure is not the only way of looking at information artefacts and it is important to recognize that other approaches are important for different purposes. For example, ERMIA will not provide any information about how long it actually takes a user to do something. It can highlight where difficulties in an interface might lie, but it can only provide a symbolic representation of search time and the amount of memory which is required. Designers and choosers need to decide how important these symbolic representations are likely to be in any particular circumstance. Neither is ERMIA a fully formal method. A lot of the meaning of the model is captured in the names which the modeler chooses for the entities and relationships. The reader of the model has to supply some understanding to go with the representation.

To make it a bit clearer when ERMIA might and might not be useful, here are very brief descriptions of three other modeling techniques, each of which has been widely used. We have endeavoured to explain the nub of the techniques but we have avoided going into detail, which means that we have had to omit description of the actual notations used; there is further reading on each of these techniques listed in the Resources section.

12.1.1 GOMS

Detailed time predictions can be derived from a simplified model describing the user's cognitive processes. The user's activities are divided into *tasks*, and for each task the model sets out the *goal* of the task, any sub-goals involved, the *method* to accomplish the task, and the *operators* required. If more than one method is possible, the model also includes the *selection rule* to decide which method (hence GOMS, Goals-Operators-Methods-Selectors). This is actually a family of models at different levels of detail.

For the simple graphics package example (Fig 1.1), the goal of the user might be to rotate the rectangle. The method for doing so might be something like that shown in Figure 12.1

```
GOAL: EDIT-DRAWING
    .    GOAL: EDIT-UNIT-TASK
    .    .    GOAL: ACQUIRE-UNIT-TASK
    .    .         somehow decide to rotate the rectangle
    .    .    GOAL: EXECUTE-UNIT-TASK
    .    .    .    GOAL: SELECT-SHAPE
    .    .    .    .    REACH-FOR-MOUSE
    .    .    .    .    POINT-TO-RECTANGLE
    .    .    .    .    CLICK
    .    .    .    GOAL: APPLY-OPERATOR
    .    .    .    .    POINT-TO-MENU-HEADING
    .    .    .    .    DEPRESS-MOUSE
    .    .    .    .    DRAG-TO-ROTATE-OPERATOR
    .    .    .    .    RELEASE MOUSE
```

Fig 12.1 Simplified GOMS description of method to apply an operator such as Rotate.

In a GOMS description, the steps are arranged hierarchically; the task of 'select shape', for example, is achieved by achieving the three sub-tasks, 'reach for mouse', 'point to rectangle' and 'click'. In a full GOMS description, the level of analysis would be taken down to the individual actions, in which 'point to rectangle' would be fully described. In a full model there might be a method for searching through the menu headings looking for the Rotate operator.

Each of these actions can be assigned an approximate time: example timings include 1.10 secs for the operator 'point with mouse' and 1.35 secs for the operator of 'select from alternatives'. The approximations have been derived from timings of users. Very good time estimations have been reported using GOMS, simple though it is.

GOMS is a very detailed account of the experienced user's actions, but it is not intended to describe the explorations of learners, nor does it handle user errors. It is difficult for non-specialists to use, and because it is so detailed it is not a quick method of analysis. (See the Resources section for a simpler approach, closely related, called NGOMSL – Natural GOMS Language – that is supposed to be easier for non-specialists.) GOMS only describes the user and not the system being used. Because it focuses on the user's actions, it cannot easily be applied at an early stage of design. The emphasis in most GOMS work has been on quantitative results that can be used to assess the quality of a design, rather than using it to create or inspire a new design or a re-design.

12.1.2 UAN

For many design purposes it is necessary to define how the system responds to the user's actions. GOMS does not show how the system behaves at all; UAN (User-Action Notation) is based on the notion of user tasks, like GOMS, but for each user action it records what the interface 'replies'. It is usual to present a UAN model as a table (Fig 12.2).

TASK: Select and rotate the rectangle			
User actions	*Interface feedback*	*Interface state*	*Connection to computation*
Move mouse to rectangle	Cursor tracks		
Click mouse	Rectangle highlighted	Rectangle selected	
Move mouse to menu heading 'Arrange'	Cursor tracks		
Depress mouse button	Menu items are pulled down		
Move mouse to 'Rotate'	Cursor tracks		
Release mouse button	Rectangle rotates		Menu item action executed

Fig 12.2 An English version of a UAN description of rotating a rectangle.

Figure 12.2 uses English descriptions but there is a special terse notation for user actions and system responses, such as $M\lor\land$ which means 'depress mouse button then release mouse button' (i.e. click mouse). A taste of the terse form of the notation is given in Figure 12.3. This form makes it easier to indicate preconditions (rectangle must be selected before it can be rotated), as well as allowing alternative orderings of action sequences to be indicated.

TASK: Select a file icon in Macintosh Finder		
User actions	*Interface feedback*	*Interface state*
~[file_icon-!] M∨	file_icon!, ∀file_icon'!: file_icon'-!	selected = file
M∧		

Fig 12.3 A UAN description using the UAN notation.

The UAN notation may be interpreted as follows:

~	=	move the cursor
[ ]	=	context ('spatial region')
file_icon!	=	highlighted file-icon
file_icon-!	=	un-highlighted file-icon (notice the dash before the !)
M∨	=	depress mouse button
' (prime)	=	signifies that an object has been changed

and so on.

The interpretation of the UAN description of selecting a file icon in Figure 12.3 can therefore be read like this:

Step 1: move the cursor to a spatial region surrounding a file icon that is not highlighted, and depress the mouse button. The effect on the interface is to highlight that file icon and to select the corresponding file, while all file icons that were previously highlighted become un-highlighted.
Step 2: release mouse button. No effect on interface.

12.1.3 Z

The language called Z is a specification language, originally developed to make it possible to give an exact description of what software should do. It is a 'declarative' notation, meaning that it defines the effect of each possible operation but says nothing about how the operation is achieved. The basis is set theory with some extensions and a good deal of logical notation. Models created in Z are very precise, which means that they necessarily contain a great deal of detail.

When applied to the simple drawing program, a Z model would represent it as a universe containing objects which we will call Graphic Entities – each object being a circle or a rectangle – and allowing various operations on these objects. We will only consider one operation, rotation, but obviously there would be operations to create, delete, and move objects.

Z models are built from 'schemas', which define useful parts of the model. One of the great strengths of Z is that these schemas can refer to each other, so that a Z model of a number of schemas, each of which is moderately comprehensible, instead of a single huge chunk of notation. For the drawing program, the first schema would define the idea of a drawing, which contained a set of Graphic Entities; in this very simple drawing package, there are just two kinds of graphic entities, rectangles and circles.

Another schema would define the effect of rotation. Rotation is a function operating on a (selected) rectangle and producing another rectangle. Z does not have a notion of changing an object, so the change would be modeled as removing the old rectangle and creating the new one: that is to say, the new set of rectangles is equal to the old set, minus the selected rectangle, plus the output from the function 'rotate'.

Once again, there is a special notation for saying all this tersely. The first schema would be represented thus:

```
┌─────── Drawing ──────────────┐
│                              │
│  object: GraphicEntity       │
│  rectangle: GraphicEntity    │
│  circle: GraphicEntity       │
│  ──────────────────────────  │
│  {object} = {rectangle} ∪ {circle} │
└──────────────────────────────┘
```

The sheer detail of Z makes it ideal for very exact descriptions, but at the same time makes it less useful for 'broad-brush' work where the aim is to understand the main outlines of a design

12.1.4 Summary

Each of these three modeling techniques has its own use. GOMS describes the sequence of user actions in a way that emphasizes the cognitive and motor components, allowing good time estimations to be derived. UAN also describes the sequence of user actions, but relates them to the behaviour of the interface; unlike GOMS, concurrent and interleaved action sequences can be handled. Z says nothing about the user at all, but it describes the universe that is being acted upon (such as a drawing) in very exact detail, with a full specification of the result of every possible operation.

12.2 Choosing a Modeling Method

Every modeling technique has its uses and there are many techniques in use which are concerned with evaluating designs of information artefacts. Many of these, for example UAN, are concerned only with interactive systems such as computers. Other techniques, such as cognitive walk-throughs, are concerned specifically with the cognitive aspects of computer systems and others, such as Discount Usability Evaluation, are concerned with making good principles of HCI easily available to designers and choosers.

ERMIA needs to be seen in the light of these other techniques and those described in Section 12.1. So how can people decide when a technique is most appropriate? In this section we highlight some important aspects of choosing an appropriate technique and describe where ERMIA fits in with other approaches.

12.2.1 Purpose of Model

Different modeling tools have different aims. For example, GOMS (Card *et al.*, 1983) takes a relatively extreme position, its aim being nothing less than accurate prediction of user times. At the other extreme are models whose purpose is solely to force the model-user to concentrate, to reflect, and to achieve a full understanding. Numerical calculations are not an issue. The algebraic models, such as PIE (Dix,

1991), have that flavour; the intention of their model is to find precise definitions for terms like 'reachability'. ERMIA lies somewhere between these extremes, partaking of each. It yields comparative analyses of complexity for different designs, and thereby encourages reasoning about designs, but it does not lead to precise numerical predictions; the act of building a model forces reflection and (in the authors' experience) frequently leads us to new insights about underlying structure, or exposes our misconceptions, but it does not yield expressions that are mathematically as well formed as an algebraic model. If we describe the poles of this scale as 'numerical analysis' and 'concept analysis', ERMIA lies at a point that might be labelled 'insightful analysis'.

12.2.2 Level of Detail

We regard the level of detail, or *level of focus* as an important dimension of HCI modeling techniques. Level of focus in HCI has varied over the years. Early approaches were close-focus descriptions containing extremely fine-grain detail, whether they were attempts at cognitive modeling (such as GOMS), formal analyses of system properties (such as PIE), or natural language analyses (such as 'claims analysis' – Rosson and Carroll, 1995). These close-focus descriptions tended to drown the HCI analyst in a sea of detail.

ERMIA is an attempt to find an effective long-focus approach, suppressing the unnecessary details. ERMIA focuses on the 'wood' and not so much on the individual 'trees' so that designers *can* see the wood from the trees. As we have seen, ERMIA can be used on a number of levels of detail, but it cannot compete with detailed formalisms such as GOMS.

12.2.3 Structure or Function?

Static devices such as paper timetables do not respond to their users and so there are no easily-observed events to model. Event-based formalisms, or models of function, therefore, have only rarely been used as analysis tools for static information displays. Structure-based formalisms, in contrast, are obviously in their element here.

Structural representations, however, need not be based on ER diagrams. In data modeling, the relational model developed by Codd (1982) is a well-known alternative to ER modeling, and the parallel has been developed by Raymond and Tompa (1992) who successfully applied Codd's 'normal form' analysis to document structures. The viscosity problem, in which a writer wishing to change every occurrence of word A to word B throughout a document has to change each one individually, could be modeled as a failure to meet the required normal form, and a solution based on having a master copy of every word could be modeled as a structure that met the normal form requirements.

Although structure-based representations have the advantage that they can operate with non-interactive devices, they pay for that. Sometimes one would like to model the effects of interaction without having to adopt a new formalism. There has been some research on time-dependent ER models. Although we have not explored the possibilities in the context of ERMIA, preferring as ever to favour simplicity over expressive power, time-stamped relationships and entities can be used to model cases like limited-term driving licences which expire after a fixed term.

ERMIA describes the structure of the information that the user works on (such as the drawing) or the structure of the interface tools (such as a menu system). It has no representation of user actions and it is relatively high-level compared to the examples discussed earlier.

12.2.4 Summary

Use ERMIA for a technique that is high-level and quick to use. If you want to focus on internal structures rather than external representations then ERMIA is an appropriate modeling method. ERMIA is usable early in design, before designing the 'look and feel' and is suitable for non-specialist use. Look elsewhere for a method which shows the results of operations, the effects of surface aspects, detailed time predictions or fully formalized provable properties.

12.3 Usability Issues

ERMIA does not require extensive analysis, teams of experts with stopwatches, handbooks of expected times, or any other formal apparatus. Rather, it is a classic 'back of envelope' technique. But the authors have found it does need thought and reflection, and it can be difficult to see the structure of the information at first. Practice helps, of course.

ERMIA, like its parent entity-relationship modeling, has little expressive power; many aspects of the structure cannot be modeled. For most purposes the authors have found that natural-language annotations of the diagrams are adequate substitutes. There is a trade-off between usability and expressive power, such that truly expressive systems are fearsomely difficult to learn and use. We have, if anything, erred in the opposite direction: ERMIA is very easy to learn, but may not always be expressive enough.

As a communication tool, it is too terse to stand on its own. The diagrams need to be supported by natural language commentaries. During development of a library of examples, we spent a good deal of time talking through our models and explaining them to each other. If the diagrams are recorded without a commentary, revisiting them can occasionally be puzzling.

As an analysis tool ERMIA is well suited to collaborative modeling, with few dependencies within the diagrams and with little need to explain intentions or look ahead. But the diagrammatic notation itself is somewhat viscous if the models are drawn using a standard drawing package. Laying them out neatly, getting everything aligned and so on takes a good deal of unnecessary work. One can envision a specialist tool that would take over some of the detail of making illustrations.

Symbolic representation is feasible, leading to executable models. The authors have implemented experimental algorithms for finding cost-of-knowledge directly from symbolic representations of information structures. The application we have developed for this purpose is little more than a proof of concept, of course, but even as such we have found it useful as a means of enforcing clarity of thought about search paths.

ERMIA is not simply a sketching method with no formality; it has a well-defined semantics coming from a long tradition of data modeling. ERMIA allows different people's mental representations to be made explicit. ERMIA is applicable to distributed systems, because it can distinguish the location of different information. This helps with the 'new version' problem of identifying the effects of changing part of an information system; if we know where the dependencies are, we know which ones will get broken when the system is changed.

12.4 Future Developments

HCI is an area which is still very much 'under development'. Since the first papers on the subject were published in the early 1960s the field of HCI has grown, moving from highly detailed considerations of human motor performance to cognitive issues to social and anthropological considerations. HCI has always been chasing after technological developments, trying to make the ever increasing number of system more usable and more easily learnt by people.

Although ERMIA is not a philosophy of design, let alone a guide to good HCI practice, it has a role to play as a descriptive tool in the new approaches to HCI design now emerging. One such new approach is model-based design (e.g. Szekely *et al.*, 1993), in which the designer creates an interface for an application by describing the application at the semantic or conceptual level. The designer then chooses the various interface components which best fit the application. Interface components include interface actions, interface objects, presentation objects representing application objects, and interaction techniques to be used with presentation and interface objects. The role of structural descriptions such as ERMIA is at the stage of describing the application at the semantic level.

Another new approach is data-centred design (Benyon, 1992, 1995), an approach that is deliberately distanced from task-based or object-oriented approaches. The claim is that data-centred approaches such as ERMIA achieve a better abstraction of the whole human-computer system. To a large extent data-centred design is motivated by the need to make HCI knowledge available to software engineers. ERMIA uses the entity-relationship notation which is widely used by both the 'structured' methods of software design and by object-oriented methods. Having a common notation for both the functional 'core' of an application and for the interface to that application makes it more likely that software engineers will take on the importance of HCI.

Lastly, there are 'broad-brush' approaches, based on natural language concepts comprehensible to non-specialists, such as the 'cognitive dimensions of notations' explored by Green (1989). In these approaches, such high-level ideas as 'viscosity' are used to characterize the properties of an artefact, and the role of ERMIA is to provide an explanation and a definition of the concepts.

In these emerging approaches ERMIA offers an approach that is comprehensible to all concerned, a notation which interface designers and usability engineers can use and which software engineers will understand. We see it as a technique which plugs a gap in existing HCI design and evaluation methods, by providing an accessible, coarse-grained analysis using a notation that is familiar to at least some members of the community and that is easily learned by all.

Summary

- *ERMIA cannot do everything in the design and evaluation of information artefacts.*
- *Other methods have their strengths.*
- *Designers and choosers need to consider the purpose, level of detail and style of the modeling method which they require.*
- *Designers and choosers must also be aware of the usability of ERMIA and make their assumptions and constraints clear.*
- *ERMIA is a part of the development of HCI which focuses attention of higher level constructs and is usable by a wide range of people.*

Solutions to Exercises

Exercise 1

More than one answer is possible. The authors would choose the following entity classes: Number-Button; Operator; Clear; Decimal-Point; Equals-key; Display. (There is also an entity Close Box in the top left hand corner, but we choose to ignore that for the present.)

Exercise 2

Exercise 3

This is actually quite a tricky example, more to get you thinking about perceptual entities than really producing a detailed analysis. Our solution to this exercise is shown below. As you can see we have shown the Equals sign as a clone and as a sub-type to Operator. Number-Button has a many-to-many relationship with itself. The relationship between Clear (the button marked 'C') and Display is 1:m because the Clear button can relate to many different displays.

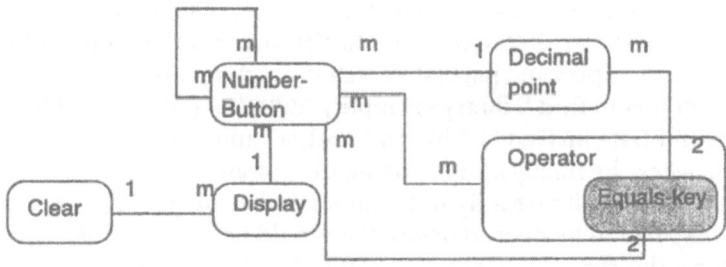

Exercise 4

Instead of, or in addition to, representing Colour as an attribute of the Flower entity, we could have shown that there is a relationship 'same-colour-as' between the entity type Flower and itself, as follows.

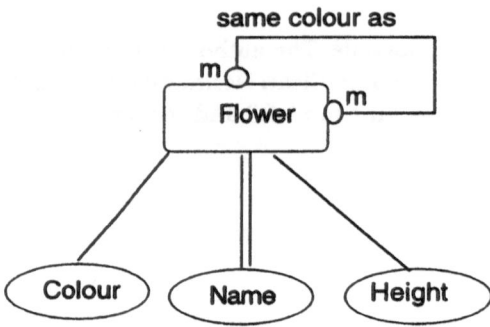

When we explore the relationship in more detail we 'discover' the entity Colour-group. We return to this feature of ERMIAs in Chapter 5.

Exercise 5

Our solution is shown below. Yours should look something similar. Of course the reason that libraries have evolved into the complex structures which they have is exactly because locating specific instances of entities – a particular piece of text in this case – is extremely difficult when there are so many millions of pieces of text which could be found. And in case you think that computers have solved all this, in order to find the figure below, one of the authors had to: search on two different computers, remember what he had called the 'top level' folder (was it in the folder 'Data' or in 'Old Data' or in 'Compacted Stuff'?), search through the folders in that to find 'ERMIA examples and papers', search through that to find 'Early examples', search through that to find 'Library example', '29/05/95' (OK, so his files are identi-fied by Title and Date instead of Title and Author) and then search through that to find page 28, where he finally located the figure he wanted. There was no facility for keyword search (since it was a figure), and a number of the files were in different formats so they had to be opened before they could be inspected. As with any large search, getting the structure right, recording the structure correctly and making that structure available to the user is what is important.

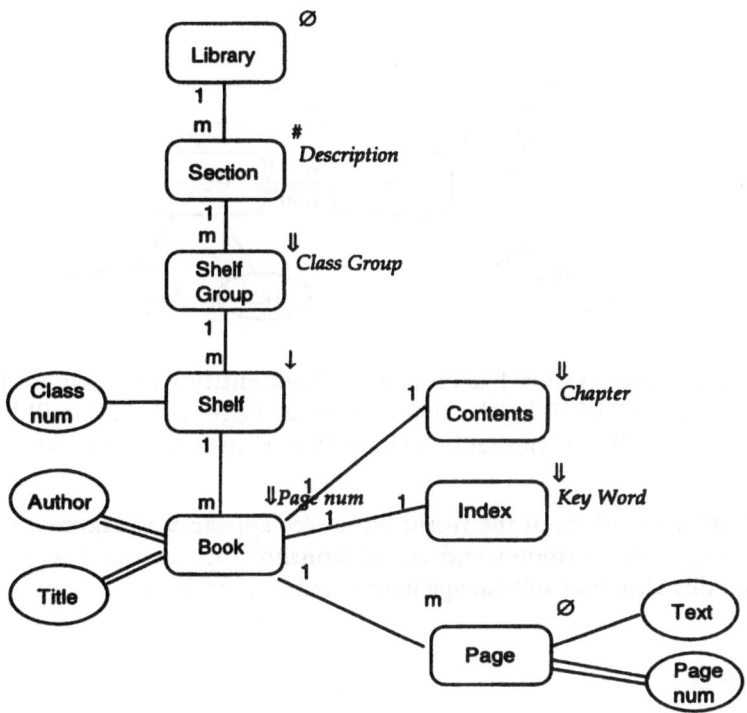

Exercise 6

Here is our solution. Yours should look very similar except you might have thought of some other attributes, or given the attributes different names. Folder should have optional participation because computer systems allow folders to be empty (i.e. contain no files). File also has optional participation since files can be kept on the desk top. Files on floppy discs are often not kept in folders.

Notice that in most operating systems the Date and the Size are attributes of File in Folder, not attributes of File. This turns out to be important because users often think that they are attributes of File. Confusion often arises as to which version of a copied file is required.

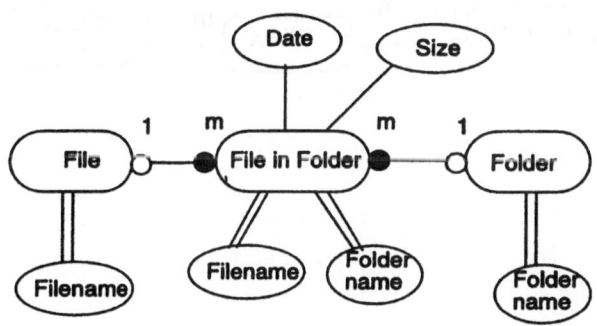

Exercise 7

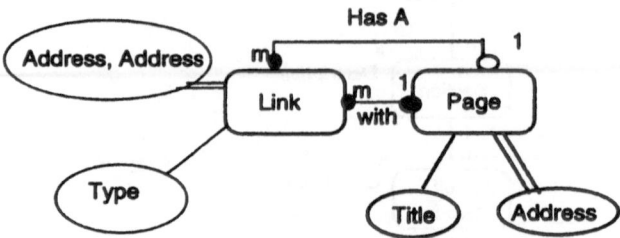

A good hypermedia system has an explicit Link entity which has (at least) one attribute – the type of link. The relationship of Page with Link will be mandatory which means that it cannot be deleted if it is involved in the 'with' relationship.

Current implementations of the World Wide Web appear as in Figure 6.5 – links do not have their own attributes and all relationships are optional. (Of course we expect that this situation will change in the next year or two.)

Exercise 8

You should have produced the following (though you may have used different names for the entities). Each of the m:m relationships has been replaced by an entity which has a mandatory m:1 relationship with the original entities.

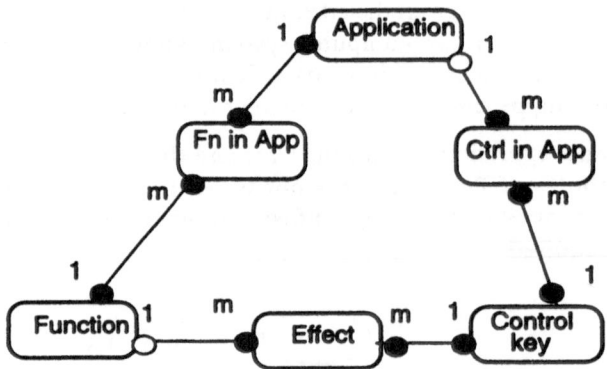

Exercise 9

There certainly are, there are connection traps all over the place! There are fan traps around Function, Control key and Application and there are potential chasm traps wherever there is an optional relationship.

They do result in lost information because to answer the question 'What is the control key in Word for importing a file?' start from Fn in App, go to Application and from there to a list of control keys in Ctrl in App. There is no way of connecting the function to the control key. If you try to traverse the structure in the other way, go to Function and from there to Effect which gives a list of all the control keys (in all applications) for the importing a file function (if any entries exist). Similarly to answer the question 'What does Ctrl I do in FrameMaker', start from Ctrl in App and the same problems arise.

Exercise 10

There is a relationship missing between Fn in App and Ctrl in App. This is a m:m relationship which we have replaced by an entity called Effect in App.

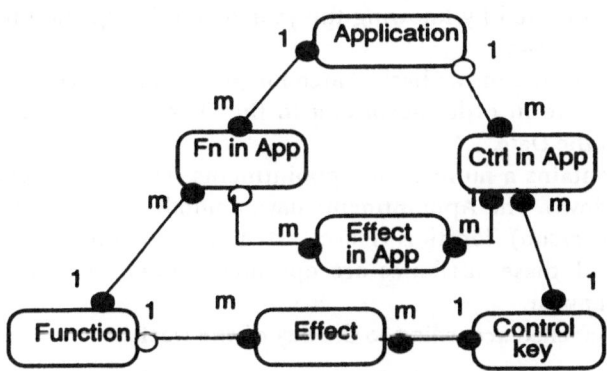

Exercise 11

The situation now is much better. To answer the question 'What is the control key in Word for importing a file?' start from Fn in App and look up Effect in App. If there is an entry then this will identify the control key. (If there is no entry then there is no control key for importing a file).

To answer the question 'What does Ctrl I do in FrameMaker' start from Ctrl in App and look up Effect in App. If there is no entry in Ctrl in App, then FrameMaker does not have a Ctrl I.

Exercise 12

Diaries are typically used to make appointments, to check that appointments do not clash, and to remember which appointments are due. They also have a use as a store of information about previous appointments.

Queries include, among others:

- What have I arranged to do today?
- When did I arrange to meet David next?
- What are all the appointments I have with David?
- Where did I go last Friday?
- Where am I meeting Jane for lunch?
- When was the last project meeting?

Exercise 13

The diary itself is the information artefact that we wish to analyse.

- A Page in the diary is a manifest entity that corresponds to a conceptual entity, a Week.
- A Day in the diary is a manifest entity, an area of the page.
- A Date is a conceptual entity that corresponds roughly to the Day. The Date itself can be inferred by knowing the year of the Diary, the month printed on the Page and the Day.
- Each Page also contains a physical area for (any number of) Notes.
- All the Pages are in order according to the Date. The Days are also in order, according to the Date.
- Each Day contains a number of Appointments. These are manifest when they are written down. The Appointments have a number of attributes, such as who is involved (Person), location (Place), what is happening (Activity), and when (Time). All of these attributes are optional, though at least one of them is expected to appear.
- Each Day is labelled according to the day of the week.

Other arrangements are possible. For instance, we might treat Person, Place, Location or Time as entities in their own right. We have chosen to treat them as attributes to make it very clear that this diary does not present any information about Persons, Places, Locations or Times except as aspects of Appointments. Other diaries might do so. For example, we might say that a diary with an address book attached to it definitely treats Persons as entities whose attributes are their Addresses and Telephone Numbers. This difference has implications for the kind of information that we can easily get from the diary. In our diary, it might not be easy to find out where a person lives. If their home is the Place of an Appointment, we would have to repeat the address for each Appointment with them, or else look through all the Appointments with that Person to find the address. If addresses or other information about a Person are important, then we need a diary that allows this information to be grouped into entities.

Exercise 14

Here are two alternatives.

The first layout shows that Page and Day are real areas of the page, whereas Person, Place etc. are just snippets of information written down. The status of Appointment is a bit more shady. The diary does not have specific areas set aside for each separate appointment in the day. We represent it as a manifest entity because Appointments are areas of the page, even though they do not each have a pre-allocated space.

Possibly the solution would be better showing separate perceptual and conceptual ERMIAs.

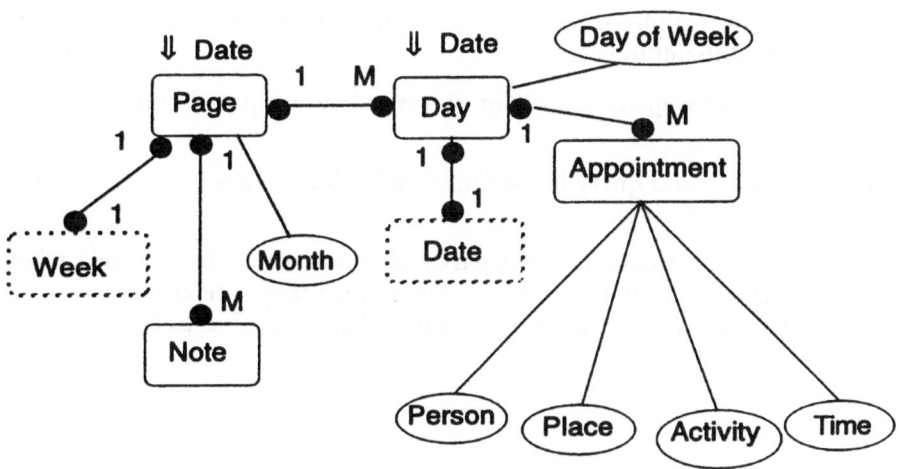

The second ERMIA treats Person, Place, and Activity as significant entities in their own right. It might be more useful in considering a diary that also had an address book, so that Person might be linked to an entity that represents their addresses.

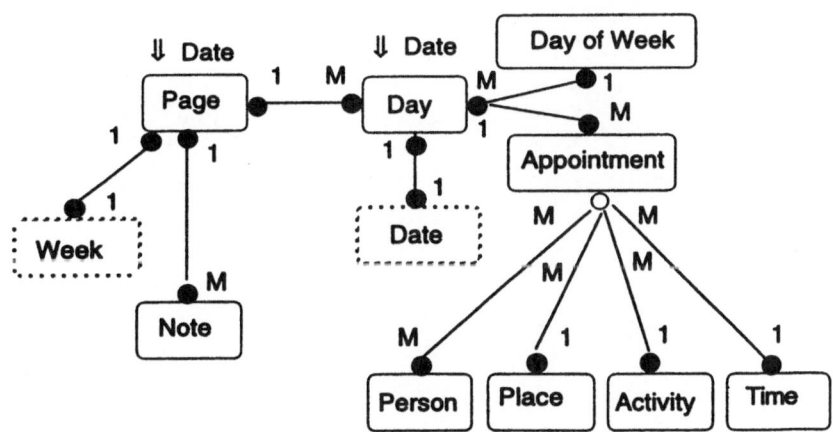

As we have drawn it here, this ERMIA does not capture the asymmetry of the many-to-many relationship between Person and Appointment. An Appointment may include a list of Persons, but there is no store for Person that includes all their Appointments. This could be added to the ERMIA by breaking down the many-to-many-relationship into an intermediate entity, and showing that the intermediate entity is ordered by Appointment.

Exercise 15

With a diary that has this (very common) layout, a diary user needs to look up dates to see who an appointment is with, what time it is, where it is, and what they plan to do. Queries about what is happening on a particular date are easy to answer, but queries about people or activities where the date is not known, or on many dates, are more difficult to answer.

The trail for the first query is a chain of 1:m relationships, all confined within a single page.

The trail for the second query is a chain of m:1 relationships, possibly distributed across many pages (weeks).

The difficulty of the second query is partly revealed by the chain of m:1 relationships. This ERMIA does not directly represent which items are visible at once – i.e. that items on different pages are harder to find. The reader has to know this.

Summary of Notation

Entity store/class set – items, objects or concepts, all of a kind

Individual entity, occurrence – one item, object or concept in an entity store

Not drawn – ERMIA models do not include indivudal entities

Attribute – property or characteristic of an entity.

Identifying Attribute – attribute that uniquely identifies one entity in the class

Relationship – connects entities

Degree of a relationship – number of entities participating, e.g. one-to-one, one-to-many, many-to-many, or numbered

Mandatory Participation of an entity in a relationship – all instances of the entity A take part in relationship with B

Optional Participation of an entity in a relationship – some instances of the entity A take part in relationships with B, others may not

Perceptually-coded or Behavioural Attribute – attribute of a manifest entity that can be directly perceived, such as colour, or which changes as a result of some interaction

Manifest Entity – entity that has some physical manifestation

Conceptual Entity – entity that is conceptually important but has no physical manifestation

Clone – entity class with instances that
cannot (easily perceptually) be told
apart

Sub-type – entity B is a sub-type of entity A
and hence inherits attributes and
relationships of A

Encapsulation – entity E is a complex object
constructed from the entities A, B, C and D
and their associated relationships

Exclusive relationship – entity A may
participate in only one of two or more
relationships

Inclusive relationship – entity A must
participate in both of two or more
relationships

Manifest entity structures

Pile – entity class with no organizational
structure imposed on the entity occurrences,
no help with searching the store

Chain – entity class in which the instances
are in an unordered sequence, search the
store from the start

Sorted list – entity class in which the occurrences
are in a sequence ordered by one of the
entity's attributes. Binary searching can be
used

Hash – entity class in which the location of
an occurrence is directly related to the value
of some attribute, search can use the value of
the attribute provied the way that it is related
to location is known

Unsearchable – no way to identify contents

Trail – a chain of 1:1 or 1:M relationships

Table – a manifest structure of rows,
columns and cells

Tree – a manifest structure with one class,
connected 1:M with itself

Network – a manifest structure with one
class connected M:M with itself

Fan trap – may be unable to relate instances
of A to C. NB There may be intervening 1:1
relationships

Chasm trap – may be unable to relate
instances of A to C owing to missing
occurrences of the relationship B:C

Replacing a many-to-many relationship

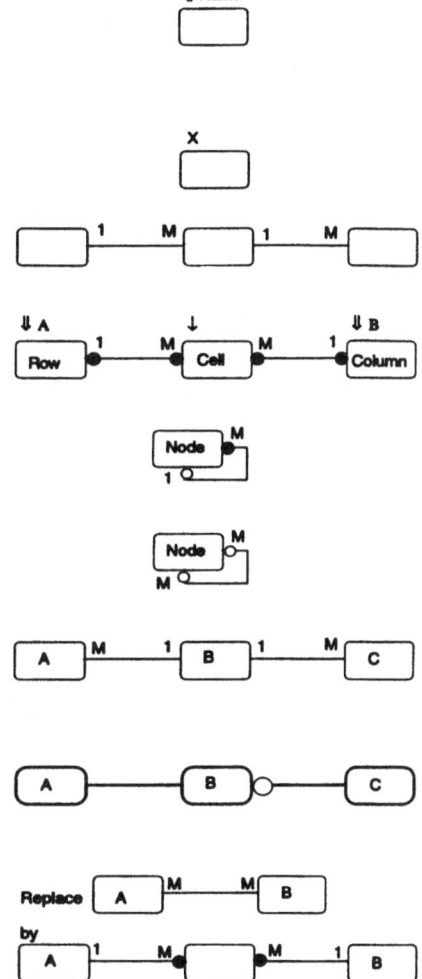

Resources

Human-Computer Interaction

There are many books on human-computer interaction and user interface design, but you have to be choosy – some are very shallow, and not very rewarding. For general views covering many aspects of the field, including sections on HCI formalisms such as GOMS, good choices might be Eberts (1994) or Preece *et al.* (1994).

Task-based approaches are covered by Lim and Long (1994), though it is quite theoretical in places. Browne (1994) gives a practical task-based method design to fit in with structured approaches to systems development.

ER Modeling

The original source paper for conventional entity-relationship modeling is Chen (1976). A voluminous literature has accumulated since then. The books by Howe (1989), Benyon (1997) and Veryard (1992) are general introductions to data modeling, with sections on ER modeling.

ERMIA Modeling

The original idea was proposed by Green (1991). A more developed version was presented by Benyon and Green (1995). Those are both conference papers, so they are necessarily brief. A full-length journal paper is *The Skull beneath the Skin: Entity-Relationship Modeling of Information Artefacts* (Green and Benyon, 1996) which includes many of the examples presented in this book.

Object Modeling

The Unified Modeling Language (UML) appears to dominate the market at present. Apart from the book by Booch, Rumbaugh and Jacobson (1998), Booch (1994) is comprehensive and Sully (1994) gives a good clear introduction and shows how object models relate to entity-relationship models.The commercial arm of the UML fraternity has a Web site at www.rational.com.

Other Formalisms

Several other notational techniques were introduced during the book.

GOMS: The book that made GOMS famous was Card *et al.* (1983). Not an easy read. Short introductions can be found in Preece *et al.* (1994) and Eberts (1994).

There has been much work using GOMS. Olson and Olson (1990) survey its development up to that date. Unlike most HCI methodologies and techniques, GOMS has been used in anger in a large commercial project, described by Gray *et al.* (1993). The CHI conference series, published by ACM, usually contains papers describing new applications of GOMS.

NGOMSL, the 'Natural GOMS Language', is a second-generation GOMS, more comprehensible, more compactly explained, and fitted with some useful extensions; see Kieras (1988). Eberts's book (1994) gives a whole chapter to NGOMSL, with lengthy examples.

User-Action Notation: The standard source for UAN is Hix and Hartson (1993).

Z: The definitive reference book on the Z language is Spivey (1992) but that is not a book for the casual reader. Several more approachable introductions are available (e.g. Imperato, 1991), and anyone seriously interested in learning Z would be well advised to start with one of those.

Bibliography

Benyon, D.R. (1990) *Information and Data Modelling*, Blackwell Scientific Publishers, Oxford.

Benyon, D.R. (1992) Task Analysis and System Design: The Discipline of Data. *Interacting with Computers*, 4(2) 246-259.

Benyon, D.R. (1995) A Data-Centred Approach to User Centred Design, in Nordby, K., Helmersen, P.H., Gilmore, D.J, and Arnesen, S.A. (eds.) *Human-Computer Interaction: INTERACT-95*, Chapman and Hall, London.

Benyon, D. (1997) *Information and Data Modelling*, 2nd Edition, McGraw-Hill, Maidenhead, UK.

Benyon, D.R. and Green, T.R.G. (1995) Displays as Data Structures, in Nordby, K., Helmersen, P.H., Gilmore, D.J, and Arnesen, S.A. (eds.) *Human-Computer Interaction: INTERACT-95*, Chapman and Hall, London.

Bertin, J. (1981) *Graphics and Graphic Information Processing*, (trans. W. J. Berg) de Gruyter, New York.

Booch, G., Rumbaugh, J. and Jacobson, I. (1998) *Unified Modeling Language User Guide*, Addison-Wesley, Cambridge, MA.

Booch, G. (1994) *Object Oriented Analysis and Design with Applications*, Addison-Wesley, Cambridge, MA.

Browne, D. (1994) *STUDIO: Structured User-interface Design for Interaction Optimisation*, Prentice-Hall, London.

Card, S.K., Moran, T. P. and Newell, A. (1983) *The Psychology of Human-Computer Interaction*, Lawrence Erlbaum.

Card, S.K., Pirolli, P. and Mackinlay, J.D. (1994) The Cost-of-Knowledge Charistic Function: Display Evaluation for Direct-Walk Dynamic Information Visualizations, in Adelson, B., Dumais, S. and Olsen, J. (Eds.) *CHI '94: Human Factors in Computing Systems*, ACM Press, New York.

Chen, P.P-S. (1976) The Entity-Relationship Model: Toward a Unified View of Data, *ACM Trans on Database Systems*, 1, 9-36.

Codd, E.F. (1982) Relational Database: A Practical Foundation for Productivity. *Communications of the ACM*, 25(2).

Dix, A.J. (1991) *Formal Methods for Interactive Systems*, Academic Press, London.

Downs, E., Clare, P. and Coe, I. (1991) *Structured Systems Analysis and Design Method: Application and Context*, Prentice-Hall, New York.

Eberts, R.E. (1994) *User Interface Design*, Prentice Hall, Englewood Cliffs, NJ.

Gray, W., John, B., and Atwood, M. (1993) Project Ernestine: Validating a GOMS Analysis for Predicting and Explaining Real-World Task Performance, *Human-Computer Interaction*, 8, 237-309.

Green, T.R.G. (1989) Cognitive Dimensions of Notations, in Sutcliffe, A. and Macaulay, L. (eds.) *People and Computers V*, Cambridge University Press, Cambridge.

Green, T.R.G. (1991) Describing Information Artifacts with Cognitive Dimensions and Structure Maps, in D. Diaper and N. V. Hammond (eds.) *People and Computers VI*. Cambridge University Press, Cambridge.

Green, T.R.G. and Benyon, D.R. (1996) The Skull beneath the Skin: Entity-Relationship Modelling of Information Artefacts, *International Journal of Human Computer Studies*, 44(6), 801-828.

Hix, D. and Hartson, H.R. (1993) *Developing User Interfaces*, Wiley, London.

Howe, D.R. (1989) *Data Analysis for Database Design*, 2nd edition, Edward Arnold, London.

Imperato, M. (1991) *An Introduction to Z*, Chartwell-Bratt, Bromley, UK.

Jackson, Benyon, D.R. and Lowe, Using ERMIA for the Evaluation of a Theorem Prover Interface, in *Proceedings of User Interfaces to Theorem Provers, UITP98*, Eindhoven, July 1998.

Jacobson, I. (1995) The Use Case Construct in Object-oriented Software Engineering, in J. M. Carroll, (ed.) *Scenario-based Design: Envisioning Work and Technology in System Development*, John Wiley, New York.

Jacobson, I., Chistensen, M., Johnson, P. and Overgaard, G. (1993) *Object-Oriented Software Engineering*. Addison-Wesley, Cambridge, MA.

Kieras, D.E. (1988), Towards a practical GOMS Methodology for User Interface Design, in M. Helander (ed.), *Handbook of Human-Computer Interaction*, Elsevier, Amsterdam, pp. 67-85.

Lakoff, G. (1987) *Women, Fire and Dangerous Things*, Chicago University Press, Chicago.

Lewis, C., Polson, P., Wharton, C. and Rieman, J. (1990) Testing a Walk-through Methodology for Theory-based Design of Walk-up -and-use Interfaces, in J. C. Chew, and J. Whiteside, (eds.) *Empowering People, Proceedings of CHI '90*, ACM Press, New York.

Lim, K.Y. and Long, J. (1994) *The MUSE Method for Usability Engineering*, Cambridge University Press, Cambridge.

Olson, J.R. and Olson, G.M. (1990) The Growth of Cognitive Modeling in Human-Computer Interaction since GOMS, *Human-Computer Interaction*, 5, 221-65.

Payne, S.J. (1991) A Descriptive Study of Mental Models, *Behaviour and Informal Technology*, 10(1), 3-21.

Payne, S.J. and Green, T.R.G. (1986) Task-Action Grammars: A Model of the Mental Representation of Task Languages, *Human-Computer Interaction*, 2, 93–133.

Preece, J., Rogers, Y., Sharp, H., Benyon, D., Holland, S. and Carey, T. (1994) *Human-Computer Interaction*, Addison-Wesley, Wokingham.

Raymond, D. and Tompa, F. (1992) *Applying Normalization to Notations*, Department of Computer Science, Waterloo University, Ontario, Canada.

Rosson, M.B. and Carroll, J.M. (1995) Narrowing the Specification-Implementation Gap in Scenario-based Design, in Carroll, J.M. (ed.) *Scenario-based Design: Envisioning Work and Technology in System Development*, John Wiley, New York.

Szekely, P., Luo, P. and Neches, R. (1993) Beyond Interface Builders: Model-Based Interface Tools, in *Human Factors in Computer Systems, InterCHI '93 Conference*, ACM Press, 383-390.

Spivey, J.M. (1992) *The Z Notation: A Reference Manual*, 2nd edition, Prentice Hall, New York.

Sully, P. (1994) *Modelling the World with Objects*, Prentice-Hall, London.

Veryard R. (1992) *Information Modelling, Practical Guidance*, Prentice-Hall, London.

Wittgenstein, L. (1953) *Philosophical Investigations*, Basil Blackwell, Oxford.

Index